HIGH SCHOOL SOFTBALL

UMPIRES MANUAL
2024 and 2025

DR. KARISSA NIEHOFF, Publisher
Sandy Searcy, Editor
NFHS Publications

Produced and published by

Referee Enterprises Inc., publishers of Referee magazine.
2017 Lathrop Ave., Racine, WI 53402

National Federation of State High School Associations
P.O. Box 690, Indianapolis, IN 46206

ISBN-13: 978-1-58208-575-3
Printed in the United States of America

Table of Contents

Definition of Terms

90-degree angle (tag) — The umpire's location on tag plays. The path of the runner into a base or the application of the tag on a play not involving a base, together with the umpire's line of vision from a location 10-12 feet away, form a 90-degree angle.

90-degree angle (throw) — The umpire's location on force plays. The path of the thrown ball to a base, together with the umpire's line of vision from a location no closer than 18 feet from the base, form a 90-degree angle.

Acknowledge partner — When one umpire communicates moving to cover a potential play ("I'm going," I've got third," "I've got the ball," etc.). Partner(s) should acknowledge the communication. Specifics of an acknowledgment vary widely among crews, often according to the situation. Depending on the crew, the acknowledgment can be as simple as pointing in the general direction of a base or as concise as a specific verbal reply. How umpires will acknowledge their partner(s) should be determined during the pregame conference.

Between play mechanics — Once the play is completed, the ball is returned to the pitcher inside the circle and all runners have returned to their base or advanced as desired, the plate umpire will take responsibility for all runners while the base umpire(s) hustle to the next starting position. The base umpire(s), after reaching the desired position, should turn and take responsibility for the runners until the next pitch (legal or illegal) while the plate umpire hustles to position for the next pitch. Umpires should keep a set of eyes on the field at all times during a live ball and enforce the look-back rule as needed. It is also acceptable to call time when all action is completed so all umpires can move at once.

Calling depth — The preferred distance from a play that enables the umpire to see all the necessary elements of the play.
  • A force play should be viewed from no closer than 18 feet, allowing the umpire to see, without moving their head, all three interactions of a force play: the ball in the fielder's glove and not juggled, the runner touching the base and the fielder's foot on the base.
  • A tag play should be viewed from an approximate distance of 10-12 feet, allowing the umpire to see the elements and interactions of a tag play: the ball, the defense, the runner and the base, the application of the tag, or the application of the tag and the runner touching the base. There may be times when the need to see multiple, diverse angles or the position of the player's bodies necessitates moving to maintain an unobstructed view.

Calling position — The primary position or the subsequent adjustment from it to see the elements of the individual play and make a call.

Chase — The act of a base umpire who abandons normal infield duties and assumes the responsibilities for a fly ball (fair/foul, catch/no catch, dead ball).

Clear the catcher — The plate umpire (P) will clear the catcher when a play follows a pitch. That will increase the distance between the umpire's body and the catcher. Observe the catcher's shoulders and move as necessary to avoid contact.

Counter-rotated position — The starting position of the base umpires (three-umpire system) with runners on:
- Second base only;
- First and second base;
- First and third base;
- Second and third base;
- First, second and third base.

The first-base (U1) umpire is positioned between first and second base, usually behind the second baseplayer and at calling depth if possible. U1 is no closer to first or second base than 15 feet. The third-base umpire (U3) is on the third-base line in foul territory, 12-15 feet from the base so that one step forward puts the umpire 10-12 feet away for a tag play and one step back puts the umpire at 18 feet for a force play. There is no rotation when counter-rotated.

Crewness — The unspoken awareness, understanding and acknowledgment that umpires are a team that functions most successfully and efficiently when each member is truly caring of the appropriate performance of each other member and works for proficiency of, and respect for, the crew. Crewness is working with and supporting partners. An example would be at the end of a play always keeping one set of umpire eyes on the runner(s) and pitcher. Another example might be consistent use of umpire-to-umpire signals.

Efficiency of movement — Starting and ending all movement in a good "base" — feet parallel to one another and at least shoulder width apart, with weight evenly distributed. Mastery of the pivot and reverse pivot. Using crossover steps — not side to side, not backpedaling. Choosing a position before moving. Move with a purpose from point A to point B. Achieving angle first, then adjusting distance. Keeping the ball in front. Moving parallel with runners. Disciplining and controlling the body.

Elements of Play — There are four elements of every play that the umpire must keep in front of them: Offense, defense, the ball and the base.

First-base line extended — An imaginary line that extends the first-base fair/foul line into foul territory behind home plate an unlimited distance.

Heel/toe plate stance: The legs/feet are wider than shoulder width apart. The shoulders and body are somewhat square to the front outside corner of the plate where a line drawn down from the umpire's navel would bisect the front outside corner of the plate. The slot foot should be in the slot pointing directly at the pitching plate or angled outward. Place the first foot behind the catcher then up and out with the slot foot to be heel/toe. The non-slot foot is behind the catcher in line with an imaginary line extending from the heel of the slot foot to the toe of the non-slot foot. The non-slot foot is angled no more than 45 degrees. Be no deeper behind the catcher than a closed fist between the non-slot knee and the catcher's back. Drop set by bending the knees. Drop only far enough so the eyes remain at the top of the strike zone.

Holding zone — An area from which the plate umpire assesses the next move and is located in an area halfway between third base and home plate, far enough away from the foul line to allow a clear view of all the action on the field.

Opening the gate — A basic umpire movement which allows continued observation of a batted or thrown ball as the ball passes the umpire. To "open the gate," begin in an upright stance with the feet comfortably apart; keeping the chest to the ball, take an initial step backward while pointing the foot toward the ball's destination; as or before the ball passes the umpire's location, turn by stepping with the opposite foot and focus on the developing play.

Pause, read and react — A three-step method that helps determine where umpires should go and what their responsibilities will be during a developing play. Pause: observe the initial action; Read: determine what play is going to develop and what position adjustment to make; React: move into position for the anticipated play and, as appropriate, communicate intentions to partner(s). "Pause, read and react" is important in coordinating umpiring coverage. It ensures that the umpires identically evaluate each developing play.

Play — The action that develops as a runner, the ball and a fielder arrive at the same place at approximately the same time. A play usually occurs at or near a base and normally requires an umpire's decision. Umpires should let the ball take them to the play and maintain an unobstructed view of all four elements.

Pre-pitch preparation — The thought process umpires should use to anticipate a play prior to each pitch to better understand where they may or may not need to move. This includes but is not limited to: the count, position of the runners, defensive positioning and recognition of any situations that may occur.

Rotation — The movement of umpires in the three-umpire system clockwise to have an umpire at a base prior to the runner arriving (keep an umpire ahead of the runner) culminating with U1 taking position for a play at home plate.

Rotated position — The starting position of base umpires (three-umpire system) with a runner on first base only. The first-base umpire (U1) is on the first-base line in foul territory 12-15 feet back. The third-base umpire (U3) is on an imaginary line straight out from the first-base side of second base toward right center field, 12-15 feet back.

Runners — Players from the team at bat are identified by their locations on base at the beginning of a play or sequence of plays: R1 is always the lead runner, R2 is the second runner and R3 is the third runner.

Secondary position — The next primary position assumed by the umpire after the initial play during continuous action. The action dictates the secondary position. Action that follows the defensive team's first attempt to retire a runner and is reasonably predictable. For example, when the batter-runner hits a ground ball and the defense overthrows first base, the play at first base is the initial play. If the batter-runner advances on the overthrow to first, the ensuing play at second base is a secondary play.

Set (plate) — From the stance, a plate umpire drops into the set position just prior to the release of the pitch. The amount of drop necessary is determined by the width of the feet in the stance. The umpire's head is at the top of the strike zone. The umpire must be able to see the outside edge of the plate and the batter's knees. Some torso lean may be needed to achieve proper height. The hands/arms should be in front of and in close to the body. Their placement provides balance and assists in locking in (not moving) during a pitch. The umpire must be completely set when the pitch is released and remain motionless as the pitch is delivered. The same position should be mirrored on both sides of the plate. The set position must be balanced and comfortable, but it is not a relaxed position.

Set (bases) — Prior to a pitch, the body position of a base umpire who is positioned off the line or has responsibilities for a runner leaving before the pitch is released, or U1 and U3 with runners on base, or any umpire prior to a play. The body is stopped, not moving, the feet are comfortably wider than shoulder width apart and parallel to each other. The hands are drawn into or placed on the body in a locked position. The head may be forward to achieve more focus. Set refers to either a ready set or hands-on-knees set position.

Slot — The area between the inside corner of the plate and the batter when the batter is in a natural stance and the catcher is in a normal crouched position behind the plate. The slot affords the umpire an excellent line of sight for seeing the zone, checked swings, hit batters, hit with batted ball and catch/no catch by the catcher.

Set for the play — Come to a complete stop before the critical moment of any play, if possible, and remain stationary until making a decision. Just like a camera taking a picture, the eyes must be stationary to produce a clear image. A play may dictate umpires to move in order to see all the elements of that play. Stop, see the play and make the call.

Starting depth:
- With no runner on base: 18-21 feet, on the line in foul territory.
- With a runner(s) on base: 12-15 feet from the base if on the line or 12-15 feet from the base line, if possible, when off the line.

Square to the base — When set for a play at any base, the head, shoulders and feet should be in line and perpendicular to a line from the umpire's location to the base. By taking a position square to the base, umpires will avoid a tendency to turn away from the play before it is complete.

The V (three-umpire system) — The area within the imaginary lines drawn from the plate to the right fielder and the plate to the left fielder. This is the chase area for U3 when in the rotated position and U1 when counter-rotated.

Third-base line extended — An imaginary line that extends the third-base fair/foul line into foul territory behind home plate an unlimited distance.

Timing play — Situation involving two outs and runners on base. If the batter-runner or another runner is retired on something other than a force play, the umpires must know if a runner(s) touched the plate before the third out was recorded.

Tracking (bases) — Letting the ball bring the umpire to the play. Umpires should observe the fielder release the ball. Track the flight of the ball until just before it reaches the targeted receiver, then switch focus to the play as all four elements of the play come together.

Tracking (plate) — See the release of the pitch, follow it into the catcher's glove. Observe the entire flight of a pitch with only slight head movement. Head movement will occur as the ball is followed in. Head movement is not used as an indication of pitch location.

Trail the batter-runner — A plate umpire's activity with no runners on base or with a runner on first base only. When no other responsibilities conflict, follow the batter-runner no more than one-third of the way to first base in fair territory to observe the developing play at first base.

Working between pitches — Movement of the umpire toward a possible play after a pitch is not hit. If there is no immediate play to a base by the catcher on a pitch not hit, the umpire should move toward a position for a possible delayed play on a runner for whom that umpire is responsible.

Part 1

Prerequisites for Good Umpiring

Any umpire representing a state high school association is performing a service to fellow umpires, to the coaches, student-athletes and fans of softball. A competent umpire performs duties with established signals and procedures. A thorough knowledge of the rules is important, but more important is the understanding of their purpose, and the ability to interpret and enforce these principles.

Good game management begins with the umpire's appearance at the game site. Players and coaches alike base many of their actions during the contest on the amount of confidence they have in the arbiter. Umpires who perform their duties in a brisk, business-like manner upon their arrival at the field, who are courteous with players and coaches (without being overly friendly) prior to the game, whose calls are made promptly and confidently and with an emphasis which dissuades argumentation, yet are non-dictatorial, and who cooperate with their partner(s) in the efficient coverage of all situations, are rarely questioned.

When umpires enter a ballpark, their sole duty is to umpire a ball game as the representative of the state association. In all actions and conduct, umpires should keep in mind that the position calls for the settling of controversies on the ball field and not in starting them elsewhere. It is a trying position, which requires the umpire to exercise patience and good judgment. Do not forget that the first essential item in solving a bad situation is to maintain temper and self-control. If umpires are courteous, but firm, they will gain respect from all. Never lose sight of the fact that friendship for the umpire, appreciation for the duties and cooperation in decisions rarely exists when a difficult situation occurs on the ball field.

The proper handling of any softball game demands each member of the umpire crew to hustle at all times. In addition, the following three factors are essential to the success of any umpire:

1. Judgment;
2. Philosophies of mechanics and technique;
3. Knowledge, application and intent of the playing rules.

1. JUDGMENT may appear to be an inherent factor of officiating. The calm demeanor that an experienced umpire displays when confronted by a spontaneous uprising, seems to support this assumption. However, the truth is the umpire, through a trying apprenticeship, has become casehardened to a degree that enables the good umpire to take a most disagreeable incident in stride. Early in a career, the average umpire will likely respond to rowdy tactics or abusive language with some show of fear, but the umpire who advances in the game learns a tight rein must be kept on temperament. No provocation, not even physical attack, should cause an umpire to lose sight of the primary responsibility — keeping the game under control. An angry umpire is never a master of the situation. To properly control the game, you must first have control of yourself.

2. PHILOSOPHIES OF MECHANICS AND TECHNIQUE are factors appreciated in some degree by even the most difficult player. A lack of good mechanics is one thing that separates an amateur umpire from a professional umpire. Mechanics of umpiring deal with the who, what, where and often the why of it all, while technique deals primarily with the "how" of umpiring. Understanding the philosophies behind the mechanics helps the umpire to react and adjust to secondary positions when required. Technique deals with the amount of flair or individualism employed by the umpire in any given situation. Hustle is an integral part of good umpiring mechanics and technique. Acceptance of any umpiring assignment requires the complete attention and energy of an umpire for the entire game. Hustle is the spirited application of the principles of good umpiring. Aimless running about is not hustle or at least is not productive hustle; one should always move with a purpose. Briefly, good mechanics and technique consist of being in the right place at the right time coupled with strict attention to detail. Umpires should work on improving their mechanics during every game.

a. Angle-over-distance theory: Obtain the proper angle, then close the distance as much as possible.

Angle. Your line of sight must provide you with an opportunity to view the interactions of a play. On a tag play, you must view the defense controlling the ball, the offensive player contacting the base and the defense applying the tag. On a force play, you must view the defense controlling the ball, the offensive player contacting the base and the defense contacting the base.

For example, on a tag play, try to look at the space between the fielder's hand or glove (holding the ball) and the runner's body. Assume for a moment that the fielder has the ball and is waiting with the glove extended to tag the runner. As the runner slides, that movement establishes the line of action. A standard "90-degree angle" would place your line of sight perpendicular to the runner's slide. You may have to adjust your angle to maintain an unobstructed view of the tag.

Distance. In theory, once you establish the proper angle, you have a reasonable opportunity to accurately view the action, regardless of the distance between your position and the play. The theory holds as long as you do not have to adjust your angle.

In reality, the final moments of virtually every play require some amount of adjustment. The greater your distance from the play, the more difficult it will be to make that adjustment.

Proximity. How close you want to be to a developing play depends on several variables, including the type of play, your mobility and your peripheral vision. Begin by moving to a position 10-12 feet from a tag play and no closer than 18 feet from a force play. Then work to improve your position to get in the best spot possible to see every element of the play.

Do not get too close as you can lose sight of the runner contacting the base if you are too tightly focused on the defensive player applying a tag to the runner.

b. Timing. Timing is essential for believable umpiring. A call made before the umpire has seen the "entire play" can be a mistake. A call made after an extended delay is often viewed as a lack of confidence in the call by the umpire. Calls made too quick or too late have the same effect on players and are less credible. Good timing is equally important on the bases and at the plate. A successful umpire will allow themselves to see the whole pitch or play. Then after a slight hesitation, make the call. Another important aspect to timing is waiting to see the play develop before adjusting your position. Adjusting before you know how the play is going to develop could place you in a worse location.

3. KNOWLEDGE OF THE PLAYING RULES is expected of every umpire. New and experienced officials should devote ample time to routinely read and study the rules book.

OTHER PREREQUISITES

Including the points just described, following are 10 prerequisites which will go a long way toward helping umpires gain the respect and confidence they are striving to attain in becoming a top-rated umpire:

1. Physical Conditioning. All umpires should be physically fit at the start of each season and then make certain that they maintain that condition. An umpire who is not physically fit is a detriment to the game. Today's athletes are well conditioned. Umpires must be able to keep pace with the athletes and be able to move quickly to get into the best position to cover a play.

2. Make Decisions Positively and Promptly. Decisions must be made positively and promptly, but an umpire must not be too hasty in calling a play. Umpires must guard against rendering decisions prematurely. An umpire has to run to get into position on a play and yet come to a stop in order to see all of the action clearly, before making a ruling. Whenever possible, do not make a fair/foul decision while in motion. Always go out on the foul line as far as possible. Stop just prior to the ball being touched and indicate fair or foul prior to making the catch/no catch ruling. It is necessary to know where the ball is when a decision is made. The fielder may drop the ball on a tag play in pivoting during a double play, or the fielder might juggle the ball on a force play. After a momentary hesitation for the purpose of making certain the play is complete, the call should be made forcefully. A timid call by the umpire will be perceived in a negative manner and reflects a lack of confidence. All plays should be called with an air of confidence. That goes a long way toward having the umpire's judgment accepted. Good umpires cultivate their voices to increase the authority implied by the spoken word. A strong voice is a valuable asset. All calls should be made loudly and clearly so that players of both teams can hear them.

3. Umpire Crew Cohesiveness (Crewness). Umpires working together must communicate and have mutual respect. The best rapport is obtained when there is a friendly attitude toward each other. Friendliness and respect for members of the crew (and profession) contribute to confidence in one another. All umpires should strive to support their partner(s) throughout the entire contest. When one umpire requests an opinion from another concerning a play which has been ruled upon, the opinion should be given honestly and courteously and the request should be made only to that umpire. Never offer an opinion, though, unless asked. Unsolicited advice is never appreciated and will cultivate a lack of confidence in the umpire(s).

Umpires must make a conscientious effort not to infringe on the duties and responsibilities of each other. There is no cause for greater embarrassment than to have opposite decisions made by umpires on a play. If proper mechanics are followed, there should be no conflicting decisions. Umpires must communicate with one another vocally, letting their partner(s) know the base they are covering.

Umpires should not discuss decisions with anyone but their partners and then only in private. They should be in a position to help if requested. The umpire is there to see everything possible. If the umpire has an alibi, the umpire loses the respect of not only partners, but of the coaches and players as well.

4. Complete Knowledge of Rules. Good umpiring is dependent, to a large extent, upon a complete knowledge and understanding of the rules. To be a competent umpire, it is necessary to know the rules thoroughly. Some decisions are repeatedly made so that, with experience, they come by reflex. The correct way to prepare oneself for effectively making decisions is through continued study of all possible situations. Then, basic fundamentals become second nature and correct interpretations are virtually automatic. To know the rules thoroughly requires constant and analytical study. It does not suffice to only read the rules. They must be studied so that mental pictures of plays and situations result. Having developed clarity in the mental pictures, the umpire will then be able to immediately recognize the situation and correctly rule on it automatically. Umpires who guess and who don't know the rules soon lose the confidence of peers, players, coaches and spectators. Veteran and new umpires alike should attend rules clinics whenever possible and learn how and when to apply the rules.

5. Proper Mechanics. Proper umpiring mechanics are essential in attaining the best coverage. Many umpires who know the rules well fail to be accepted because their mechanics are poor. Mechanics, or play coverage, must be mastered if the umpire is to be successful. First, a proper position for various situations must be learned, and then the coverage must be practiced. Position and coverage should be discussed and reviewed regularly at clinics with the opportunities to practice the mechanics being made available to all umpires, including both the veteran and the novice. It is important that all umpires obtain the best position possible for any given play without being in the way of any player or a thrown or batted ball.

6. Tune Out Spectators. Umpires must tune out statements that are heard from spectators and not react to critical comments. Every crowd will include a number of people who believe it's their right to make comments to an umpire. High school umpires must keep in mind that certain language and behavior/actions are inappropriate at any school activity. When language/behavior/actions become inappropriate, the umpire should notify the site administration of the problem and let them handle the situation.

7. Sell the Call without Showboating. Good umpires can effectively execute their duties without showboating. The umpire who discharges responsibility with dignity and in conformance with accepted signals and procedures will encourage the players and spectators to accept decisions. Being overly dramatic on routine plays too often does not accomplish the purpose for which it is intended, and such actions frequently cause coaches and players to lose confidence in the decision made by the umpire. Selling the call with dignity is much more effective. Umpires should be part of the game but never the center of attention. In no case should an umpire ever attempt to coach a player. Umpires don't want players telling them how to do their jobs, and umpires should never tell players how to do theirs. Negative comments about a player's ability or judgment on a play by the umpire can only cause hard feelings and bring trouble to the umpire.

8. Keep the Game Moving. Players should hustle on and off the field between innings and it should be a case of "do as I do" rather than "do as I say." Enforcing five pitches or one minute between innings will speed up the game significantly. Good players usually hustle, as do good umpires. Umpires and players should move quickly to and from their positions. Lead by example.

9. Keep a Dignified Attitude. Umpires must be courteous to players and coaches but avoid visiting with them immediately before, during or after the game. A businesslike attitude and atmosphere must prevail. Do not get into arguments with players, coaches or team representatives. Any discussion should be brief and to the point. A dignified attitude will often preclude and prevent an argument. Be polite and professional at all times.

10. Make Decisions Based on Fact. The judgment necessary in making a decision is acquired through proper positioning. Each and every decision must be made on the basis of fact. First, cover the play as accepted mechanics provide, and rule on the play exactly as it was seen. Umpires must realize that they will at some time err in their judgment no matter how conscientious and efficient they are and regardless of their position and rules knowledge. The fact that umpires make mistakes need not cause them to drop their head or be embarrassed. After an error, the umpire must never attempt to even it up. Each call is made on its own merits. Frequent errors in rule interpretation or in judgment quickly cause the players, coaches and spectators to lose confidence, but no one wants the umpire to attempt to even things out.

SOFTBALL UMPIRE GAME MANAGEMENT

To be successful, an umpire will have to be proficient in appearance, rule knowledge, mechanics and game management.

The ability to manage the game and to handle situations as they arise are concepts difficult to teach.

There are guidelines an umpire should or should not follow, but what works for one umpire may not work for another umpire.

There are no rules etched in stone that will make umpiring problem-free, or for that matter, will work in every game situation, but listed below are guidelines that have proven to help many umpires manage their games while developing character and stature as a respected umpire. Respect must be earned and this can only come from hard work and dedication.

1. Do not allow team personnel to swarm around a partner to dispute a call. Clear everyone away from the umpire involved except the coach, allowing the conversation to remain one on one.

2. Do not have "rabbit ears." Umpires must learn that there will be some things they need to hear and some things they do not want or need to hear. In most cases, people are talking to the position or the uniform and not the umpire personally.

3. Do not get into a shouting match with anyone on the field. Be calm. Collect your thoughts on the play and your interpretation while the person is speaking, but remember to listen as well. The umpire should be professional in replying.

4. Use a third party to handle an irate person if needed. For instance, if the player is the pitcher, the umpire should have the catcher talk to the pitcher and calm the pitcher down before continuing.

5. Do not ask a player what was said. This is baiting and intimidating the person. If you did not hear the player the first time, ignore it until you do hear something that merits enforcement.

6. Umpires should not stay on top of a close play after making the call. Watch the play until it is completed and the signal has been seen, and then move away from the area.

7. Umpires should never touch players, coaches or other team personnel; and umpires should not permit anyone to have physical contact with them.

Game management starts when the players and spectators watch the umpires take the field. First impressions are so important — sometimes even in the parking lot when the umpires are talking with one another. An umpire will never get a second chance to make a first impression. An umpire's appearance should be impeccable and pregame duties performed in a friendly yet business-like manner.

No one wants a dictator for an umpire, but everyone wants an umpire who effectively manages the game.

UMPIRE GENERAL RESPONSIBILITIES

Physical conditioning is a prime requisite of umpiring and requires a certain amount of discipline. Preseason conditioning should include exercises designed to strengthen the legs, such as jogging, running in place, etc. Basic forms of training to prepare one's self for hours of work behind the plate should begin well before the first game. The back and leg muscles can be easily conditioned for the season by steadily working up to the point where knee bends are easily endured. Conditioning during the season itself boils down to a matter of weight control and hydration. Fluids must be replaced between innings during those hot days to prevent even the best umpires from running out of energy.

To discuss why mental attitude and emotional makeup are favorable to being a good umpire touches many bases. Why did you go into umpiring? Many umpires wish to continue an association with the game beyond their playing days. Others find the contribution umpires make to the game a source of great satisfaction. Many have heard the expression that the game cannot be played without the umpires. Others, however, think of umpiring as a major source of added income. These constitute a large portion of the dropouts each season. Often times, they do not have a mental attitude that involves an understanding of the rules and purposes of the games they are officiating. Nor do they always respect the players, coaches or their partners. Frequently, they are in a hurry to get the game over. Rarely do they involve themselves in affairs of their association designed to increase their overall development as an umpire.

To remain calm in the face of adversity is an essential part of an umpire's makeup. Coolness must not be confused with complacency. It must be expected that there will be disagreements during the course of a competitive ball game. The closer the call, the greater the likelihood that a player or coach will have something to say. Many of us forget how coaches have a moral obligation to defend their players or their own actions. To request an interpretation of a rule is not to question the umpire unnecessarily. Do not interpret questioning as a personal attack. An umpire must be ready to respond to legitimately raised points of the rules. To clarify a coach's misunderstanding of a rule quickly and concisely requires a thorough knowledge of the rules. In addition, it must involve some understanding of the questioner's role in the game.

Forfeits

The plate umpire has authority to forfeit a game, but should exhaust every means to prevent it. It is the responsibility of all umpires to do everything possible to prevent a forfeit. Consult partner(s) before making the final decision to declare a forfeit.

Appeals

The appeal is a unique part of the game of softball that is initiated by the defensive team only. It occurs a) when a batter bats out of order, b) when a runner misses a base, c) when a runner leaves a base on a caught fly ball before the ball is first touched, or d) when a batter-runner attempts to advance to second base after overrunning first base. This action is brought to the attention of the administering umpire prior to the next pitch, before the defense has left the field or before the umpires leave the field at the conclusion of the game.

If the appeal is requested (during a live or dead ball), the administering umpire whose responsibility it was to observe the base and runner will step forward and make the safe or out call.

If the appeal is directed toward the wrong umpire, that umpire should point to the responsible umpire, call the umpire's name and indicate that the defense wishes to make an appeal. The responsible umpire should then step forward and make the call.

Fraternizing with Players, Coaches and Spectators

Many of the players, coaches and spectators for whom we umpire are our friends and it is difficult not to fraternize with them; however, prior to a game a friendly hello should suffice. Remember it is possible to be friendly without appearing to be friends.

Communication and Signals

Communication signals for umpires are essential. These signs enable one umpire to let a fellow umpire know the game situation on a specific play. Umpires should review the NFHS signals prior to the start of the game and utilize these, and only these, throughout the game.

Signaling is a very important aspect of umpiring. Decisions are relayed to the players, coaches and spectators by their proper use. The adopted signals are dignified, informative, meaningful and, therefore, shall be used by all umpires. Poorly executed and unauthorized signals serve only to confuse both players and coaches, as well as the umpire's partner(s). The manner in which a signal is given determines, at least to a degree, its acceptance by players, coaches and spectators. By using signals that are clear, distinct and meaningful, an umpire can communicate the results of the play while reducing the likelihood of being questioned.

Umpire-to-Umpire Communications

Besides individual signals provided by the umpire, there are several signals between umpires that assist in communication and help the game run smoothly. These include:

1. Plate umpire requesting help on a half or check swing. (Remove mask, step away from the catcher and point to the first-base umpire for a right-handed batter. If it is a left-handed batter, the plate umpire should point to the third base umpire, if working a three-umpire system.)

2. Base umpire indicating yes, if it is a strike (give a definite strike signal).

3. Base umpire indicating no, if the batter did not swing (give a safe signal).

4. Indicating an infield fly situation is in effect (right hand to your left chest).

5. Indicating an infield fly situation is no longer in effect (tap your left forearm with your right hand).

6. When requesting the count or the number of outs, use a verbal communication request, and a partner should reply with the count verbally.

Clear, concise communication during each play will help eliminate coverage errors and ensure at least one umpire is watching everything that happens on a field. That includes the plate umpire telling the base umpire, "I've got third." It also includes a base umpire alerting the crew when going out on a fly ball and the plate umpire echoing "two umpire." Using good communication techniques allows you and your partner(s) to flow with the action and gives a strong appearance of confidence and promotes crewness.

Pregame Responsibilities

Arrive at the playing field no less than 45 minutes before the scheduled starting time. The umpire should notify the coaches or game administration upon arrival at the site. Prior to the game, the host administration shall give each team a game ball to warm up with to remove the manufacturer's gloss.

Make sure the field is properly marked, and the pitcher's plate and bases are legal and at proper distances. The entire umpire crew should tour the field together so that any questions concerning the ground rules can be considered and the conclusion made known to all. All obstacles that may create a dead-ball situation should be specifically noted. Ground rules should take care of situations for the particular playing field. Always try to make all ground rules to keep the ball in play as much as possible. In ballparks that are not completely fenced in, the umpire should establish an out-of-play area down the left-field and right-field lines, usually paralleling the foul lines and starting at the backstop to the team bench/ dugout area and then from the team bench/dugout area on out. Umpires should try to sight a permanent object from the end of the bench to make it easier to determine whether a ball is in or out of play. Make sure that all equipment is kept behind the out-of-play line and everyone stays in the dugout/bench area.

Ground rules define the playing area, not the enforcement procedures stated in the official NFHS playing rules of softball. Remember, ground rules cannot supersede a book rule.

Review the ground rules with the home team prior to the pregame conference. If there is a conflict, the umpires should resolve it before the pregame meeting. If there is a doubleheader, ask how much time there will be between games.

SOFTBALL UMPIRE-TO-UMPIRE PREGAME CONFERENCE REVIEW

Date Prior to Game Day —
- Confirm game time and site with the school and partner(s).
- Review the state association approved umpires' uniform that will be worn (dress alike).

Pregame Once at Game Site —
- Review new rules — Have a rules book, case book and umpires manual available for reference.
- Discuss foul-line coverage and dead-ball area coverage.
- Review pitching and illegal pitch rules and who is responsible for what calls.
- Review proper tag-up responsibility, missed base coverage and proper appeal procedures.
- Review check swing mechanics.
- Review keeping track of balls, strikes, outs and warmup pitches.
- Review communications between partners; if you deviate, communicate.
- Review procedure for pregame conference with head coaches.
- Review field ground rules.
- Know if there will be a national anthem and introduction of players, or other pregame ceremonies.
- Be courteous, considerate and professional.
- Bring a brush, indicator, ball bag(s) and plate umpire equipment if necessary.
- Arrive on the field in enough time to perform these duties.

PREGAME CONFERENCE WITH HEAD COACHES AND GROUND RULES

No less than five minutes before game time, all umpires meet the coaches and captains (and game administration if tournament play) at home plate for ground rules. Discussion at the plate before the game should be handled by the plate umpire. It is not necessary for the other umpire to enter the discussion, except to ask a question for clarification. The plate umpire (P) should be positioned behind home plate facing the outfield with each team's head coaches on each side of home plate. The base umpire(s) (B) will be opposite the plate umpire facing the backstop. Team captains and assistant coaches may also attend the pregame conference. Items to be covered:

1. The plate umpire should introduce themself and their partner(s) to all in attendance. Then have all others introduce themselves.

2. Ask the head coaches to verify that players are legally equipped and the players and equipment are in compliance with all NFHS rules.

3. Review the ground rules. Begin by outlining dead-ball areas then proceed to home plate, third-base dugout / bench area, outfield fence and foul poles and the first-base dugout / bench area. Cover all openings and obstacles.

4. Ask if there are any questions on the rules, especially the re-entry, DP/FLEX and the EP rules.

5. Remind teams if there are any questions, only one person — the coach or captain — approaches the umpire responsible for the call in a sporting manner.

6. Check the lineups from the respective teams. Check each lineup card, including first initial, last name, defensive position and number of each participant, and hand it back to the coach for a last inspection. When returned to the plate umpire, the lineup is now official. Any changes that take place now will be substitutions and should be marked on the lineup card as such. Remind the coaches the importance of reporting all substitutions to the plate umpire. Once the lineups are confirmed, ask the head coaches whether they wish to make any changes (DP/FLEX rule).

NOTE: (F.P.) Make sure if there is a DP/FLEX there are 10 players and if no DP/FLEX there are only nine players. (S.P.) Make sure there are 10 players listed or 11 if using an EP.

7. Review with all in attendance the expectations regarding sporting behavior and wish them all the best of luck.

Following the pregame discussion with the head coaches, the plate umpire should double-check the data with the scorer so that if an error in recording or completing the lineup card is made it can be corrected. It is good to briefly discuss with the official scorer such matters as how the appearance of pinch hitters, courtesy runners and substitutes will be handled. This matter is particularly important because of the re-entry rule, and in fast pitch games, the DP/FLEX rule and in slow pitch games, the Extra Player (EP) rule.

End-of-Game Procedures

Umpires should leave the field together after giving the defensive team reasonable time for a possible appeal play. When the game is completed, umpires should take care of their responsibilities and leave the field together on the side where the least resistance will be received, normally the winning team.

The plate umpire should return the game balls to the person responsible for them and report at once to the proper authority any flagrant conduct or irregularity associated with the game.

Often, coaches, players and fans will make comments to umpires as they leave the field. Do not stop to answer questions or enter into a discussion about any controversial play that occurred in the game. Politely tell them, "I cannot discuss the play with you now," or, "I am sorry I cannot talk with you now." Umpires should not kid themselves into thinking they will be able to explain the play to them or make them understand a call. If they did not agree with you at the time the play happened, they most often would not agree with you after the game either. Some coaches, players and fans want the umpire to stop and make a rebuttal to their comments, but for the umpire to do so is both unprofessional and inexcusable. Umpires must learn to keep their composure at all times. This may mean not commenting on occasion, but the umpire does not have to have the last word. Be polite to everyone and quickly leave the area as businesslike and inconspicuously as possible.

If you are confronted by the press, refer them to the game administration. Again, be polite with your answers to questions and be certain to keep emotions in check. Do not say anything that may be embarrassing later, for such things could easily result in the situation being blown out of proportion and even more difficult for everyone.

When the game is over, the crew should find a location to be by themselves to review the game just completed. Cover unusual situations that occurred in the game to see if the play could have been covered better and review any uncertain rule situations. Umpires must not dwell on the games in the past but learn from their mistakes and concentrate on doing an even better job in the future. Umpires cannot hold a grudge or remember the comments made in an earlier game. Each game is a new game and a fresh start for everyone. Do not go on the field looking for trouble.

HELPFUL HINTS FOR UMPIRES DO'S AND DON'TS
DO . . .
1. Hustle.
2. Study rules regularly.
3. Be neat and well-groomed at all times.
4. Study why bad situations occur and work to correct them.
5. Be courteous but firm.
6. Be punctual.
7. Forget the bad days.
8. Be truthful.
9. Call your own plays.
10. Keep your hands off the players and coaches at all times.
11. Keep home plate, the pitcher's plate and the bases clean.
12. Get the recommended angle and distance on plays.
13. Back up your partner.
14. Keep your eye on the ball.
15. Use the energy necessary to make a call believable, but never embarrass a player.
16. Be alert to game situations.
17. Always strive to improve yourself.
18. Stay in shape.
19. Be pleasant and professional at all times.
20. Know the ballpark and ground rules.
21. Take pride in your work.
22. Avoid unnecessary conversation with the players and coaches.
23. Use preventive umpiring whenever possible.

DON'T . . .

1. Kid with the coaches, players, team personnel or fans at any time.
2. Call the pitch until it is caught or hits the ground behind the plate.
3. Make a verbal call when the batter obviously swings at and misses a pitch.
4. Second guess your partner at any time, on or off the field.
5. Make decisions too soon. Take a good look first to be sure the play is completed, then make the call.
6. Tell the coaches or players what to do or how to play their position.
7. Call the runner out (sell out) with the mask in your dominant hand. It might slip out of your hand and hit the runner or fielder making the play.
8. Let the coaches, players or team personnel be disrespectful. Be patient and tolerant but assertive when necessary.
9. Be doubtful. Always know what is going on.
10. Stand in a player's way.
11. Have rabbit ears. Ignore what they say or do in the stands.
12. Look for trouble.
13. Be overly technical. Use common sense.
14. Talk about anyone else, unless there is something good to say.
15. Go out on the field with a chip on your shoulder.
16. Use tobacco products in the vicinity of the playing field.
17. Locate the ball for the players or let on where the ball is.
18. Alibi to anyone at any time. It won't help.
19. Carry messages to your partner from a coach.
20. Allow the players to keep anything hanging out of their pockets when they bat.
21. Get lazy. No one respects or appreciates an umpire who doesn't hustle.

UNIFORM — EQUIPMENT

The appearance of officials is most important, for both the respect of players, coaches and spectators, as well as for comfort and safety. It is imperative that all umpires wear identical color combinations. The proper uniform for an umpire consists of a powder blue shirt (pullover style), heather gray or navy blue slacks and a navy blue fitted cap. With regard to slacks, the NFHS recommends either color; however, umpires should work with their state association to determine the color combinations approved for their state. If an undershirt is worn under the powder blue shirt, it shall be white and short sleeved. If a long-sleeve undershirt or turtleneck is worn, it shall not be exposed. Pullover style jackets or knit sweaters shall be navy blue. No patch other than the state association patch shall be worn on the uniform.

Equipment for the plate umpire should offer the best in protection, mobility and comfort. A mask with a throat protector is required in fast pitch and recommended in slow pitch. The inside-style chest protector and leg guards are strongly recommended in both fast pitch and slow pitch. Slacks should fit comfortably over leg guards. Shoes for the plate umpire should offer the maximum in protection with a hard shell or steel reinforced toe and steel or reinforced tongue. Soles should provide good traction. Shoes should be solid black with no white or colored markings. The plate and base umpire(s) should use a ball/strike indicator and plate brush. A ball bag(s) the color of the slacks is mandatory for the plate umpire. The fitted cap is mandatory and shall never be worn backwards. Black socks that are at least mid-calf length should be worn. A black belt with a small buckle completes the uniform requirements.

Umpire(s) should dress according to weather conditions and have additional or backup equipment at their disposal. Male umpires shall wear a protective cup. State associations may adopt other uniform options, as long it does not compromise umpire(s) safety and all umpires are dressed alike.

Part 2

Plate Mechanics

Plate mechanics begin with calling balls and strikes and end with any required movement by the umpire to complete other duties. This includes the elements of the stance, the set position, the pitch and movement from the plate when required. A plate umpire who keeps these elements in perspective has a better chance of having a solid game behind the plate. These elements are similar in both slow pitch and fast pitch. Attention to detail in these areas will make a better plate umpire.

A. Calling the Pitch in Slow Pitch:

Stance: The stance is the foundation of good plate mechanics. The elements of a good stance are as follows:

1. The umpire must set their feet with the heel of the foot closest to the batter in a straight line with the toe of the foot closest to the catcher. Do this by setting a foot behind the catcher first and squaring the shoulders to the outside front corner of the plate. Then bring in your foot behind the batter so the feet are in a heel-toe alignment, making sure your ear closest to the catcher is lined up with the inside corner. Both feet should be turned slightly outward so your knees are over your toes. On a right-handed batter, set your right foot first, then your left foot. On a left-handed batter, set the left foot first, then the right foot. This will provide the same stance on both a left-handed batter and a right-handed batter. The feet should be at least shoulder width apart or wider, if comfortable, keeping in mind that you will have to move when needed.

2. Umpires should position themselves so that they are not too close or too far from the catcher. Remember this rule of thumb: The umpire must see the complete plate and then the ball from the pitcher's hand to the catcher's glove or the ground as it passes through or out of the strike zone.

3. Rotating your head and eyes toward the pitcher will assist in seeing the ball from the pitcher's hand to the catcher's glove or the ground.

4. Be sure to bend at the knees, not at the waist. This allows the back to be as straight as possible with a slight tilt forward to bring the head into the proper position. This will reduce the pressure on the lower back and the top of the legs.

Set Position (PlayPic 1): The plate umpire assumes the set position to call balls and strikes. To be in a good set position the plate umpire should follow these guidelines:

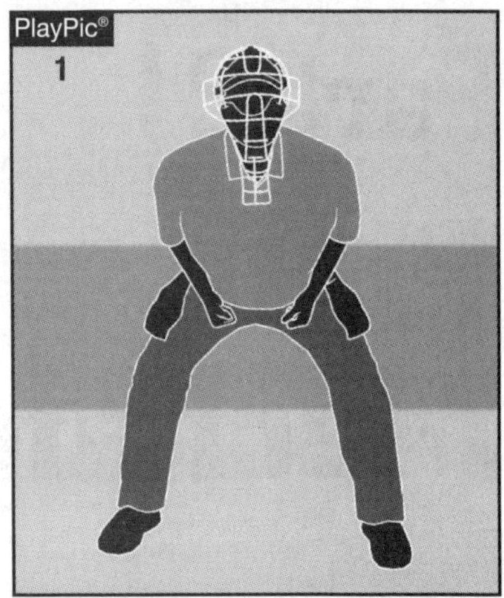

1. The umpire must start in the slot. The slot is defined as the position the umpire assumes prior to going set in which they are behind the catcher, slightly inside the inside corner of the plate with your ear closest to the catcher lined up with the inside corner, and outside the perimeter of the strike zone.

2. The umpire must have good pelvic alignment, referred to as GPA. This position is achieved when the umpire has the pelvis aligned with the outside front corner of the plate. This allows the umpire to look down and through the strike zone.

3. Set no lower than the top of the strike zone in relationship to the batter. The umpire's body should be locked in a stationary position to see the ball released from the pitcher's hand and travel all the way to the catcher's glove or the ground. Hands should be placed in a comfortable position in front of the body.

4. Drop to the set at the start of the pitch. In slow pitch, this is when the pitcher makes any motion with the ball after the required stop. Each pitcher is different and the time to go set can vary accordingly.

5. Be sure to bend at the knees, not at the waist. This allows the back to be as straight as possible with a slight tilt forward to bring the head into the proper position. This will reduce the pressure on the lower back and the top of the legs.

6. Being in the correct slot and set position on both sides of the plate gives the umpire an unobstructed view of the strike zone on every pitch from the same angle.

The Pitch: Calling the pitch is where a plate umpire puts the stance and set position to work. To call the pitch, the plate umpire should follow these guidelines:

1. To start the game or any time after the umpire has prevented a pitch from being delivered, the umpire should direct the pitcher to play ball. When holding up play, simply hold up the hand opposite the batter with your palm facing the pitcher. When the umpire is ready for the pitch, point at the pitcher and say "play" or "play ball." At this point, it is imperative that the umpire picks up the ball with the eyes while the ball is in the pitcher's hand.

2. The umpire then tracks the ball from the pitcher's hand to the catcher's glove or to the ground. Tracking the ball is the act of watching the ball from the pitcher's hand into the catcher's glove using a slight movement of the head guided by the nose. Tracking is not an exaggerated head movement or just an eye movement. It is a movement of the nose which simultaneously brings the head with the pitch as the eyes are locked on the ball.

3. Good timing is crucial when calling the pitch. After the ball is in the glove or hits the ground in slow pitch, make sure to pause, and then call the pitch.

4. The verbal call is always made from the down position. The strike call should be

elongated and made briskly and loudly. The umpire should then rise to an upright position without moving the feet and bring the right arm up to a 90-degree angle so the elbow can be seen with the umpire's peripheral vision. The fist should be closed with the palm facing the umpire's ear. A strong hammer adds certainty to the call. Any swinging strike should be a signal only (PlayPic 2).

5. In Slow Pitch on a called third strike, a 90-degree hammer is used with a louder verbal call. For further emphasis, verbalize the words "strike three."

6. Ball calls should be short and crisp and made in the down position. Use volume to indicate closeness of the pitch.

7. In Slow Pitch when the ball hits in front of the plate, hits the plate or hits the batter, the proper mechanic is a dead-ball signal followed by a verbal "ball."

8. The count should be given by the plate umpire anytime the next pitch could end the batters time at bat, anytime there has been a long delay in playing action or anytime it is requested. Signaling the count is done by raising both arms above the head indicating balls with consecutive fingers on the left hand and strikes with consecutive fingers on the right hand. Give both the number of balls and strikes every time the count is given. Rotate the hands, not the body, so everyone can see the count.

9. After each pitch step back, relax, reset and restart the process. This allows the umpire the time to refocus and reset for the next pitch.

B. Calling the Pitch in Fast Pitch:

Stance: The stance is the foundation of good plate mechanics. The elements of a good stance are as follows:

1. The umpire must set feet with the heel of the foot closest to the batter in a straight line with the toe of the foot closest to the catcher. Do this by setting the foot behind the catcher first and squaring the shoulders to the outside front corner of the plate. Then bring in the foot behind the batter so your feet are in a heel-toe alignment, making sure your ear closest to the catcher is lined up with the inside corner. Both feet should be turned slightly outward so the knees are over the toes. On a right-handed batter set the right foot first, then the left foot. On a left-handed batter, set the left foot first, then the right foot. This will provide the same stance on both a left-handed batter and a right-handed batter. The feet should be at least shoulder width apart or wider, if comfortable, keeping in mind that you will have to move when needed.

2. Umpires should position themselves so that they are not too close or too far from the catcher. Remember this rule of thumb: The umpire must see the complete plate and then the ball from the pitcher's hand to the catcher's glove or the ground as it passes through or out of the strike zone.

3. Rotating the umpire's head and eyes toward the pitcher will assist in seeing the ball from the pitcher's hand to the catcher's glove or the ground.

4. Be sure to bend at the knees, not at the waist. This allows the back to be as straight as possible with a slight tilt forward to bring the head into the proper position. This will reduce the pressure on the lower back and the top of the legs.

Set Position (PlayPics 3A and 3B): The plate umpire assumes the set position to call balls and strikes. To be in a good set position the plate umpire should follow these guidelines:

1. The umpire must start in the slot. The slot is defined as the position the umpire assumes prior to going set in which the umpire is behind the catcher, slightly inside the inside corner of the plate with ear closest to the catcher lined up with the inside corner, and outside the perimeter of the strike zone.

2. The umpire must have good pelvic alignment, referred to as GPA. This position is achieved when the umpire has the pelvis aligned with the outside front corner of the plate. This allows the umpire to look down and through the strike zone.

3. Set no lower than the top of the strike zone in relationship to the batter. The umpire's body should be locked in a stationary position to see the ball released from the pitcher's hand and travel all the way to the catcher's glove or the ground. Hands should be placed in a comfortable position in front of the body.

4. Drop to the set at the start of the pitch. In fast pitch, this is when the hands separate after the hands have been placed together. Each pitcher is different and the time to go set can vary accordingly.

5. Be sure to bend at the knees, not at the waist. This allows the back to be as straight as possible with a slight tilt forward to bring the head into the proper position. This will reduce the pressure on the lower back and the top of the legs.

6. Being in the correct slot and set position on both sides of the plate gives the umpire an unobstructed view of the strike zone on every pitch from the same angle.

Left-hand Slot

Right-hand Slot

The Pitch: Calling the pitch is where a plate umpire puts the stance and set position to work. To call the pitch, the plate umpire should follow these guidelines:

1. To start the game or any time after the umpire has prevented a pitch from being delivered, the umpire should direct the pitcher to play ball. When holding up play, simply hold up the hand opposite the batter with your palm facing the pitcher. When the umpire is ready for the pitch, point at the pitcher and say "play" or "play ball." At this point, it is imperative that the umpire pick up the ball with their eyes while the ball is in the pitcher's hand.

2. The umpire then tracks the ball from the pitcher's hand to the catcher's glove or to the ground. Tracking the ball is the act of watching the ball from the pitcher's hand into the catcher's glove using a slight movement of the head guided by the nose. Tracking is not an exaggerated head movement or just an eye movement. It is a movement of the nose which simultaneously brings the head with the pitch as the eyes are locked on the ball.

3. Good timing is crucial when calling the pitch. After the ball is in the glove or hits the ground make sure to pause, and then call the pitch.

4. The verbal call is always made from the down position. The strike call should be elongated and made briskly and loudly. The umpire should then rise to an upright position without moving the feet and bring the right arm up to a 90-degree angle so the elbow can be seen with the umpire's peripheral vision. The fist should be closed with the palm facing the umpire's ear. A strong hammer adds certainty to the call. Any swinging strike should be a signal only. (PlayPic 4)

5. In fast pitch on a called third strike, both a strong verbal call and signal should be given. For further emphasis, verbalize the words "strike three."

6. Ball calls should be short and crisp and made in the down position. Use volume to indicate closeness of the pitch.

7. On a foul tip, the umpire should rise and brush the fingers of the right hand over the left hand, at least shoulder high in front of the body followed by the strike signal.

8. The count should be given by the plate umpire anytime the next pitch could end the batters time at bat, anytime there has been a long delay in playing action or anytime it is requested. Signaling the count is done by raising both arms above the head indicating balls with consecutive fingers on the left hand and strikes with consecutive fingers on the right hand. Give both the number of balls and strikes every time the count is given. Rotate the hands, not the body, so everyone can see the count.

9. After each pitch step back, relax, reset and restart the process. This allows the umpire the time to refocus and reset for the next pitch.

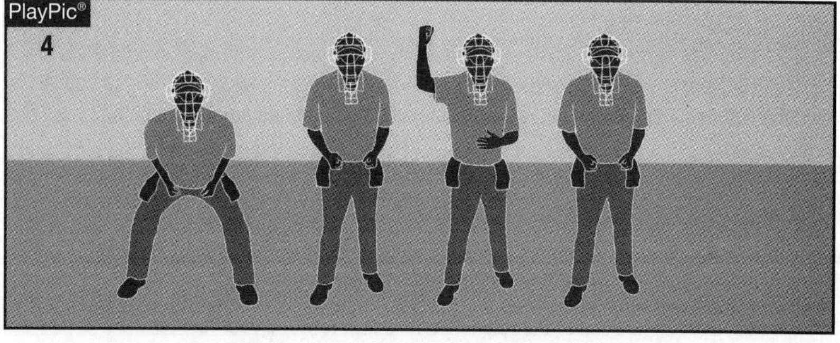

C. Movement from the Plate in Slow Pitch and Fast Pitch:

Movement: Good plate umpires realize that they are not only required to call balls and strikes, but must be able to move to cover other responsibilities. The plate umpire must be ready and able to move during the game.

   1. On a ball that eludes the catcher, a passed ball, a foul fly ball behind the catcher or a dropped third strike in fast pitch, the plate umpire should be ready to move to clear the catcher.

     a. Umpire movement is based on reading the shoulders of the catcher.

     b. On either a right- or left-handed batter, pivot and drop step to allow the catcher to take you to the ball.

     c. After the umpire has cleared the catcher, move to the next area of responsibility such as a possible catch of the foul fly ball, help on a throw to first base on the batter-runner, a play at third base, or the plate.

   2. On a batted ball with no runners on base or a single runner at first base, the plate umpire should always exit to the left of the catcher to trail the batter-runner, unless the play takes you elsewhere.

     a. Trail the batter-runner slightly inside the foul line approximately one-third of the way to first base to help the first-base umpire with a pulled foot, swiped tag or a bobbled ball.

     b. After trailing the batter-runner to first base, the umpire may need to move to the holding zone or third base.

     c. When moving to third base, move directly across the diamond to a location 90 degrees to the path of the runner, just short of the base the runner is trying to reach and a minimum of 10-12 feet from the base.

     d. When moving to the holding zone, move directly to an area in foul ground about halfway to third base and read the play.

   3. The plate umpire has fair/foul responsibility on ground balls near the foul line. Position yourself on the foul line:

     a. If the ball is foul, give the dead-ball signal and a verbal call of "foul" or "foul ball."

     b. If the ball is fair, point toward fair territory with the arm closest to fair ground; no verbal call is given.

   4. On fly balls to the outfield not near the foul line, move parallel to the flight of the ball to obtain a good angle to the catch versus straight at the fielder catching the ball.

     a. If the ball is caught, give an out signal and a verbal "out" call.

     b. If the play is very close but the ball is not caught, it is permissible to give a safe or no-catch signal if needed.

   5. On a fly ball to the outfield near the foul line when your partner does not turn their back, the plate umpire has fair/foul and catch/no catch responsibilities. When the ball is near the foul line with no runner at third base, move up that foul line to a position to see the ball.

     a. When the ball is close to the foul line and is touched, whether caught or not, the umpire must first give the ball status by pointing fair or foul.

     b. When the ball is close to the foul line and is first touched over fair territory point fair, and if the ball is not caught the point is followed by a strong fair-ball signal. If the ball is caught, give an out signal.

     c. When the ball is close to the foul line and is first touched over foul territory, point foul and if the ball is not caught, give a strong dead-ball signal and strong verbal call of "foul" or "foul ball." If the ball is caught, give an out signal.

    d. If the ball is near the foul line and lands in fair territory untouched, give a "fair ball" signal.

    e. If the ball is near the foul line and lands in foul territory untouched, give a dead-ball signal and verbal call of "foul" or "foul ball."

    6. When the ball is hit over the fence in fair territory, give a home run signal by raising the right arm above the head, fist closed and rotate the fist.

    a. The plate umpire should hustle to achieve the best angle and distance based on the scenario to see the ball clear the fence.

    b. The plate umpire should assume a position to watch the runners touch home plate in foul territory so they have all action in front of them.

    c. If the ball hits the ground before clearing the fence and then bounces over the fence, give the two-base award signal by raising the right arm above the head, hand open with two consecutive fingers extended and verbally call "two bases."

Movement to Third Base: Once the umpire has exited to the catcher's left, there are several situations where the umpire should move to third base:

    1. After going to the holding zone and a play develops at third base, move inside the diamond about two-thirds of the way to third base, to a minimum of 10-12 feet from the base, obtaining a 90-degree angle. Stop, read the play, then make the call.

    2. When exiting the catcher with a play immediately at third base, move up the foul line in fair territory to a minimum of 10-12 feet from the base, obtaining a 90-degree angle. Stop, read the play, then make the call.

Plays at Home Plate: There are specific mechanics used by the plate umpire when making calls at home plate.

    1. On throws from the outfield or the infield assume a position in foul ground, 90 degrees to the path of the runner, at a minimum of 10-12 feet from home plate in line with the outside deepest corner of the right-handed batter's box (MechaniGram 5). Adjust as needed to obtain an unobstructed view of the play. If the ball gets away from the catcher and goes behind you, move as the play dictates to get an unobstructed view. Avoid going inside the diamond except as a last resort.

    2. When returning to home plate from a play at third base and the ball is in foul ground, remain inside the diamond and move parallel to the base line, to a minimum of 10-12 feet from home plate, obtaining a 90-degree angle to the path of the runner.

    3. On a timing play when the runner touches the plate prior to the last out of the inning and the run will count, point to the plate emphatically and say "run counts" or "run scores."

    4. On a timing play where the runner does not touch the plate before the last out of the inning is made and the run will not count, say "run does not count" or "no run."

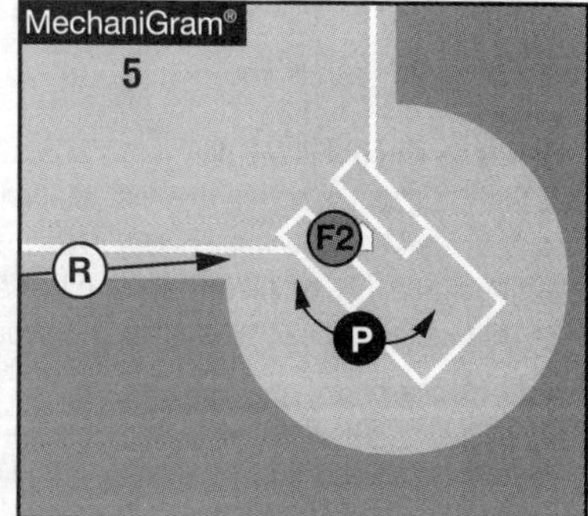

D. Difficult Situations:

Slow Pitch:

• Illegal Pitches: A slow pitch plate umpire will normally make more illegal pitch calls than a Fast Pitch plate umpire due to the differences in the pitching rule. An illegal pitch must be called when it becomes illegal by the plate or base umpire. To signal an illegal pitch raise the left arm horizontal with the fist closed and verbally say "illegal" or "illegal pitch" loud enough for the closest defensive player to hear you. In slow pitch, if the batter does not swing at the illegal pitch, it is ruled a ball. If the batter swings at the pitch, the illegal pitch is ignored and the result of the swing stands.

Fast Pitch:

1. Illegal Pitches/Catcher's Obstruction: When catcher's obstruction or an illegal pitch is called, the umpire should give the delayed dead-ball signal. Give the signal by extending the left arm straight out to the side of the body with the fist closed while verbalizing "obstruction" or "illegal pitch." The illegal pitch can be called by either umpire. The plate umpire calls the timing elements and stepping outside the 24-inch-width of the pitcher's plate. The base umpire is responsible for infractions involving the feet being in front or behind the pitcher's plate and a replant. The batter may swing at or hit an illegal pitch after it's been called. If the batter reaches first base safely and all runners advance at least one base, the illegal pitch is ignored and no option is given. If not, the head coach of the offended team is given the option of taking the result of the play, or having a ball awarded to the batter. If an illegal pitch hits a batter, the batter is awarded first base and all runners are advanced one base only if forced.

Catcher's obstruction: Is the act of a catcher that hinders or prevents the batter from striking at or hitting a pitched ball. If the batter reaches first base safely and all runners advance at least one base, the obstruction is canceled. All action as a result of the batted ball stands. No option is given. Once a runner has passed a base the runner is considered to have reached that base. If all runners, including the batter-runner do not advance at least one base, the head coach has the option of taking the result of the play, or enforcing obstruction by awarding the batter first base and advancing all runners if forced. If the catcher steps on, or in front of home plate without the ball and prevents the batter from hitting the ball, the umpire will call "dead ball." The batter is awarded first base and all runners are advanced one base, if forced. On a swing or attempted bunt, the catcher or any other fielder prevents the batter from hitting the ball, touches the batter or their bat with a runner on third base trying to score on a squeeze play or a steal, the ball is dead. The runner shall be awarded home plate and the batter shall be awarded first base on the obstruction. All other runners shall advance if forced.

2. Hit by Pitch: Kill the play as soon as the batter is hit, with a strong "dead ball" verbal call. Now review the action that just happened.

a. If the pitched ball was entirely in the batter's box, award the batter first base. No attempt to avoid being hit by the pitch is required.

b. If the pitched ball was entirely in the batter's box and the batter made an obvious attempt to get hit, call the pitch a "ball" or "strike" depending on the location of the pitch and the batter remains at the plate unless it is either ball four or strike three.

c. If the pitch was not entirely in the batter's box and the batter attempted to avoid getting hit, award the batter first base.

d. If the pitch was not entirely in the batter's box and the batter did not attempt to avoid getting hit, call the pitch a "ball" or "strike" depending on the location of the pitch and the batter remains at the plate unless it is either ball four or strike three.

e. If the pitch was not entirely in the batter's box and the batter made an obvious attempt to get hit, call the pitch a "ball" or "strike" depending on the location of the pitch and the batter remains at the plate unless it is either ball four or strike three.

3. Hitting the ball a second time: When a batted ball hits the bat a second time or hits the batter, a dead ball is declared using the dead-ball signal and a strong verbal call of "dead ball." While making the dead-ball call, review in your mind what you just saw. Then, ask yourself the question, "Did the second hit occur in fair or foul territory?" If the answer is foul territory, the ball is foul and a strike is called on the batter. If the ball is fair, the next question you need to ask yourself is whether the batter was in or out of the batter's box. If the batter was in the box, it is a foul ball and a strike is called on the batter. If the second hit occurred out of the batter's box, the batter is out. In each case give a strong dead-ball call and point to where the second hit took place. Then announce to all the result of the action "foul ball, strike on the batter" or "the batter is out." The base umpire should assist the plate umpire by making a dead-ball signal and a strong verbal call immediately, indicating only that there was a second hit. Remember, as a plate umpire take charge of this call and sell it.

4. Check Swing: When asking for help on a check swing, the umpire should step out from behind the plate to be visible to their partner, remove the mask, point to their partner and ask with a loud verbal "swing?" or "did they go?" Step back in behind the plate and give the count.

5. Batted ball off of a batter's foot:
   a. When the batter is in the batter's box:
      1. Raise both hands above the head and call "dead ball" to stop all action.
      2. Verbalize "foul ball."
   b. When the batter is out of the batter's box:
      1. Raise both hands above the head and call "dead ball" to stop all action.
      2. Point to the play, give an out signal and verbalize "batter is out."

6. Three-Foot Running Lane: A three-foot running lane violation is an example of an interference call. The plate umpire should:
   a. Give the dead-ball signal while giving a strong verbal "dead-ball" call.
   b. Point in the direction of where the interference occurred.
   c. Take charge and give a strong out call, sell the call.

7. Appeal at the Plate: If a runner misses home plate and the catcher misses the tag, the umpire should hesitate slightly to allow the players to finish the play, either the runner reaches to tag the plate or the catcher reaches to tag the runner. If no tag is made, the umpire should declare the runner safe. If a proper appeal play is made by the fielder, by either touching the runner or the plate with the ball prior to the runner touching the plate, the umpire should then declare the runner out. There are two reasons why this procedure is advocated:
   a. The umpire does not want to tip either team that the play may not be over; and
   b. A runner is assumed safe until put out. If a proper appeal is not made, the runner is safe.

E. General Responsibilities:

Infield Fly Situation: When an umpire signals to their partner that the infield fly rule is in effect, do so prior to the pitch. The signal is made by placing the right hand and arm across the chest with the hand over the heart. It is the plate umpire's responsibility to call the infield fly. When an infield fly is judged by the umpire:

1. The umpire should judge the infield fly when the ball reaches its highest point.

2. Give the infield fly signal by raising the right arm above the head with fist closed and verbalize "infield fly, the batter is out," or if near a line verbalize "infield fly if fair the batter is out."

3. When the infield fly is no longer in effect, simply tap the left forearm with the right hand to signal to your partner the infield fly has been removed.

Hold-Up Play: To hold up play on a right-handed batter, raise the right arm above the head with the palm open and facing the pitcher. On a left-handed batter raise the left arm above the head with the palm open and facing the pitcher.

Time-out — Suspension of Play: To suspend play raise both arms high above the head with palms facing the pitcher while moving out from behind the batter and catcher. If the pitcher has started the pitch, time-out should not be granted. If the batter steps out of the batter's box and the pitch is delivered, the pitch shall be called a "strike" regardless of its location.

Cleaning Home Plate or the Pitcher's Plate: If time has not been declared, call "time." Move to a position facing the backstop with your back to the field of play. Use your brush to clean the plate using short, crisp strokes.

Conferences: There are two types of conferences: offensive and defensive. It is the plate umpire's responsibility to document conferences.

1. Offensive Conferences:

a. An umpire should only allow one offensive conference per half-inning.

b. At the end of the conference, the umpire should notify the coach that the conference was the last offensive conference for that inning.

c. A coach who insists on having a second offensive conference during the same half-inning should be removed from the game.

2. Defensive Conferences:

a. Each team is permitted three defensive conferences during a seven-inning game.

b. All of the defensive conferences can take place during the same inning without removing the pitcher from the pitching position.

c. Umpires should not penalize an offensive team for having a conference while the defensive team is having a defensive conference provided the offensive team is ready to play when the defensive-charged conference is over. The same is true if the defensive team has a conference while the offensive team is having a charged conference.

d. Once the umpire instructs the team that is charged with the conference to play ball, both teams must immediately play ball or be in jeopardy of a conference being charged to them and enforcement of the appropriate penalty.

Ball Rotation: According to NFHS procedure, the current game ball is in play until such time as it goes out of play. However, if both game balls do not get into play during the first half of the first inning, the pitcher in the bottom half of the first inning must throw the unused ball.

　1. If both game balls have been used, the pitcher has a choice of which ball to use during that half of the inning.

　2. The pitcher cannot have both game balls for the purpose of making a choice.

　3. The pitcher may request another ball prior to the start of warmup pitches.

　4. The umpire should require the pitcher to relinquish possession of the ball and then put a replacement ball into the game. The umpire has sole authority to determine if a ball is playable or not.

Lineup Card Management: In order to prevent problems during the game, the plate umpire should keep an accurate lineup card throughout the game. Here are some suggestions to help properly manage the lineup card:

　1. Use a lineup card holder to protect each individual lineup.

　2. At the pregame conference with the coaches, inspect each card:

　　a. To see that all starters have the first initial, last name, number and positions listed.

　　b. To see that all substitutes have first initial, last name and numbers listed.

　　c. Count the players in the starting lineup to make sure they have the proper number of players. (i.e., fast pitch — 9 or 10 if the DP/FLEX is used, slow pitch — 10 or 11 if the EP is used).

　　d. In fast pitch, identify the DP's position to indicate that this is the only place in the batting order to which the FLEX may enter.

　　e. Return the card to the respective coaches for their final review.

　　f. Accept them as "official" when they are returned to you.

　3. During the game, record the following information on the lineup card:

　　a. Substitutions.

　　b. Re-entries.

　　c. Movement of the DP and FLEX in and out of the lineup.

　　d. Defensive conferences.

　　e. Offensive conferences.

　　f. Courtesy runners.

　　g. Any changes to the pitcher or catcher positions.

　4. In order to properly manage the lineup card, understand the principles of re-entry and substitutions as well as playing short-handed.

　5. Understand when a player is permitted to be added to the lineup card and what to do about an incorrect number or position on the lineup card.

　6. Managing the lineup card is an integral part of overall game management.

Part 3

The Base Umpire

Base Mechanics begin with the fundamentals of positioning, followed by timing, judgment, signals and a verbal call.

A. General Responsibilities:

Base Umpire Starting Positions Terminology: Language to describe where the starting positions are on the field, for example, first base line, rotated to second base, counter-rotated between first base and second base, and third base line. These positions are not X's on the field, they are general areas.

Some Specific Examples:
No R's on base:

Two-Umpire System:	BU — first base line
Three-Umpire System:	U1 — first base line
	U3 — third base line

R1 on first base:

Two-Umpire System:	BU — counter rotated between first base and second base
Three-Umpire System:	U1 — first base line
	U3 — rotated to second base

R1 on second base:

Two-Umpire SP System:	BU — counter rotated between first base and second base
Two-Umpire FP System:	BU — counter rotated between second base and third base
Three-Umpire System:	U1 — counter rotated between first base and second base
	U3 — third base line

R1 on third base, only:

Two-Umpire SP System:	BU — first base line
Two-Umpire FP System:	BU — counter rotated between second base and third base
Three-Umpire System:	U1 — first base line
	U3 — third base line

Starting Positions: In slow pitch with no runners on base or a runner on third base only, start on the foul line 18 – 21 feet behind the base and walk the line. Walk the line by taking one or two steps toward home plate, pushing off with your foot farthest from the foul line to move into fair territory when the ball is batted. Umpires should stay upright throughout the entire process to allow for quicker movement, smooth transition and maximize their field of view.

In fast pitch with no runners on base, start on the foul line 18 – 21 feet behind the base and walk the line. Walk the line by taking one or two steps toward home plate, pushing off with your foot farthest from the foul line to move into fair territory when the ball is batted. Umpires should stay upright throughout the entire process to allow for quicker movement, smooth transition and maximize their field of view.

When starting off the line or starting on the line with runners on base, the base umpire will take the "ready position or stance" prior to a pitch being delivered to the batter. Do this by:
a. Standing upright in a comfortable position, placing your feet at least shoulder width apart or wider to create a firm foundation.
b. Go to the ready position at the start of the pitch by leaning forward and placing your hands comfortably in front of your body in a position that allows you to move as the play dictates. This position transfers your body weight from your heels to the balls of your feet for better balance providing an athletic response much the same as a defensive player.
c. Rise from the ready position at the end of the pitch and be prepared to move as the situation dictates.
NOTE: Remember, the ready position is an athletic position, you should not be locked in place.

A counter rotated slow pitch base umpire between first base and second base in the two-umpire system, with no runner on second base, will take a starting position shading first base and off of or behind the Infielder. Anytime a runner is on second base the umpire will take a position shading the runner at second base and off of or behind the infielder. This positioning will allow the umpire to move to their primary position when the ball is put into play. Adjustments should and may be made based on the fielder's positions. Fielder's often position themselves several feet behind the baseline. This positioning starts the base umpire too deep to effectively move to their primary position either inside or outside the diamond. Therefore, an option available to the base umpire is to draw an imaginary line between the appropriate infielders. The umpire should make every effort not to take a position that puts them in the line of sight of a defender and a pitched ball to the batter. Furthermore, the base umpire that uses the imaginary line as a guide needs to have pre-pitched and be prepared for the inherent risk of being in a potential throwing lane and must be ready to immediately move parallel to the baseline and out of the throwing lane on any batted ball.

General Techniques on the Bases: Umpires must be students of the game in preparation for handling decisions on the bases. The game situation will include the presence of runner(s) on base(s), the number of outs and the count on the batter. These factors will dictate the base umpire's primary responsibility as a play develops and all should be a part of the umpires pre-pitch preparation prior to each pitch. The umpire's complete concentration, full energies and undivided attention is required from the first pitch to the last out. Work for the best angle and distance possible on all plays and do not let the players or coaches make the call. On a close play, sell the call; but on an obvious play use only a routine signal.

Whenever possible, stop to allow time to see the entire play before making a decision. See the play to its completion and give both a strong verbal call and a visual signal simultaneously. This will help timing and reduce the possibility of the dreaded "out/safe" call. On a ball that is hit to the outfield that could possibly be trapped, go out on it, even with runners on base. Remember to communicate with your partner(s). On home runs hit out of the park, know where and when the ball left the playing field.

Points Governing Decisions on the Bases: Base umpire decisions are governed by the game situation and the actions of offensive and defensive participants. The four elements of a play consist of:

1. Ball;
2. Base;
3. Offense;
4. Defense.

The base umpire must hustle to get into the correct position to see these elements come together before making a call. Umpires should say "safe" while giving the safe signal when a runner beats the ball to a base on a force-out attempt and likewise say "out" while giving an out signal when the ball beats the runner to the base. A good verbal call and strong signal should be given simultaneously. The volume of the voice should reflect the closeness of the play. If you think that you were blocked out of seeing the entire play and are asked to go for help then go to your partner for information to get the call correct. **Always make the call and then go for help, if needed.**

Going for Help: Always make the call based on the information you have and then go for help if needed due to a missing element of the play. Should you feel you were blocked out of seeing the entire play, go to your partner(s) without being asked or, if you are asked to go for help and you feel you may have not clearly seen one of the four elements of the play, go to your partner(s) for information to obtain the correct call.

Watching the Ball: Watching the ball aids a base umpire in reading where the play is likely to develop. The umpire must watch the ball as it is fielded on the infield while moving to the proper position for their primary call. Let the ball take you to the play, turning your head into the play as the four elements of the play come together, move to obtain, and maintain an unobstructed view, stop, read the play and make the call.

On batted balls to the outfield, the base umpire is required to pick up the ball and glance at the runner while hustling inside the diamond to button hook, at a minimum of 10-12 feet. Continue to alternate between the ball and the runner keeping all four elements in front of you. As the runner gets close to the base, change your focus to glancing at the ball and watching the runner to see the runner touch the base. Know where the ball is at all times; no live-ball play can be made on a batter, batter-runner or runner without the ball.

B. Base Calls:

Force Plays/Plays at First Base/Tag Plays: Tag plays, force plays and plays at first base require movement to the proper position to see the entire play.

1. On a routine out call (PlayPic 6), keep the feet at least shoulder-width apart and bring the body to an upright position. Raise the right arm to a 90-degree angle with the fist closed, so the elbow can be seen with peripheral vision. On a routine safe call (PlayPic 7), keep the feet at least shoulder-width apart and bring the body to an upright position while bringing the hands chest high with palms down. With forearms parallel to the ground, extend the arms straight out keeping palms down.

2. On a play at first base, with no runner on base and a ground ball to the infield, without taking eyes off the ball, move inside the foul line to a position that is 90 degrees to the throw but no farther than a 45-degree angle from the foul line and no closer than 18 feet from the base. When the runner is out on a very close play, use the sell-out signal (PlayPic 8). This signal is nothing more than simulating a throw by a fielder. Move your feet as if you were fielding

a ground ball and give the signal and a strong "out" call simultaneously. When the runner is safe on a very close play, use the "sell-safe" signal. This signal is made by stepping toward the play, giving an emphatic "safe" signal and a strong "safe" call simultaneously. Finish the call by bringing the rear foot forward and squaring up to the play.

3. With a runner at first base and a ground ball to the infield for a possible double play, make two movements from the starting position. When the play goes to second base, take one or two parallel steps toward second base to watch the play and push off with the right foot and make the call while moving parallel to the baseline toward first base. Without taking eyes off the play, let the ball turn your head to the play at first base. Stop, read the play and then make the call.

4. On a tag play, take a position 90 degrees to the path of the runner just short of the base the runner is trying to reach at a depth of 10-12 feet from the play. All four elements will be in front of the umpire. As the play develops, move to obtain and maintain an unobstructed view, read the play, hesitate slightly and then make the call.

Swipe Tag/Pulled Foot: Adjustment from primary position: Once the umpire has obtained the best angle to see the play, further actions may dictate the need to move. Sometimes movement from the primary position will help the umpire obtain or maintain an unobstructed view of the play.

1. After obtaining 90 degrees to the path of the runner on a tag play, the umpire should adjust as necessary.

2. After obtaining an angle on the play at first base and the throw takes the defense off the base for a possible swipe tag, move with the play to keep an unobstructed view. A slight adjustment will put the umpire in a position to see the possible tag. Once the umpire sees the tag, the umpire should point with the left hand and say "tag" followed by an "out" call and signal.

3. After obtaining an angle on the play at first base and there is a possible pulled foot, move with the play to keep an unobstructed view. A slight adjustment can put the umpire in a better position to see the foot off the base. If the fielder pulls a foot, point with the left hand and say "off the base" and give a strong "safe" call and signal.

Inside/Outside Theory: The inside/outside theory is simple.

1. If the ball is hit inside the diamond, stay outside the diamond;

2. If the ball is hit outside the infield, pick up the ball and glance at the runner while you hustle inside the infield. This allows the four elements to be in front of you: the ball, the base, the offense and the defense.

3. For the purpose of the inside/outside theory, the umpire will consider the diamond as the area of the infield inside the baselines forming a diamond shape. The infield is defined as that portion of the field that is normally covered by the infielders.

4. The key to the inside/outside theory is movement, and the key to movement to inside the diamond is the button hook. When moving from the starting position toward the infield, concentrate on your runner responsibility. Alternate between watching the ball and glancing at the runner. Once inside the diamond at a minimum of 10-12 feet, plant the right foot and pivot into the play, watching the runner touch the base. Move parallel with the runner to the next base or return to the previous base obtaining your 90-degree angle for a possible tag play.

5. When the ball stays inside the diamond, the umpire should stay outside the diamond. This allows the umpire to keep the four elements in view while gaining the proper angle and distance to make a call.

Fly Ball Coverage: There are times a base umpire needs to go to the outfield for fly ball coverage. When going out on a fly ball, the angle the umpire obtains is very important.

1. When going to the outfield, the umpire should verbally communicate with their partner(s), using phrases such as "one umpire," "two umpire" or "going."

2. When going to the outfield, move for an angle parallel to the flight of the ball as opposed to running directly at the fielder attempting to make the catch. This allows a better view of the catch or no catch. Read the fielder so that you are stopped and set to see the play. Stop, read the play and make the call by signaling either "out" for a catch or "safe" for no catch. Once the call is made, let the ball turn you back to the infield to observe additional plays. Remain in the outfield and do not come back to the infield until all play has ceased.

3. When going out on fly balls near the foul line, stay near the foul line. You are responsible for fair or foul and catch or no catch. Position yourself near the foul line, and if foul, signal by raising the hands over the head and give a verbal call of "foul" or "foul ball." If the ball is fair, point toward fair territory with the arm closest to fair ground.

4. When the ball is close to the foul line and is touched, whether caught or not, the umpire must first give the ball status by pointing fair or foul.

5. When the ball is first touched over fair territory, point fair and if the ball is not caught the point is followed by a strong fair ball signal. If the ball is caught, an out signal is given. When the ball is first touched over foul territory, point foul and if the ball is not caught give a strong dead-ball signal and strong verbal call of "foul" or "foul ball." If the ball is caught, give an "out" signal.

C. Difficult Situations:

Live-Ball Running Violations: There are violations by runners that require a signal and a verbal call when they occur, while allowing the ball to remain live.

1. Running out of the base path to avoid a tag:
   - Point at the runner with the left hand and loudly verbalize "out of the base path ... out" while giving the out signal.
   - Let the play continue.
2. Passing a runner:
   - Point at the runner who passed their teammate and loudly verbalize "out" while giving the out signal.
   - Let the play continue.

Rundowns: When a player is caught in a rundown, it is important that the umpire(s) responsible for the coverage move(s) to get the best perspective of both ends of the play. Most rundowns are covered by only one umpire.

1. Stay approximately 12-15 feet from the rundown and move parallel to the baseline.
2. Know where the ball is at all times.
3. Move quickly toward and around the play to achieve the best angle as the tag is applied.
4. Be alert for obstruction or interference.

When covering rundowns with two umpires, each umpire should take a position at their end of the rundown. This is referred to as "bracketing." When bracketing, one umpire should be outside the diamond and the other umpire should remain inside the diamond whenever possible.

For example, in a two-umpire system, if the runner is between first base and second base, the plate umpire should take the trail position closest to first base. The base umpire should take the lead position at second base. The plate umpire should be inside the diamond while the base umpire should be outside the diamond.

If the runner is between second base and third base, the plate umpire should take the lead position closest to third base inside the diamond, while the base umpire takes the trail position closest to second base outside the diamond.

If the rundown is between third base and home plate, the plate umpire will take the lead position nearest home plate outside the diamond, while the base umpire takes the trail position nearest third base inside the diamond.

In all cases, communication is a must. When two umpires are covering a rundown, the umpire with a clear unobstructed view of the tag should make the call.

To prevent both umpires from making a call, eye contact is essential prior to the call being made.

Interference: To indicate that interference has occurred the umpire should:

1. Step forward while giving a strong dead ball signal while emphatically calling "dead ball."
2. Point to the interference then give a strong out signal and a verbal "out" call.

Obstruction: The base umpire should immediately:

1. Give the delayed dead ball signal and verbally say "obstruction." The signal need not be held throughout the play, but just long enough for it to be seen.
2. If the obstructed runner is put out prior to reaching the base(s) that would have been reached had there been no obstruction, the umpire shall call "time" and award the obstructed runner and all other runners, the base(s) they would have reached had there been no obstruction.
3. When catcher's obstruction occurs, the plate umpire shall give the delayed dead ball signal and verbalize "catcher's obstruction."
4. When the play becomes dead, make the proper obstruction award. Be prepared to explain the ruling.

Collision: Contact between defensive and offensive players does not necessarily mean that obstruction or interference occurred. The field is laid out in such a manner that it puts the defensive and offensive players on a collision course. Thorough knowledge of interference and obstruction rules and their application will assist in making a prompt and accurate decision. Consider the following:

1. Did the offensive player alter direction in a way to draw contact with the defensive player in an attempt to draw an obstruction call?
2. Did the defensive player alter an attempt to field the ball to draw an interference call?
3. Could the defensive player actually make a play?
4. Did the defensive player have possession of the ball? Thorough knowledge of interference and obstruction rules and their application will assist in making a prompt and accurate decision.

Helping on Fly Balls in Foul Territory Between Home and First or Third Base:

It is permissible for the base umpires to assist the plate umpire on fly balls in foul territory when the base umpire starts on either foul line with no runner responsibilities and the plate umpire has an obstructed view of the fly ball. Reminder: this is the plate umpire's call unless the base umpire turns their back to make the call.

Part 4

Signals

An umpire's primary method of communicating is through hand or full body signals. Signals are the language of umpires. High school umpires must use this language precisely and appropriately.

Concepts
- Initiated from set position
- Visible — up, out, and away from body
- Structured
- Clear, distinct and meaningful
- Informative
- Dignified
- Timed (calculated)
- Convey strength, confidence, and authority

Philosophy

Umpires are communicators, and signals are how umpires communicate. You must use the prescribed signals to be a good, effective umpire. The universal language of umpiring is body language, and the words of this language are signals. Signals are a form of sign language. In sign language, only the hands are used. In signal language, the whole body is used. Signal language is designed to be understood immediately by anyone at any ballpark.

Signals initiate from a set position. To increase the visibility of a signal, come to a full standing position, without moving the feet (moving the feet distracts from and weakens the impending message of the signal), before executing a signal. Signals are designed to be given up or away from the body for the express purpose of being seen.

Once seen, a signal must be immediately understood. That allows for little to no variance in signal structure except for sell outs and called third strikes. Along with established, precise structure, a signal must be timed appropriate to the play, convey strength, confidence and authority, while held long enough to manifest conviction. A hammer, in signals that use a hammer, is the culmination of the power of the signal. Display the hammer long enough to convey its strength and do not unclench the fist until the arm is brought down. Any movement while giving a signal is always forward, at the play, and the signal is completed by bringing the arms and hands back into the body before moving to the next position.

Signals should never be squandered. The less a signal is seen the more effective it is when used. If there is no play, a call or signal is not needed. Do not draw attention to yourself by overusing, misusing or needlessly using any signal. Conversely any time there is a play made on a runner by the defense with the ball, a decision and signal should be made regardless of how obvious the call appears to the umpire. Except for the infield fly, there is no need to echo a partner's call.

Out — Extend an arm straight up with an open palm. Bring the forearm slightly forward while clenching it into a fist (hammer). The upper arm and forearm should both be at a 90-degree angle. Verbally call "out" if appropriate. Control the other arm by pulling it into the midsection of the body or against the body.

Punch Out — Use this signal to sell an out when you are too close to the play to do a full overhand out, if a play warrants more than a routine out but less than a full overhand out, or as a full-fledged sell out. A variety of punch-out techniques can be used so long as they embody the essential concepts of signals. To maintain visibility, a punch out should be at least shoulder height. To use a punch out that brings you no closer to the play, step back with the one foot and punch forward with the same arm (right or left) as the foot you stepped back with. The initial stepping back is overshadowed and compensated for by the strength and forward trust of the punch.

Overhand Out — While moving at the play, maintain dignity and control of the body and eyes on the play throughout the signal. Bring the right or left arm high above the head as in a throwing motion and bring it down toward the play with force while making a fist. A verbal call of "out" (usually drawn out- ooouuutt) accompanies the signal typically starting when the arm is directly overhead and finishing with the thrown fist. End in a balanced position facing the play. Some individuality is allowed with this signal so long as you don't make yourself the center of attention.

Safe, No Catch, No Tag — Bring both arms into the chest at shoulder level then immediately pop and hold this signal by extending both arms straight out horizontally with the palms down. Do not have your hands in fists. Do not allow the extended arms to snap back in front of your body. Finish the signal with a controlled release of the arms back into the body. Do not just drop them before moving to the next position.

Sell Safe — Bring both arms into the chest at shoulder level then immediately take a forward step at the play as you pop and hold this signal by extending both arms straight out horizontally with the palms down. Loudly call "safe." Do not allow the extended arms to snap back in front of your body. Finish the signal by bringing the back foot forward, even with the front one along with a controlled release of the arms back into the body.

Dead Ball, Foul Ball, No Pitch, Time — Raise both arms straight up with palms forward. Arms should be at about a 35- to 40-degree angle from the body. Verbally call "dead ball," "foul ball," "time," "no pitch." If the call is "foul ball" and the ball is close to the line, the feet should be straddling the line. When the plate umpire signals no pitch, the signal may be accompanied by sideward movement out from behind the plate for better visibility.

Fair Ball — Extend the arm closest to the field horizontally at shoulder height and point to fair ground, with either open hand palm forward or a finger. Do not make a verbal call. Do not point across the body. If the ball is close to the line, the feet should be straddling the line.

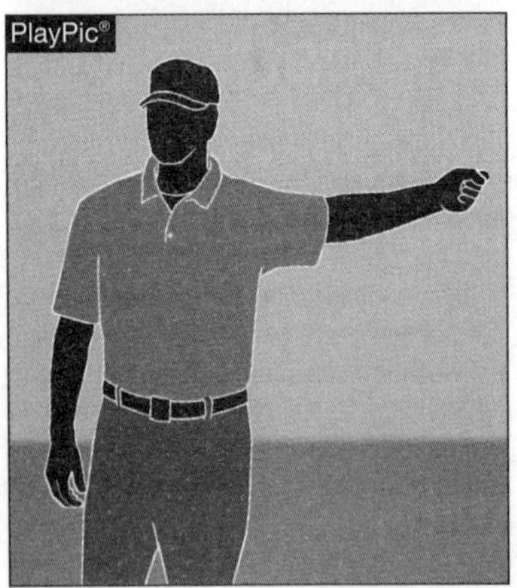

Delayed Dead Ball — Extend the left arm straight out at shoulder height, parallel to the ground. The hand is in a fist with the fingers of the fist facing forward or facing toward the ground.

Infield Fly — Fully extend an arm above the head with the hand in a clenched fist. Verbalize "infield fly, the batter is out." If the ball is close to a line verbalize "infield fly, the batter is out, if fair."

The plate umpire is responsible for making this call. If the plate umpire does not make the call (forgets or is not certain of the call) and a base umpire, after eye contact communication with the plate umpire, is certain the ball is an infield fly; the base umpire may make the call.

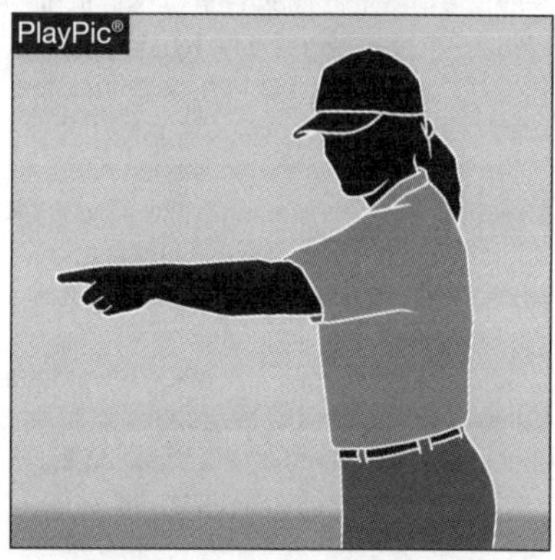

Point — Usually the left arm extended straight out at the play or player. Only the index finger is extended on the hand. The other arm should be under control in close to the body.

Use the point to indicate an abnormality in a play (i.e., a tag, a missed tag, a pulled foot, a swing attempt) or to identify a player who committed a violation. The point signal may be accompanied with a brief verbal explanation of the abnormality then is followed by another signal; either an "out," "safe" or "strike."

Home Run — Fully extend a fist high above the head and making a circling motion, counter clockwise, with the fist and arm at the elbow.

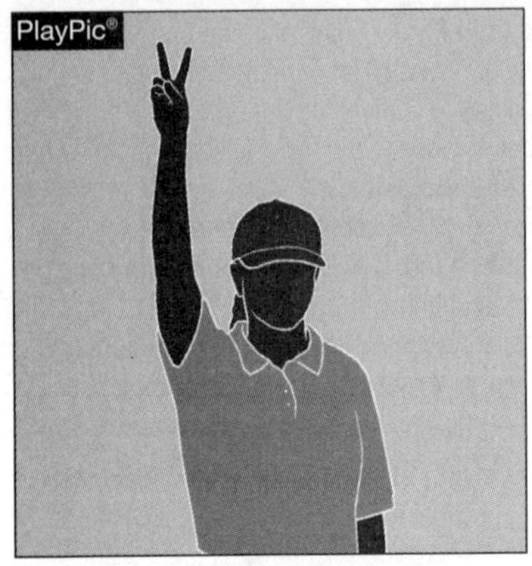

Double — Fully extend an arm above the head with the index and middle finger showing on the hand. Do not circle the arm.

Ejection — While facing the person to be ejected, step back with one foot to open the body and allow it to turn away from the person. Bring an arm with the index finger extended up across the body and point skyward. The arm should be at a 45-degree angle to the body. You will be facing away from the ejected person. It is imperative when making this signal that no aggressive move, real or perceived, is made toward the person being ejected. The signal should be moderately animated after increasing the physical distance between the umpire and the ejected person as needed. Remember to always maintain a calm demeanor and not allow the ejection to appear like an emotional decision. This signal does not have to be exact, but it must be clearly understood that someone has been ejected.

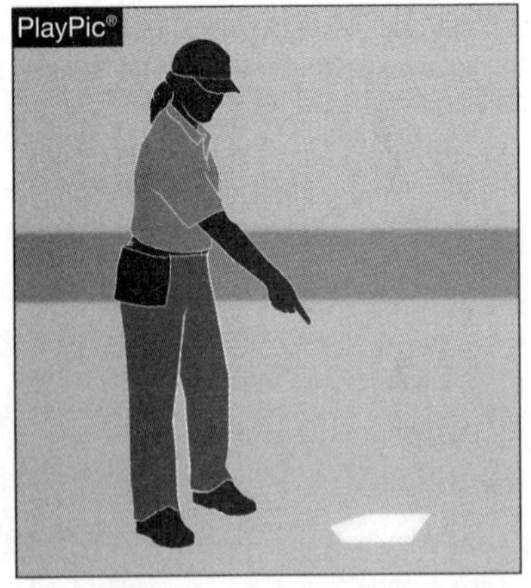

The Run Scores — Stand at the plate and emphatically point down at the plate while saying "the run scores" or "score the run." Establish eye contact with the scorer while signaling and make sure the run goes up on the scoreboard. If necessary, use a deliberate pumping motion with the arm while pointing at the plate and repeat "the run scores." Only used when there is possible doubt if the run scored on the third out of the inning.

The Run Does Not Score — Stand at the plate. Raise both arms above the head like a foul ball signal. Cross the arms back and forth (not too quickly) while saying "no run" or "the run does not score." Establish eye contact with the scorer while signaling. Watch the scoreboard to make sure a run is not recorded. Only used when there is possible doubt if the run scored on the third out of the inning.

Play Ball — With an arm extended toward the pitcher, the umpire may use a beckoning motion with an open hand, a pointing motion with an open hand or a pointing motion with one or two fingers extended to indicate the ball is in play. The signal may be accompanied with the verbal call "play ball." The verbal call may be used without any signal.

Do Not Pitch — Either arm of the plate umpire extended straight out directly at the pitcher with the hand open and the palm of the hand facing the pitcher. Use the hand opposite the batter to give this signal better visibility. Do not move from behind the plate.

Strike — The verbal call of "strike" is made in the down/set position and is followed by the signal, which is made in the "up" position. Do not move the feet during the signal. The right arm is extended straight up with an open palm then brought slightly forward while clenching the hand into a fist (hammer). The right upper arm and forearm should be at a 90-degree angle. Control the left arm by pulling it into the midsection of the body or against the body. The signal is finished by bringing the right arm back into the body before stepping back or moving the feet.

Swinging Strike — Should not be verbalized but should be clearly signaled. If strike three, verbalize a simple "three" loud enough for the catcher and batter to hear while signaling the strike call to insure both are aware the third strike has been called in case of a dropped third strike. Do not show up the batter who is swinging at pitches. In case the swing is questionable but ruled a swing by the plate umpire, with the hand closest to the batter point at the batter and verbalize "yes, yes, you did swing" or "swing" and signal strike. Under no circumstances should a pitch ruled a strike be changed to a ball. If no swing is ruled by the plate umpire and the action is questionable, but the pitch is in the strike zone a called strike should be enunciated. If no swing is ruled by the plate umpire and the action is questionable, verbalize "ball." Be prepared for a request for help when all action has stopped. Unless you are certain the situation does not call for it, request help from your base umpire if asked to do so. If in doubt of a swing/no swing ask for help as soon as the playing action allows. Live with the call.

Called Third Strike — A called third strike signal differs from a called strike one or strike two signal because it is not only a strike but is also an out. A more demonstrative signal and additional emphasis is always used for a called third strike. The normal verbal for a strike should be given in the down position with a second verbal given with the signal to indicate this is the third strike. Individuality is allowed with this signal. A popular style is the bow-and-arrow signal. The feet may move while making the signal, but the eyes must stay focused in the plate area and the body be under control.

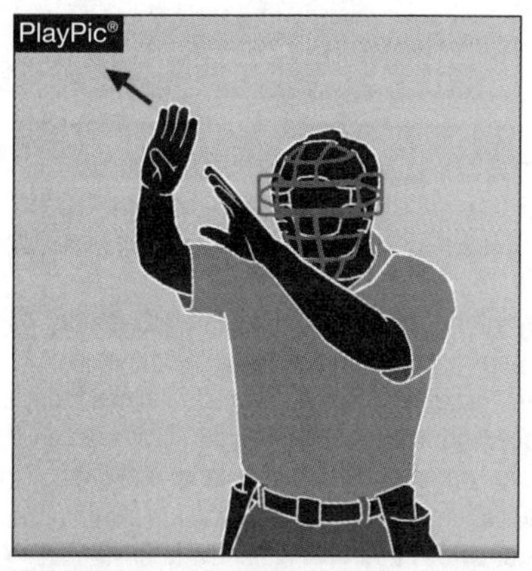

Foul Tip — The signal should be used every time the ball is a foul tip. Bring the left hand in front of your body, shoulder height or higher, with the palm or back of the hand facing you. With an upward motion, brush or tap the fingers of the left hand with the fingers of the right hand. This signal is always followed by a standard strike signal.

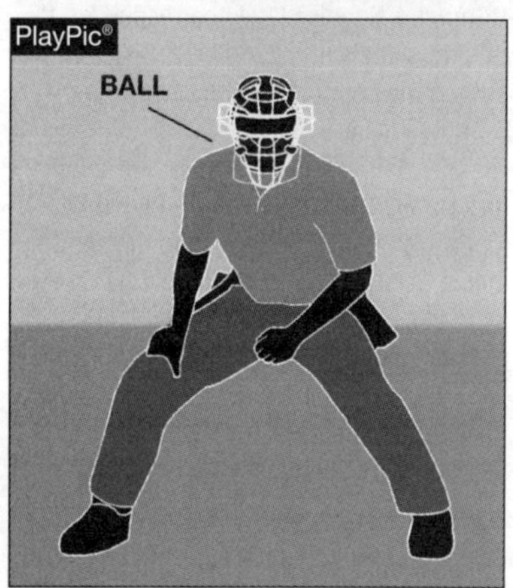

Ball — Remain locked in the normal down position while vocalizing "ball." Use volume to indicate closeness of the pitch. Stand up after the verbal call is made and back away from the catcher.

Count — Raise both arms up, in front of the body so that your fingers are above your eyes. Balls are shown with the fingers of the left hand. Strikes are shown with the fingers of the right hand. Consecutive fingers should be used in displaying the count. A verbal call may accompany the signal and, if used, should be "two balls, two strikes." Do not say "two and two," or "22." The count is given to the pitcher and held long enough for any other player to see it. The hands should be rotated or turned to increase visibility.

Umpire-to-Umpire Signals

Concepts
- Visible to partners
- Structured
- Used consistently
- Acknowledged
- Low or close to body

Philosophy

Whereas standard signals are used to convey information to everyone in the ballpark, umpire-to-umpire signals are meant to convey information between umpires. It does not matter if anyone other than an umpire sees them, however, no one else needs to see them besides other umpires. Because of that difference from standard signals that are given up and away from the body, umpire-to-umpire signals are given lower and closer into the body.

Those signals are vital to good crew communication; they establish an alliance within the crew, and it is crucial to good umpiring that the crew use them consistently. To ensure an unbroken flow of communication, most umpire-to-umpire signals should be responded to with the same or appropriate signal. Umpire-to-umpire signals are standardized so that any umpire working with any other umpire can understand the communication. Hence, there is room for little to no variation in the signals used or how they are displayed.

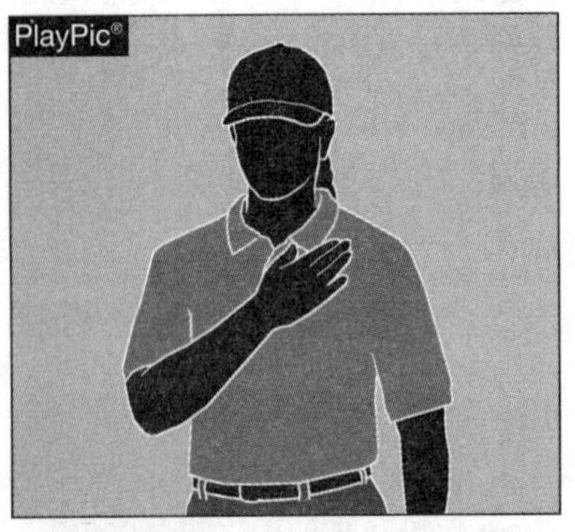

Infield Fly Situation is On — A hand, palm open, on the chest opposite to the hand being used, indicates the infield fly situation is in effect.

The infield fly signal should be initiated by the plate umpire just prior to the batter stepping in the box. Each base umpire should acknowledge, to the plate umpire, by returning the same signal. The signal should be given before every batter when an infield fly situation is possible.

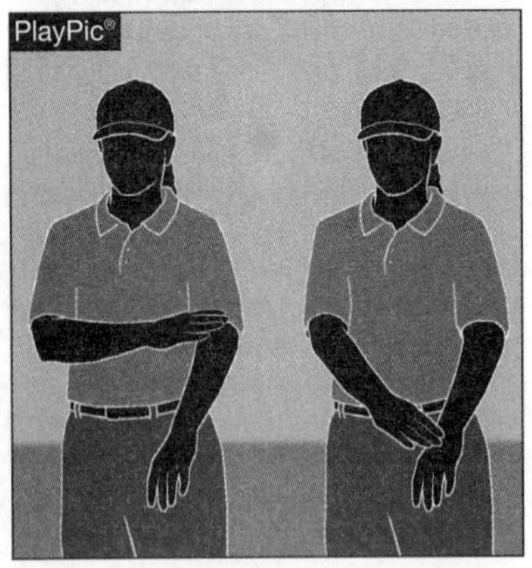

Infield Fly Situation is Off or Not On — A hand used in a wiping motion on the forearm from the elbow to the wrist indicates the infield fly situation is no longer in effect. When the infield fly rule is no longer in effect because there are two outs or, any time there are runners on at least first and second and there are two outs.

Part 5

One-Umpire System

The One-Umpire System is being used in many areas of the nation today, mostly in slow pitch. It is not recommended and should be used only when necessity demands.

Most softball authorities believe that when only one umpire is assigned to a game, the best location for the umpire prior to each pitch is behind home plate.

Single umpiring is a difficult job that takes a tremendous amount of hustle, alertness and keen anticipation. The theory of "angle over distance" and keeping your head on a swivel are paramount when working this system.

The umpire's starting position for each pitch should be from behind home plate. This is the best position for calling balls and strikes, and fair and foul balls. It also enables the umpire to have a clear view of the complete playing field.

On each batted ball or play that develops, the umpire must move from behind the plate and into the infield to obtain the best position possible for any play that develops. A key to help anticipate the play is to watch the feet of the outfielder making a throw, as fielders will step in the direction the throw will be made.

It's important that umpires keep their eyes on the ball; this is especially important when umpiring alone. In some situations, this is almost impossible. The umpire must make the call and still see if the runner coming home touched the plate before the out was made. When this happens, there is the possibility of the ball being dropped or bobbled on the tag. As soon as it is determined whether the runner scored or not, turn back to the tag play to be sure the ball was retained by the fielder.

Try to position yourself as close as possible on all play situations, especially tag plays. With no other runners on base, make sure all calls are made from inside the diamond.

If there is a play at home plate, position yourself near the back of the right-hand batter's box at a 90-degree angle to the runner. Then adjust your position to allow an unobstructed view of the play. It is important to get close to the play to obtain the best angle and be able to see the ball, the base runner and defensive player. Not only is this important to make the calls, but also to watch runners tag the bases.

On situations where a call is made at a base and a subsequent play develops at another base, the umpire should make sure to watch the ball so as not to be hit with a thrown ball.

Movement to cover the other bases is based on judgment. Hustle to the best position possible to make a call. If the ball is live when a runner is on base, such as after a base hit, the umpire should call "time" when the ball is held by a player in the infield area and in the umpire's opinion, all play has ceased.

There is no excuse for calling a play from behind or just in front of the plate. When the ball is hit the umpire should move out from behind home plate and toward the pitching circle, unless the first play is developing at home, where they can read the play and adjust as needed to obtain the best angle and distance possible. In the following diagrams, the starting position for the plate umpire is designated as "P." Movement for each situation is then depicted as "A through D."

GROUND BALL

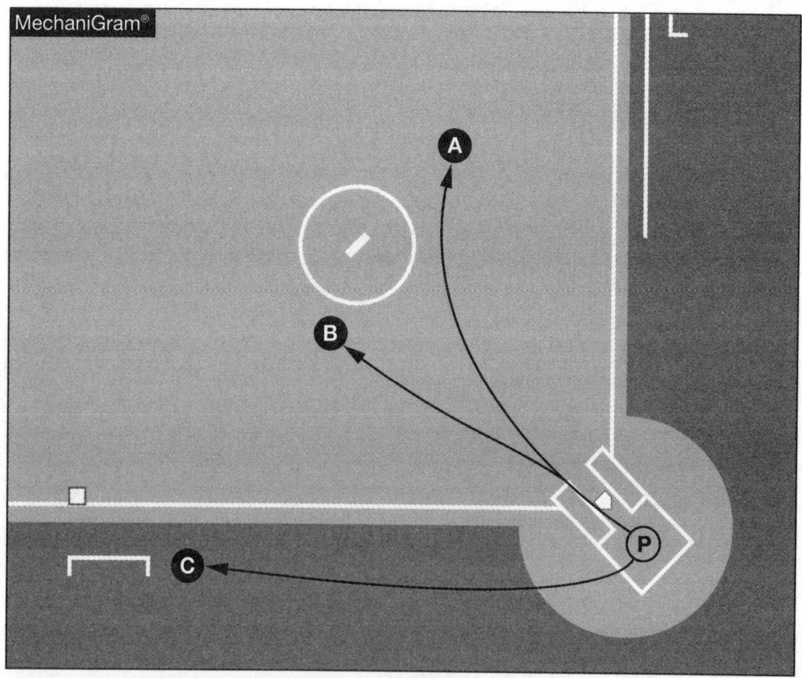

A. No runners on. Play at first base. Move up the line toward first base, get the best angle and distance. Stop, read the play and make the call.

B. Runner on first base or second base only, or runners on first and second base. Move out from behind the plate toward the middle of diamond and read the play. Be prepared for a subsequent throw to take you to your next play. Be prepared for any additional plays by returning to the middle of the diamond. In every situation, remember to call time when all action ceases.

C. Bases loaded hit to the infield. Move from behind the plate and read the play. Move to get the best possible angle and distance.

FLY BALL

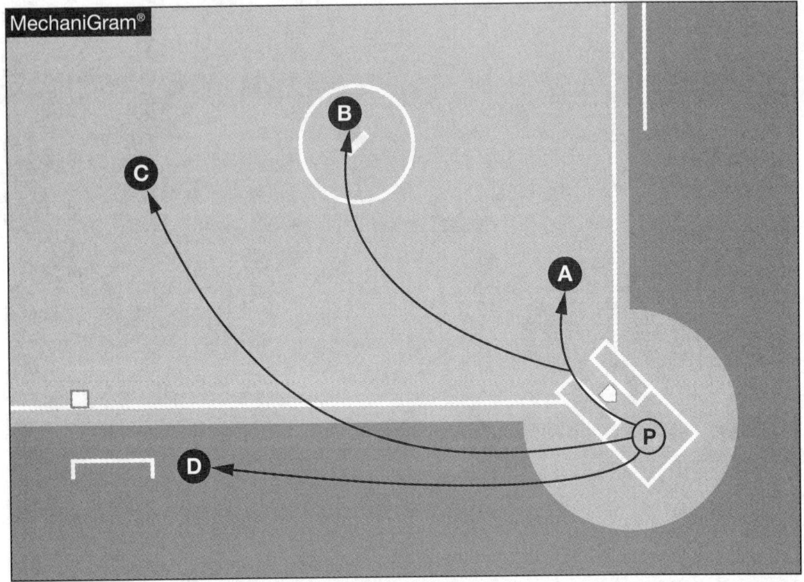

A. No runners. Fly ball to the infield or outfield and not near the foul line. Move out from behind the plate and focus on the ball. Move to obtain an angle that is parallel to the flight of the ball to see the catch/no catch. Stop, read the play and make the call.

B. Runner on first base. Move to the best angle possible to see the catch/no catch. Once the ball is touched glance at first base to see the runner tag-up. Be prepared to move to the best angle and distance possible should the runner advance to second base. Stop, read the play and make the call.

C. Runners on first and second or second base only. Move to a possible call at third or to foul territory ahead of the lead runner for a possible play at home if necessary after the catch. Responsible for watching all runners tag up. Focus on the lead runner but glance at all runners to insure they properly tag up. Read the fielder then move to get the best angle and distance possible. Be prepared to move to the next play when necessary, moving to the best angle and distance possible. Stop, read the play and make the call.

D. Runners on second and third or first and third or bases loaded. Responsible for watching all runners tag up. Focus on the lead runner but glance at all runners to insure they properly tag up. Read the fielder then move to get the best angle and distance possible. Be prepared to move to the next play when necessary, moving to the best angle and distance possible. Stop, read the play and make the call.

NOTE: On all fly ball situations where the ball is near the foul line, the umpire must stay on the foul line to determine whether the ball is fair or foul — then move into the infield to pick up runners and plays.

NO RUNNER(S) ON BASE

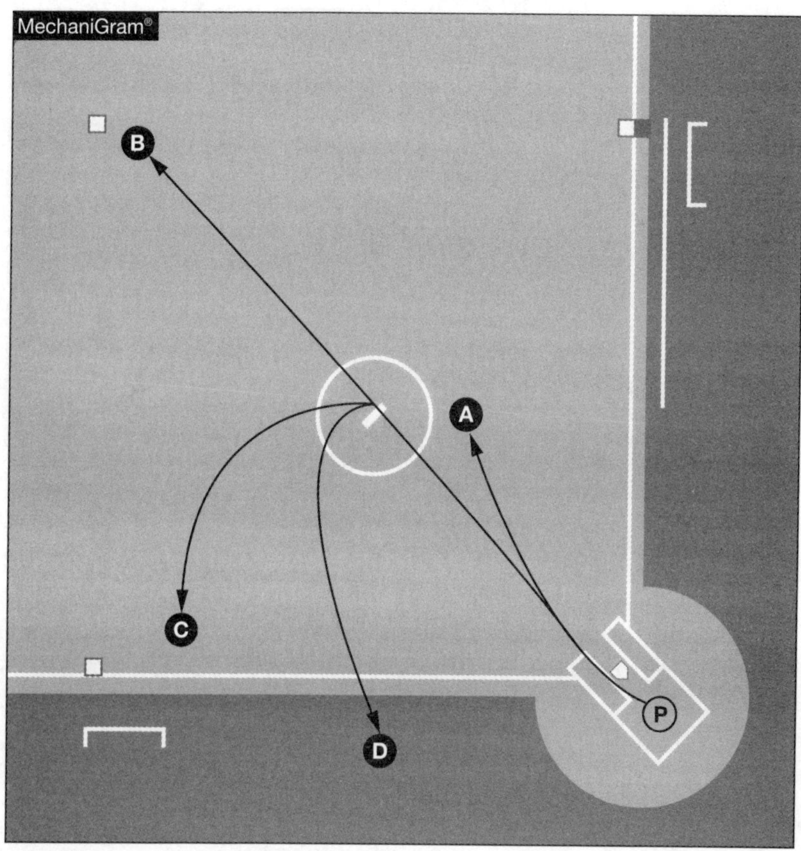

A. Single.
B. Double.
C. Triple.
D. Home run.
NOTE: On all base hit situations, the umpire must watch the runner touch bases and be aware of position of the ball.

BETWEEN INNING MECHANICS

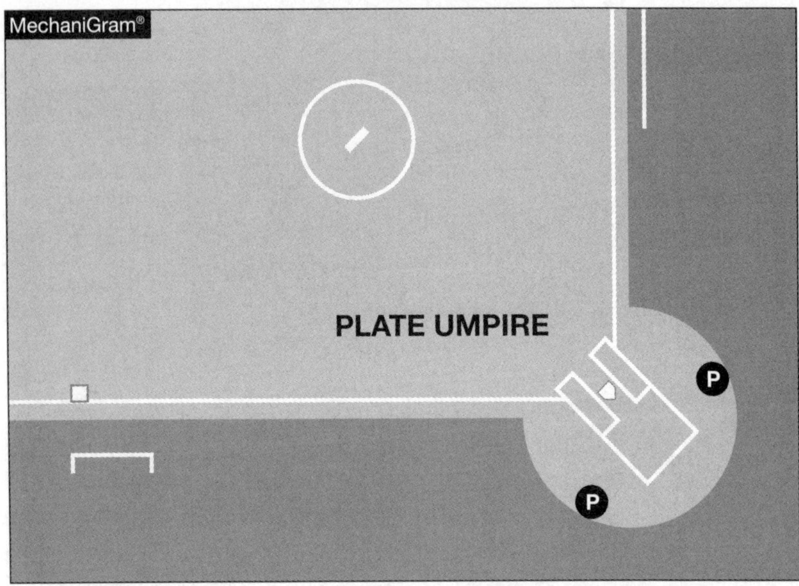

The plate umpire shall take a position on the first-base line extended facing the field when that team is coming to bat and the third-base line extended facing the field when that team is coming to bat.

Part 6

Two-Umpire System

- **Plate Umpire Responsibilities**
- **Plate Umpire Coverage**
- **Base Umpire Responsibilities**
- **Base Umpire Coverage**
- **Fly Ball Coverage**
- **Fly Ball Tag-up Responsibilities**
- **Between-Inning Mechanics**

Umpires must know where they would like to be on any given play and why one position is more desirable than another. There can be a lot of different situations because of the action, so it's best to apply the essential concepts of mechanics while figuring out the best way of obtaining the best position.

The Two-Umpire System is now standard for most games. With its use, 90 percent of the situations that will ordinarily arise may be adequately covered. Two umpires, working as a team for any period of time, can cover their plays with ease, be in the right place at the right time, and perform mechanics so smoothly that players and spectators are unconscious of their presence until the play has been made.

Plate Umpire Responsibilities

Although the first job of the plate umpire (P) is to call balls and strikes, they should be prepared to take a share of the base plays. The lead runner, if there is more than one on the bases, is the plate umpire's responsibility. To do the job properly, the plate umpire must go to the "holding zone" in foul territory between home and third base, then immediately pick up the lead runner, and prepare to make the call on the runner, whether it is at third base or the plate. If there are two runners on base and the next batter hits the ball for an extra base hit which will score the lead runner without a play, the plate umpire pays little attention other than noting (from the holding zone) that the runner touched third base and the plate.

Attention is then directed to the second runner and the play that may be made. An umpire should only move from the holding zone to cover a developing play, if there is no play the umpire should stay in the holding zone and observe the action from there. With no runners on base, or a runner on first base only trail the batter-runner near the first base line, unless the ball takes you elsewhere. Observe other plays as much as possible to be in a position to offer the base umpire help on an element of a play when asked.

Plate Umpire Coverage
- Calling balls and strikes;
- Illegal pitches covering F1's hands and outside the 24-inch width of the pitchers plate;
- Determining if the ball was legally or illegally batted;
- Checked swings;
- Fair/foul;
- Catch/no catch;
- A bunted ball when players converge (interference/obstruction);
- All plays on lead runners (except for the first play in the infield) at third base and any play at the plate;
- Interference/obstruction;
- Observing lead runners touch third base and home;
- Infield fly;
- Tag-ups as detailed below;
- All plays and tag-ups when the base umpire chases a fly ball.

Base Umpire Responsibilities
The base umpire (B) meanwhile ascertains that all runners touch second base and first base and takes whatever plays are made at first base and second base, and any play made on the last runner to third base. If the batter-runner advances as far as third base on the hit, and a play is made, it is the base umpire's call. Although each umpire has equal authority to call leaving a base too soon on the pitch, the base umpire is the most likely to rule on this infraction.

There are four times a base umpire will make a call at third base:
1. On the batter-runner on a triple with no runners on base.
2. On the last runner into third base.
3. On a lone runner on fly ball advancement.
4. On any return throw from the plate area or a throw toward the plate that is cut-off by a player.
Note: When there is a throw to home to make a play on a runner the plate umpire must position themselves to rule on that play. After this play, or if the ball is cut-off on it's way to home and then returned to third base to make a play on another runner the base umpire should cover this play.

Base Umpire Coverage
- Runners leaving base early on the pitch;
- Illegal pitches covering F1's feet;
- Help for the plate umpire when asked on checked swings;

- Runners stealing bases;
- Pickoff attempts;
- All plays at and runners touching first base and second base;
- The first play in the infield at any base;
- Plays at third base in one of the four situations listed above;
- Tag-up responsibilities as detailed below;
- Interference/obstruction;
- Fair/foul and catch/no catch when chasing a fly ball.

Fly Ball Coverage

In the two-umpire system, the plate umpire rules fair/foul and catch/no catch on all fly balls unless the base umpire chases the fly ball. Once the base umpire turns their back to go to the outfield they take fair/foul and catch/no catch responsibilities. If the ball is hit near the first base foul line with no runners on base it is acceptable for the base umpire to chase this fly ball, as they are able to rule on fair/foul as well as catch/no catch. This situation also has no runners on base so the plate umpire would only have responsibility for plays on the batter-runner. The base umpire should never chase a ball near the third base foul line or one near the first base foul line with runners on base, as they do not have the ability to obtain the proper position to rule fair/foul in these situations. With a runner on base, the base umpire could chase a ball hit toward the center of the field if it seems like it would be a difficult call for the plate umpire. Prior to chasing, the base umpire should evaluate the situation, especially with multiple runners on base. When the base umpire chases, they leave the plate umpire with all runner responsibilities. If bases were loaded, that would amount to one umpire covering three tag-ups as well as the potential of four possible plays. A quick evaluation should be conducted to determine whether the plate umpire can cover the fly ball acceptably, allowing both umpires to rule on tag-ups and possible plays, or if the base umpire will better serve the crew chasing the fly ball and leaving all other responsibilities to the plate umpire.

Fly Ball Tag-up Responsibilities - Fast and Slow Pitch: The following table shows the umpires' tag-up responsibilities under the following situations:

Runner(s) Location(s)	Base Umpire	Plate Umpire
Runner at 1B Only	R1 at 1B	N/A
Runner at 2B Only	R1 at 2B	N/A
Runner at 3B Only	N/A	R1 at 3B
Runner at 1B & 2B Only	R2 at 1B	R1 at 2B
Runner at 2B & 3B Only	R2 at 2B	R1 at 3B
Runner at 1B & 3B Only	R2 at 1B	R1 at 3B
Bases Loaded	R2 at 2B & R3 at 1B	R1 at 3B

NOTE: These tag-up procedures should be followed at all times, unless there is communication between both umpires. These responsibilities are covered in the duties listed on the following pages.

BETWEEN-INNING MECHANICS

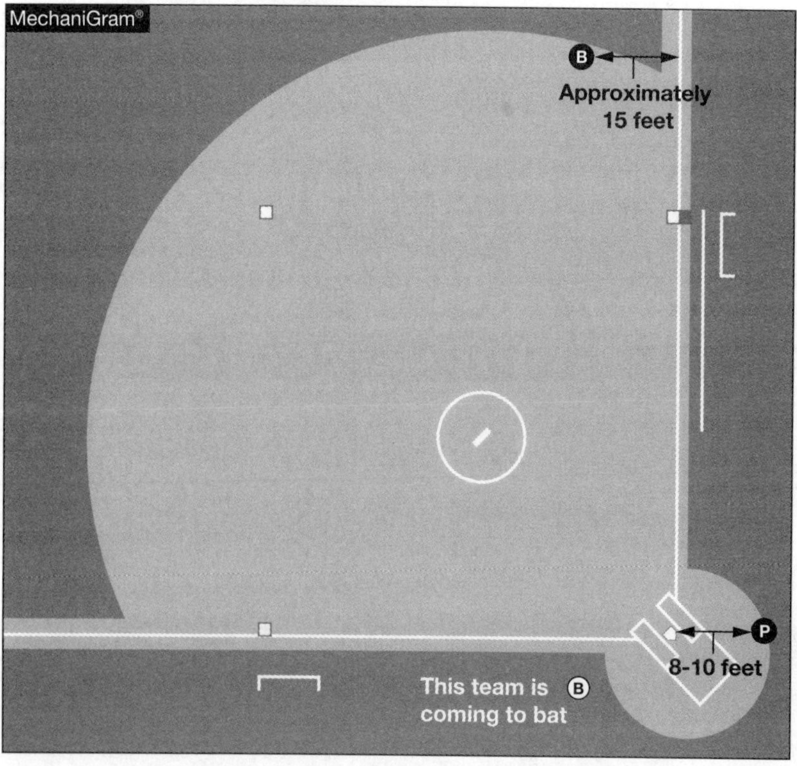

Plate: Facing the team that is coming to bat. About 8-10 feet from the line on a perpendicular line from where the foul line meets the plate.

Base: Facing the plate no more than about 15 feet off the foul line at approximately where the grass starts in front of the outfielders.

Two-Umpire System

Part 6.1

No Runners on Base

- Ground Ball in the Infield

- Base Hit to the Outfield

- Fly Ball to the Outfield, Ball Is Caught, B Does Not Chase

- Fly Ball to the Outfield, Ball is Not Caught, B Does Not Chase

- Fly Ball to Right Field, B Chases

- Bunt or Bouncing Ball Fielded in Front of the Plate

GROUND BALL IN THE INFIELD

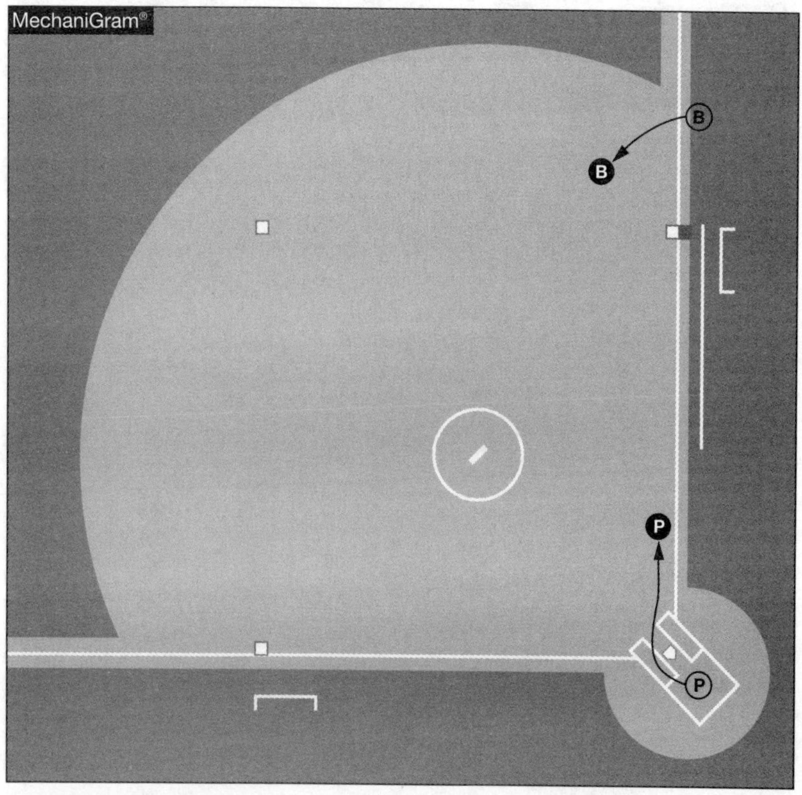

P: Trail the batter-runner no more than one-third of the way to first base in fair territory and read the play. Responsible for any play at the plate.

B: Step into fair territory, at an angle 90 degrees to the path of the throw, but no more than a 45-degree angle from the foul line and let the ball take you to the play. Responsible for any play at first base, second base or third base.

BASE HIT TO THE OUTFIELD

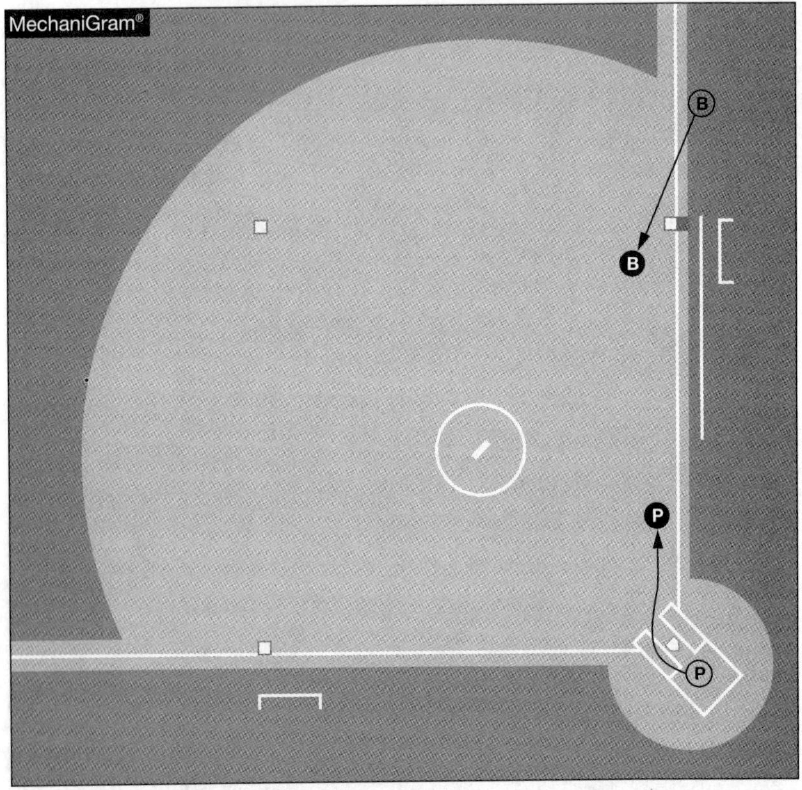

P: Trail the batter-runner no more than one-third of the way to first base in fair territory, unless the play takes you elsewhere, and read the play. As the runner approaches second base, move to the holding zone halfway to third base in foul ground to an area where you have an unobstructed view of all four elements and read the play. Responsible for any play at the plate.

B: Pick up the ball and glance at the runner as you hustle inside the diamond to button hook at a minimum depth of 10-12 feet. Continue to alternate between the ball and glancing at the runner keeping all four elements in front of you. Be prepared to move parallel to the baseline staying ahead of the runner. Responsible for any play at first base, second base or third base.

FLY BALL TO THE OUTFIELD, BALL IS CAUGHT, B DOES NOT CHASE

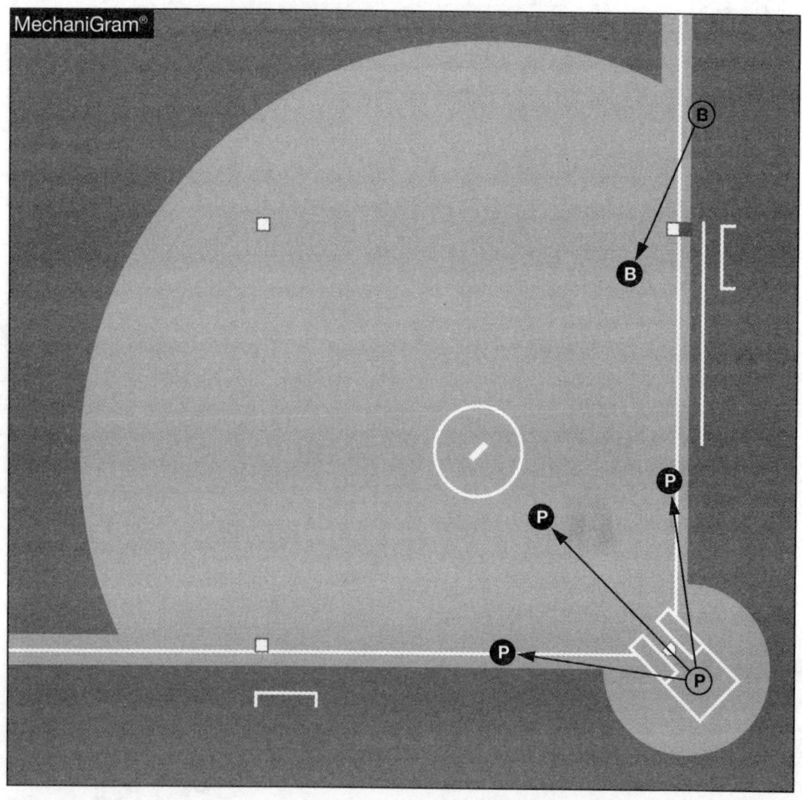

P: Move out from behind the plate to get the best angle and distance possible. As the runner approaches second base, move toward the holding zone halfway to third in foul ground to an area where you have an unobstructed view of all four elements and read the play. Responsible for fair/foul, catch/no catch and any play at the plate.

B: Pick up the ball and glance at the runner while hustling inside the diamond to button hook at a minimum depth of 10-12 feet. Continue to alternate between the ball and glancing at the runner keeping all four elements in front of you. Be prepared to move parallel to the baseline staying ahead of the runner. Responsible for any play at first base, second base or third base.

FLY BALL TO THE OUTFIELD, BALL IS NOT CAUGHT, B DOES NOT CHASE

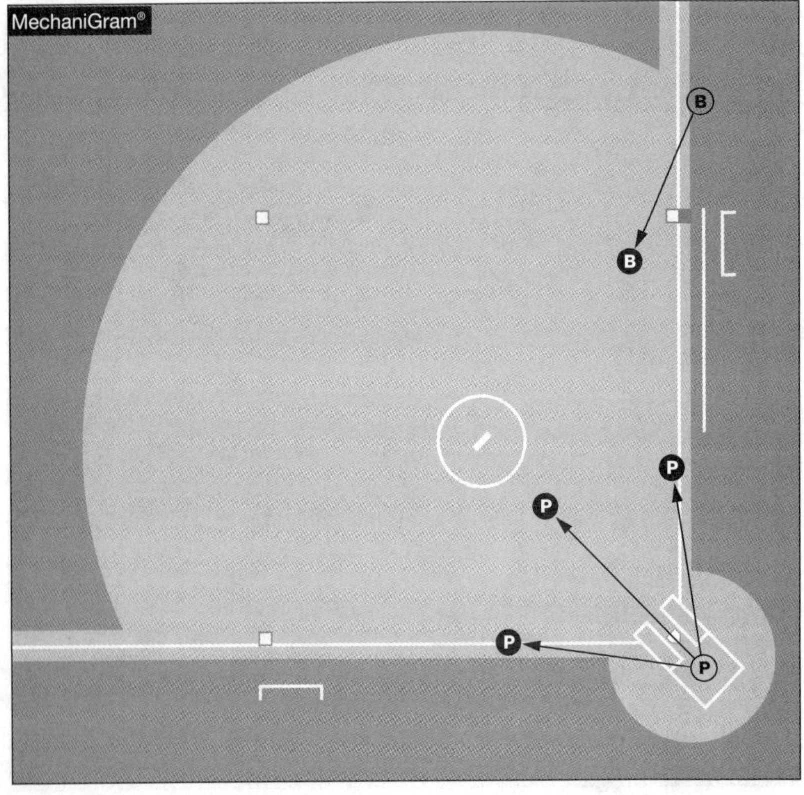

P: Move out from behind the plate to get the best angle and distance possible. As the runner approaches second base, move toward the holding zone halfway to third in foul ground to an area where you have an unobstructed view of all four elements and read the play. Responsible for fair/foul, catch/no catch and any play at the plate.

B: Pick up the ball and glance at the runner while hustling inside the diamond to button hook at a minimum depth of 10-12 feet. Continue to alternate between the ball and glancing at the runner keeping all four elements in front of you. Be prepared to move parallel to the baseline staying ahead of the runner. Responsible for any play at first base, second base or third base.

FLY BALL TO RIGHT FIELD, B CHASES

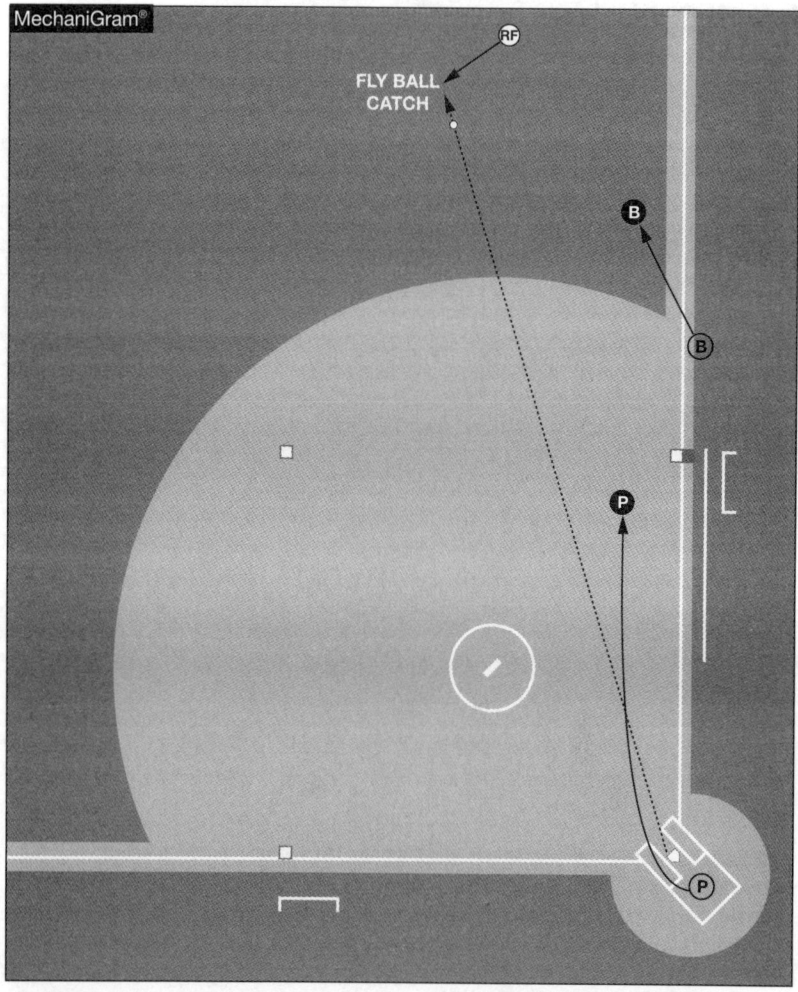

P: Trial the batter-runner then move to the best angle and distance (no closer than 18 feet) for a possible play at first base. Be prepared to move parallel with the batter-runner. Responsible for any play made on the batter-runner.

B: Move parallel to the ball facing the fielder and stop just prior to the fielder making the catch. Watch the play, come to a stop and make an out signal while facing the fielder. Do not turn around and face the diamond to make the signal. Let the ball turn you back toward the infield and observe all playing action. Return to infield when the play is completed. Responsible for fair/foul, catch/no catch.

BUNT OR BOUNCING BALL FIELDED IN FRONT OF THE PLATE

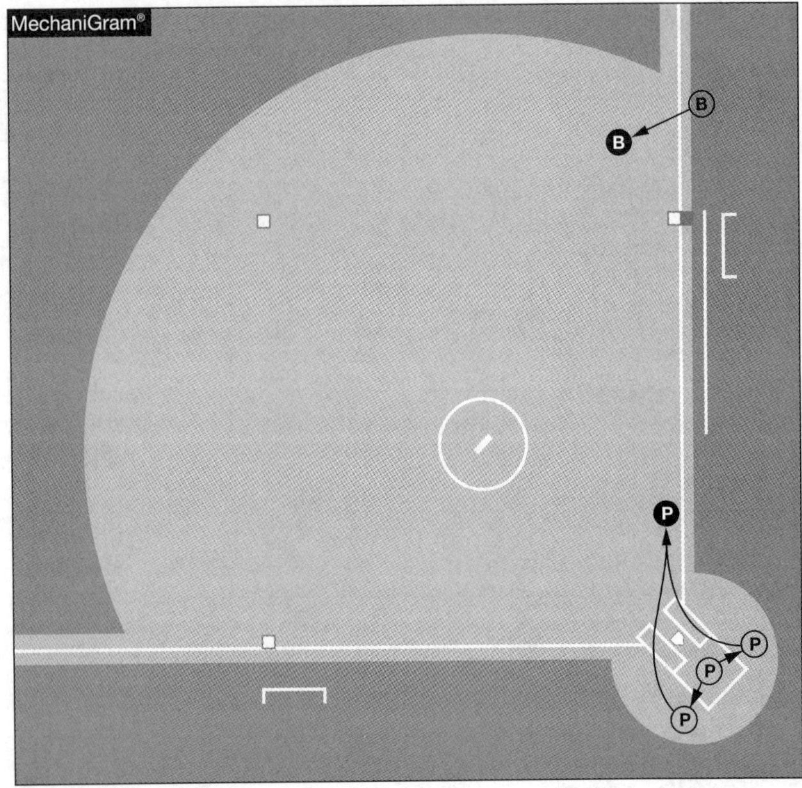

P: Move as required to view first or third baseline to rule the ball fair or foul as necessary. If the ball is fair, clear the catcher and trail the batter-runner no more than one-third of the way to first base. Be prepared to rule on a swipe tag up to the running lane. Observe the remainder of the play to offer an opinion of a swipe tag or pulled foot if requested by base umpire. Be alert for running lane interference and rule immediately if interference occurs. Responsible for any play at the plate.

B: Step into fair territory, in this case at a 45-degree angle from the foul line, and let the ball take you to the play. Responsible for any play at first base, second base or third base.

Two-Umpire System

Part 6.2

Runner on First Base

- ◆ Ground Ball in the Infield

- ◆ Base Hit to the Outfield

- ◆ Fly Ball to the Outfield, Ball is Caught, B Does Not Chase

- ◆ Fly Ball to the Outfield, Ball is Not Caught, B Does Not Chase

- ◆ Pickoff Throw By Catcher to First Base

- ◆ Batter Bunts, Play at Second or First

- ◆ Steal Attempt

GROUND BALL IN THE INFIELD

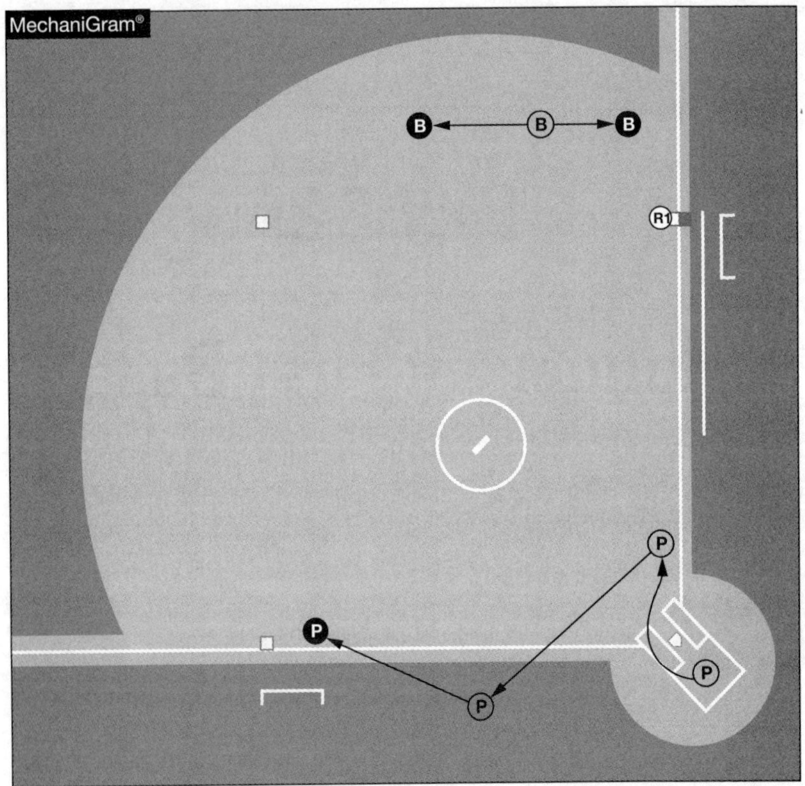

P: Trail the batter-runner no more than one-third of the way to first base in fair territory and read the play. As the lead runner approaches second base, move toward the holding zone halfway to third in foul ground, unless a play develops at third base. When a play develops at third base on the lead runner, move toward third base to first obtain the proper angle, then close your distance working to get an unobstructed view of the play and to obtain a final calling distance of 10-12 feet from the play. Remember, as the four elements come together; stop, read the play and make the call. Responsible for a subsequent throw on the lead runner (R1) at third base and any play at the plate.

B: Let the ball take you to the play, obtaining the best angle and distance possible. Responsible for any play at first base, second base and the last runner (batter-runner) to third base.

BASE HIT TO THE OUTFIELD

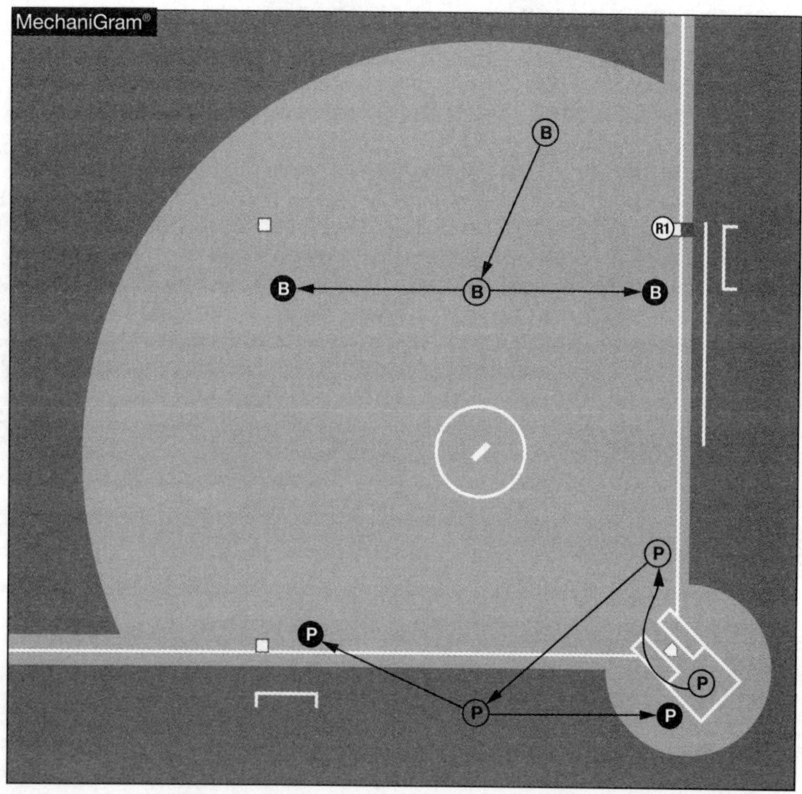

P: Trail the batter-runner no more than one-third of the way to first base in fair territory and read the play. As the lead runner (R1) approaches second base, move toward the holding zone halfway to third in foul ground, unless a play develops at third base. When a play develops at third base on the lead runner, move toward third base to first obtain the proper angle, then close your distance working to get an unobstructed view of the play and to obtain a final calling distance of 10-12 feet from the play. Remember, as the four elements come together, stop, read the play and make the call. Responsible for any play on the lead runner (R1) at third base and any play at the plate

B: Pick up the ball and glance at the runner while hustling inside the diamond to button hook at a minimum depth of 10-12 feet. Continue to alternate between the ball and glancing at the runners keeping all four elements in front of you. Be prepared to move parallel to the baseline staying ahead of the runner. Responsible for any play at first, second base and the last runner (batter-runner) into third base.

FLY BALL TO THE OUTFIELD, BALL IS CAUGHT, B DOES NOT CHASE

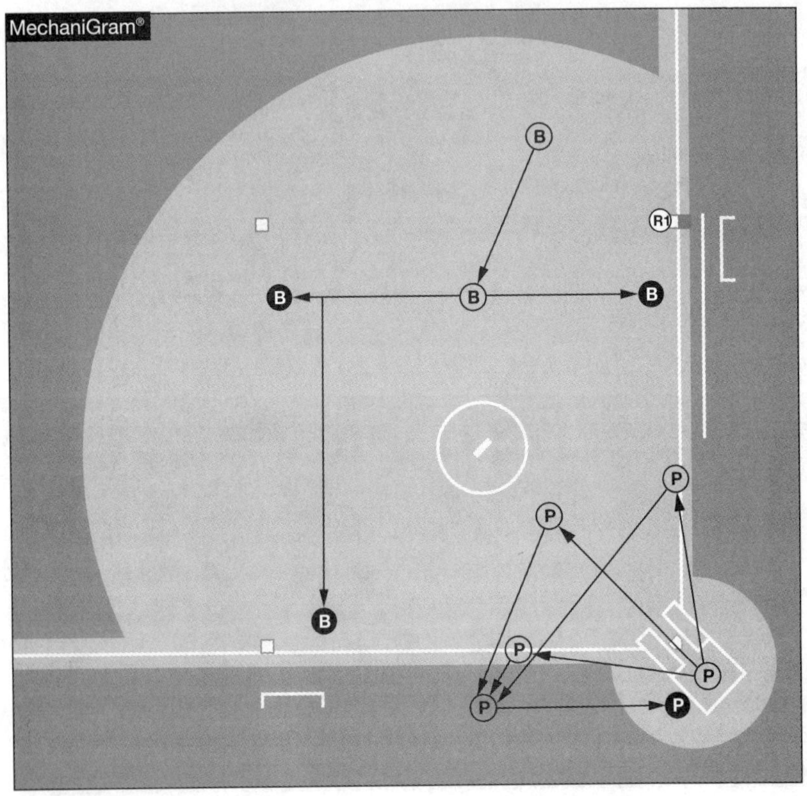

P: Move out from behind the plate to get the best angle and distance possible. As the lead runner (R1) approaches second, move toward the holding zone halfway to third in foul ground to an area where you have an unobstructed view of all four elements and read the play. Be prepared to move as the play develops as you are responsible for fair/foul, catch/no catch and any play at the plate.

B: Pick up the ball and glance at the runner while hustling inside the diamond to button hook at a minimum depth of 10-12 feet. Continue to alternate between the ball and glancing at the runner keeping all four elements in front of you. Be prepared to move parallel to the baseline staying ahead of the runner. Responsible for R1 tagging up at first base, any play at first base, second base and the last runner (R1) into third base.

FLY BALL TO THE OUTFIELD, BALL IS NOT CAUGHT, B DOES NOT CHASE

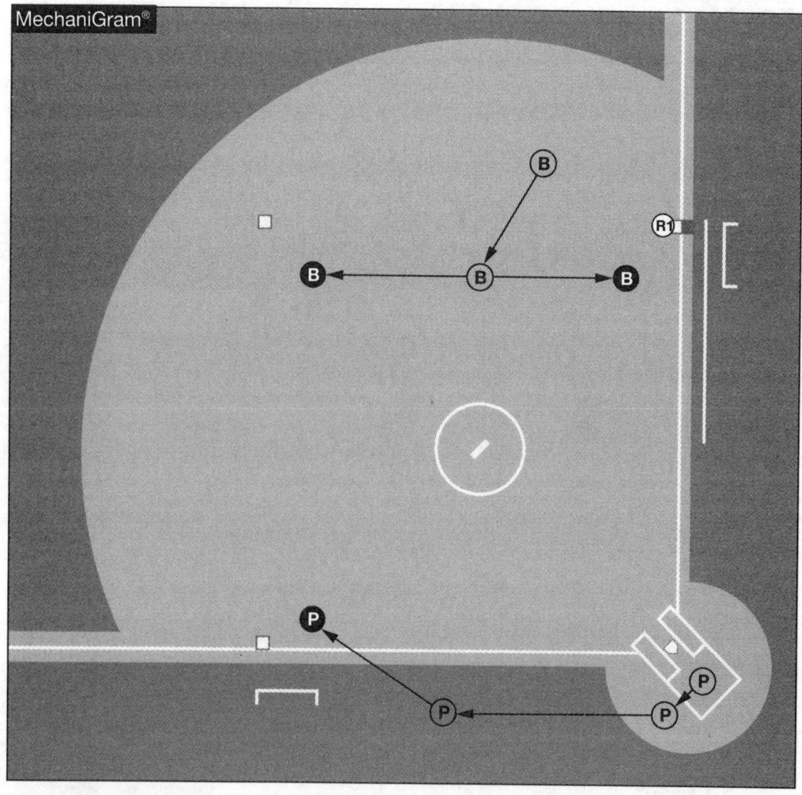

P: Move out from behind the plate to get the best angle and distance possible. As the lead runner (R1) approaches second, move toward the holding zone halfway to third in foul ground to an area where you have an unobstructed view of all four elements and read the play. Be prepared to move as the play develops as you are responsible for fair/foul, catch/no catch, any play on the lead runner (R1) at third base and any play at the plate.

B: Pick up the ball and glance at the runner while hustling inside the diamond to button hook at a minimum depth of 10-12 feet. Continue to alternate between the ball and glancing at the runner keeping all four elements in front of you. Be prepared to move parallel to the baseline staying ahead of the runner. Responsible for any play at first base, second base and the last runner (batter-runner) into third base.

PICKOFF THROW BY CATCHER TO FIRST BASE

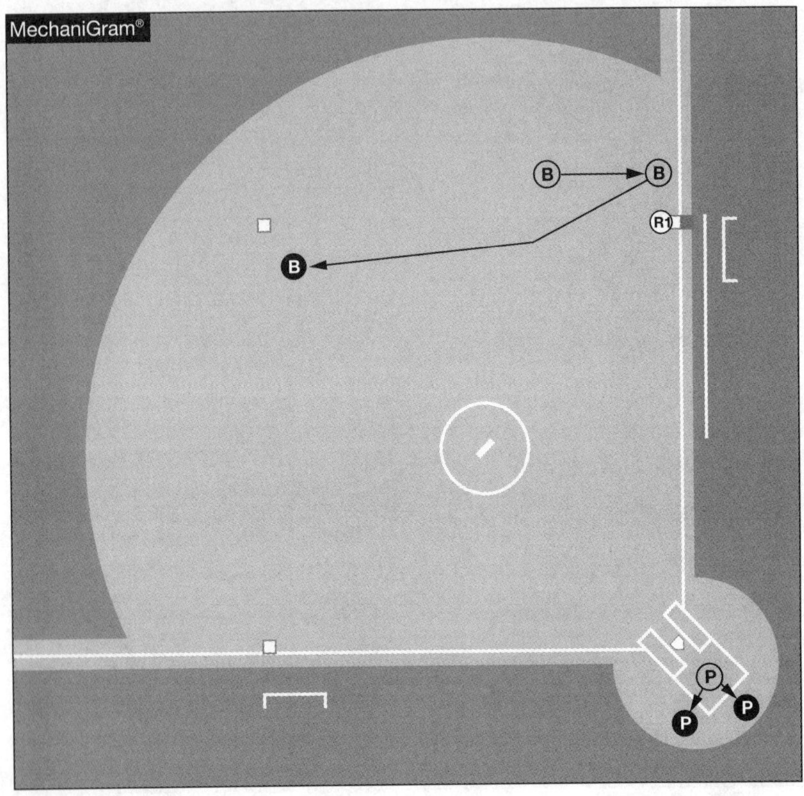

P: After ruling on the pitch, move to obtain an unobstructed view of the play at first base; observe the play. If the throw is errant, move as necessary and rule on an overthrow near a dead-ball area.

B: Move parallel to the baseline and obtain a 90-degree angle to the path of the runner just short of the base they are trying to reach. Move as necessary to maintain an unobstructed view of the play. Come to a set position and observe the play. If there is an overthrow and the ball goes outside move inside the diamond, button hook and be prepared to lead R1 to second base. If R1 is not retired, observe R1 until the ball is back in the circle or time is called.

BATTER BUNTS, PLAY AT SECOND OR FIRST

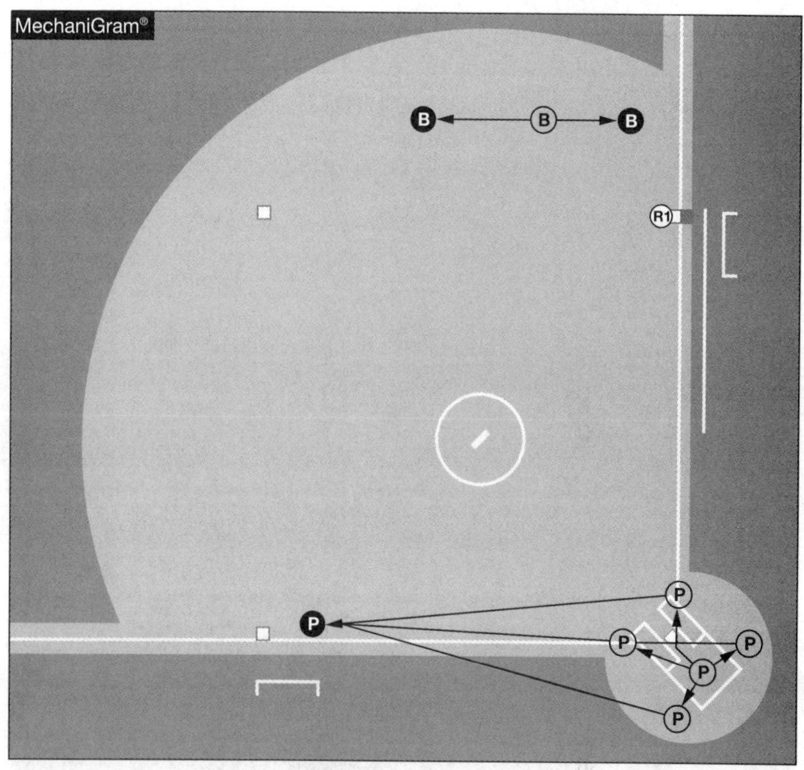

P: Move as necessary to obtain an unobstructed view of the ball to rule fair or foul. As the play develops, trail the batter runner no more than one-third of the way to first base. Be prepared to rule on a swipe tag up to the running lane. Observe the remainder of the play to offer an opinion of a swipe tag or pulled foot if requested by base umpire. Be alert for running lane interference and rule immediately if interference occurs. Be prepared to cover third base in the event of a subsequent play on R1. If the play is at second base, be prepared to cover third base in the event of a subsequent play on R1. Responsible for a subsequent play at third base on the lead runner (R1) and any play at the plate.

B: Read the play and determine where the play will develop, first base or second base. Move to obtain the best angle and distance to the play, coming to a set position to allow you to focus on the play. For a play at first base, move closer to the first-base line; for a play at second base, move toward second base and stay behind the fielder. If the play breaks down and there is uncertainty of a swipe tag or pulled foot, make a decision on the play based on the information available. After the ball is dead consult with the plate umpire if you have a question about an element of the play. Responsible for any play at first base, second base and the last runner (batter-runner) into third base.

STEAL ATTEMPT

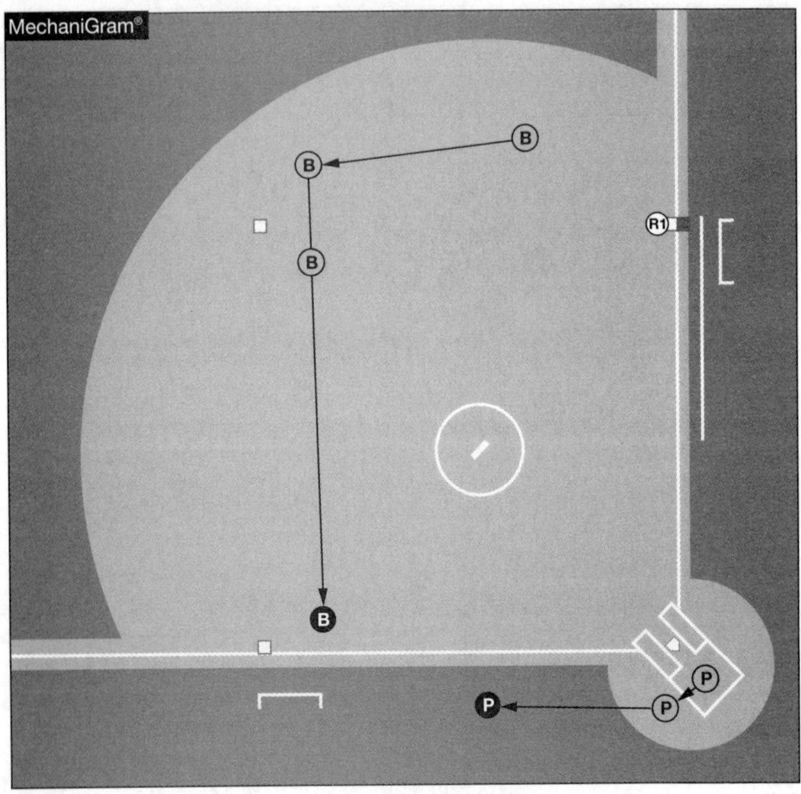

P: When the pitch is delivered, rule it a ball or strike. Step back and observe the action at home plate, watching for batter interference with F2's throw. Adjust your position, if necessary, to observe the play at second base. Move toward the holding zone if there is an overthrow at second base and be prepared to assist in a rundown or deviate if required to cover the play at third base if the base umpire is unable to.

B: Move parallel toward second base to obtain an angle 90 degrees to the path of the runner and just short of the base they are trying to reach. Move as necessary to maintain an unobstructed view of the play. If there is an overthrow, move inside the diamond and prepare to take R1 to third base.

Two-Umpire System

Part 6.3

Runners on First and Second Base

◆ Ground Ball in the Infield

◆ Base Hit to the Outfield

◆ Fly Ball to the Outfield, Ball is Caught

◆ Fly Ball to the Outfield, Ball is Not Caught

◆ Pickoff Throw By Catcher to First Base

◆ Batter Bunts, Play at First, Second or Third

◆ R1 is Stealing

GROUND BALL IN THE INFIELD

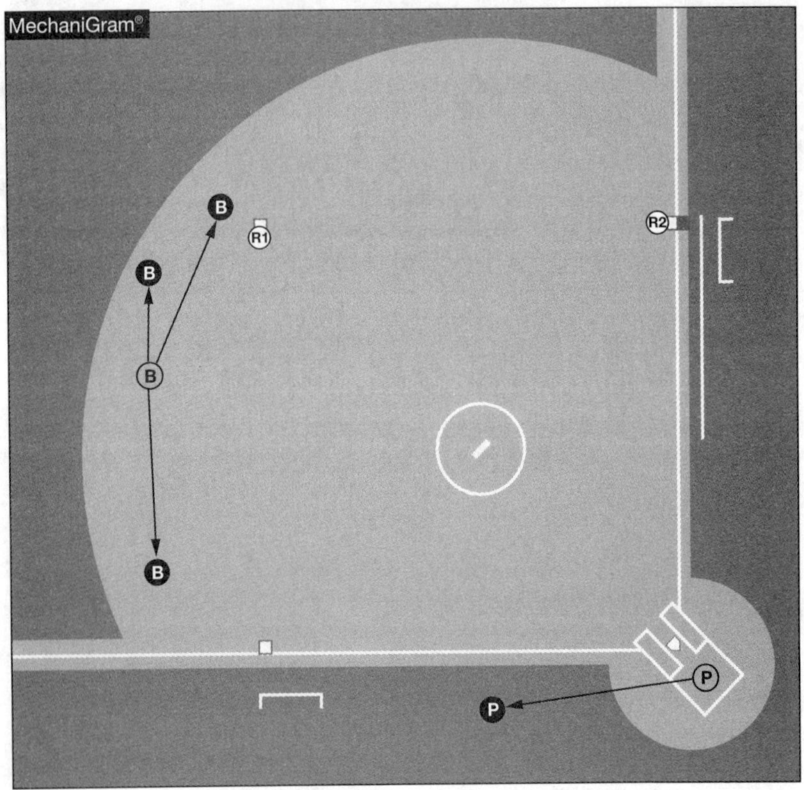

P: Move out from behind the plate toward the holding zone halfway to third base in foul ground to an area where you have an unobstructed view of all four elements and read the play. Be prepared to move as the play develops as you are responsible for a subsequent throw to third base on the lead runner (R1 or R2) and any play at the plate.

B: Let the ball take you to the play. Responsible for the first throw in the infield, any play at first base or second base and the last runner (batter-runner) to third base. Be prepared for a possible double play and move to get the best angle and distance possible being set when the play happens.

BASE HIT TO THE OUTFIELD

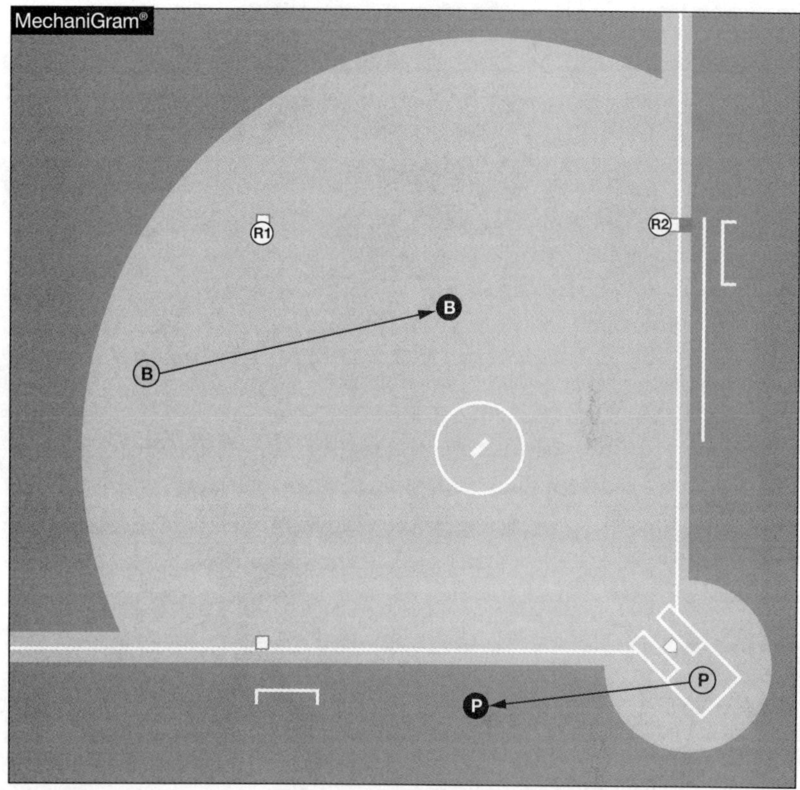

P: Move out from behind the plate toward the holding zone halfway to third base in foul ground to an area where you have an unobstructed view of all four elements and read the play. Be prepared to move as the play develops as you are responsible for any play on a lead runner (R1 or R2) at third base and any play at the plate.

B: Pick up the ball and glance at the runner as you hustle inside the diamond about halfway between second base and first base. Continue to alternate between the ball and glancing at the runners keeping all four elements in front of you. Be prepared to move parallel to the baseline staying ahead of the runner as you are responsible for any play at first base, second base and the last runner (batter-runner) into third base.

FLY BALL TO THE OUTFIELD, BALL IS CAUGHT

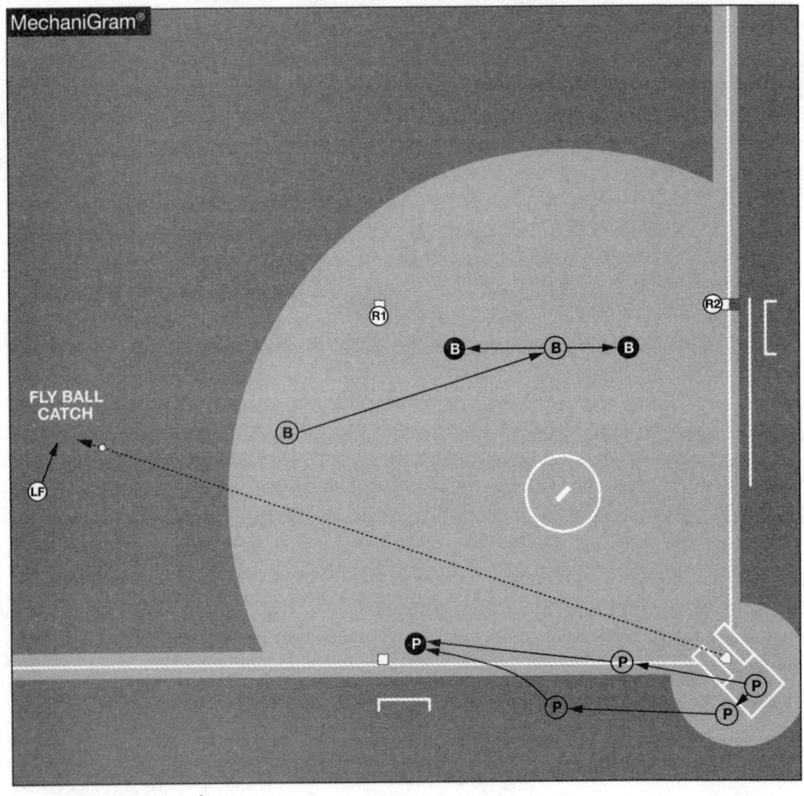

P: Move out from behind the plate to get the best angle and distance possible. Responsible for fair/foul, catch/no catch, R1's tag-up at second base, any play on the lead runner (R1) at third base and any play at the plate.

B: Pick up the ball and glance at the runner while hustling inside the diamond about halfway between second base and first base. Continue to alternate between the ball and glancing at the runner keeping all four elements in front of you. Be prepared to move parallel to the baseline staying ahead of the runner. Responsible for R2's tag-up at first base, any play at first base, second base and the last runner (R2) into third base, or a play on a runner at third base when there is a return throw from the plate area or is cut-off by a player.

FLY BALL TO THE OUTFIELD, BALL IS NOT CAUGHT

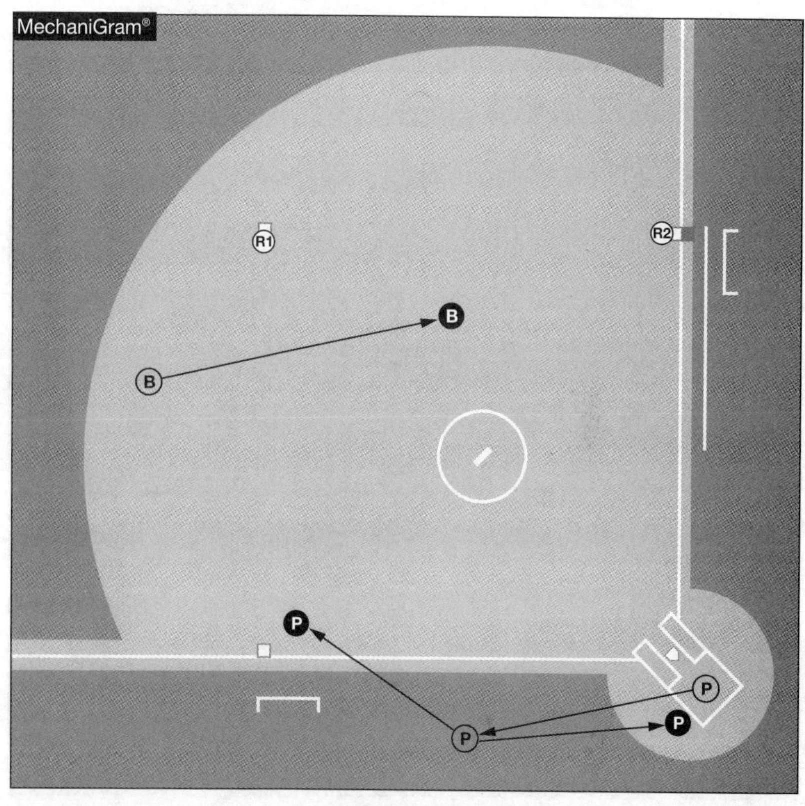

P: Move out from behind the plate to get the best angle and distance possible. Responsible for fair/foul, catch/no catch, R1's tag-up at second base, any play on the lead runner (R1 or R2) at third base and any play at the plate.

B: Pick up the ball and glance at the runner while hustling inside the diamond about halfway between second base and first base. Continue to alternate between the ball and glancing at the runners keeping all four elements in front of you. Be prepared to move parallel to the baseline staying ahead of the runner. Responsible for R2's tag-up at first base, any play at first base, second base and the last runner (batter-runner) into third base, or a play on a runner at third base when there is a return throw from the plate area or is cut-off by a player.

PICKOFF THROW BY CATCHER TO FIRST BASE

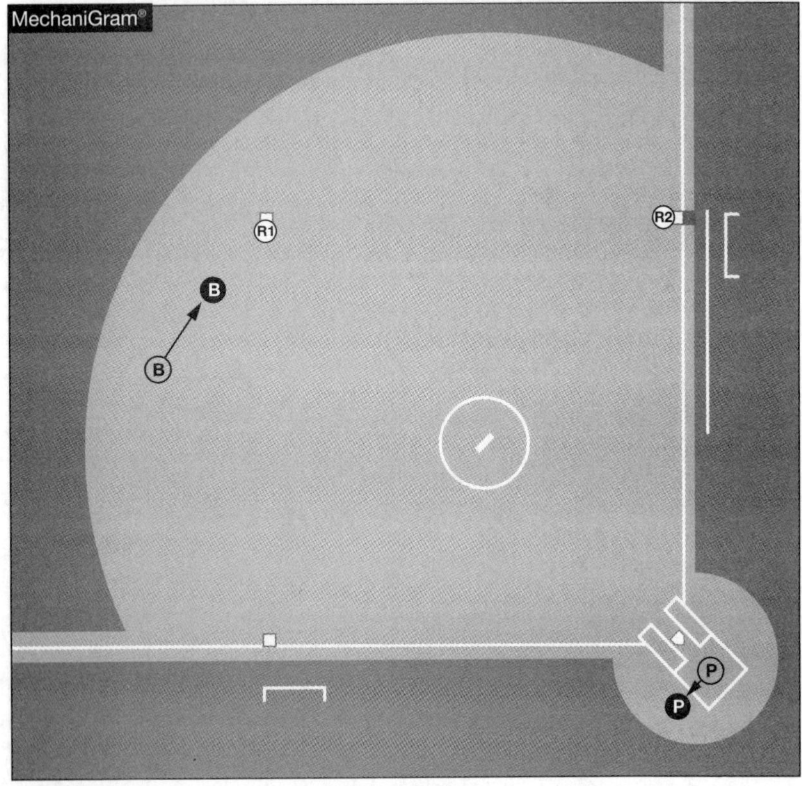

P: After ruling on the pitch, move to obtain an unobstructed view of the play at first base; observe the play. If the throw is errant, move as necessary and rule on an overthrow near a dead-ball area. Be prepared as you are responsible for a subsequent play at third base on R1 and any play at the plate.

B: Move to obtain the best angle and distance possible working to obtain 90 degrees to the path of the runner where you can see all four elements of the play. Come to a set position to observe the play; be prepared to move to a secondary position in case of an overthrow. Responsible for any play at first base, second base and the last runner (R2) at third base.

BATTER BUNTS, PLAY AT FIRST, SECOND OR THIRD

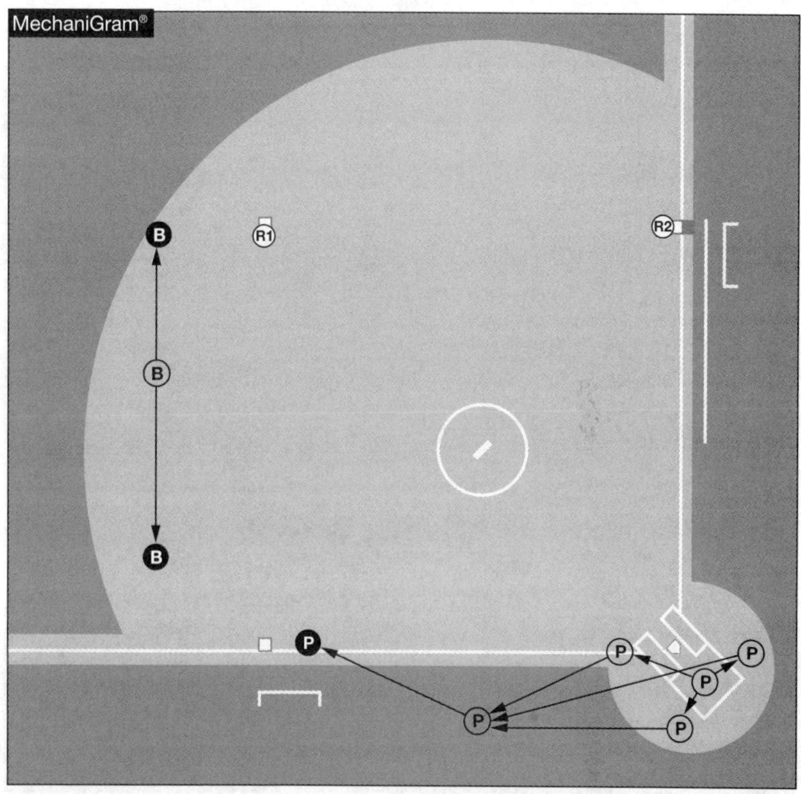

P: Move as necessary to obtain an unobstructed view of the ball to rule fair or foul. If the ball is fair, signal fair then begin moving toward the holding zone halfway to third base keeping all elements in your view. As the play develops, be prepared to offer an opinion on a swipe tag or pulled foot if requested by the base umpire. Be alert for running lane interference and rule immediately if interference occurs. If the initial play is at first base or second base, be prepared to cover third base in the event of a subsequent play on R1 or any play at the plate. Responsible for fair/foul and a subsequent play on the lead runner (R1 or R2) at third base.

B: Read the play and determine where the play will develop at first base, second base or third base. Move to obtain the best angle and distance possible to the play, coming to a set position to allow you to focus on the play. If the play breaks down and there is uncertainty of a swipe tag or pulled foot, make a decision on the play based on the information available. After the ball is dead consult with the plate umpire if you have a question about an element of the play. Responsible for the first play in the infield, any play at first base, second base and the last runner (batter-runner) at third base.

R1 IS STEALING

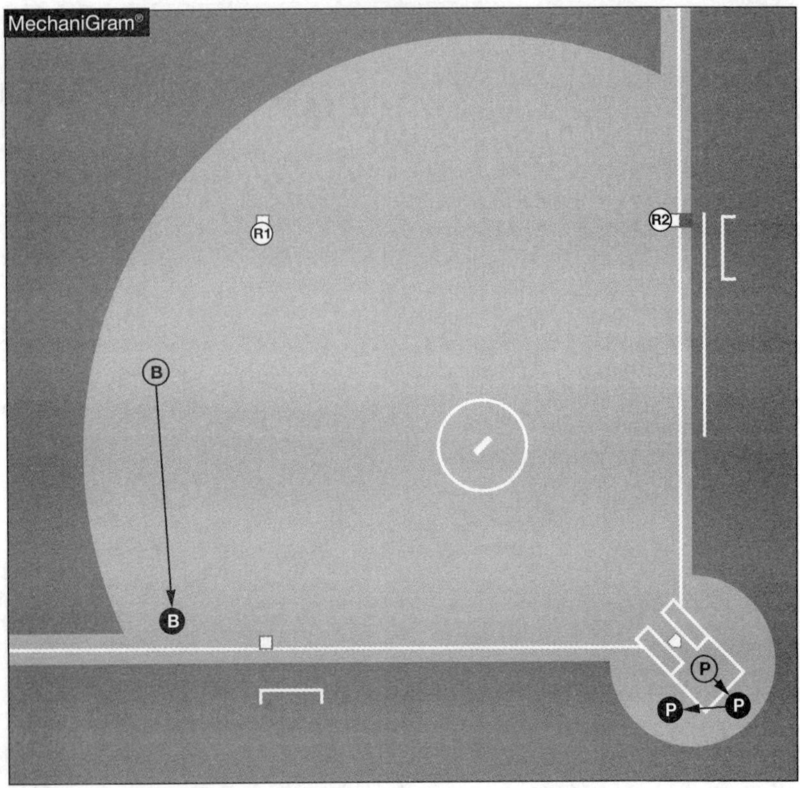

P: When the pitch is delivered, rule it a ball or strike. Step back and observe the action at home plate, watching for batter interference with F2's throw. Adjust your position, if necessary, to observe the play at third base. Move toward the holding zone if there is a potential rundown between second base and third base and be prepared to assist in a rundown covering third base.

B: Move parallel toward third base to obtain an angle 90 degrees to the path of the runner and just short of the base they are trying to reach. Move as necessary to maintain an unobstructed view of the play. If a rundown occurs and the plate umpire is there to help, cover second base.

Two-Umpire System

Part 6.4

Runners on First and Third Base

- Ground Ball in the Infield

- Base Hit to the Outfield, B Does Not Chase

- Fly Ball to the Outfield, Ball is Caught, B Does Not Chase

- Fly Ball to the Outfield, Ball is Not Caught, B Does Not Chase

- Pickoff Throw by Catcher to Third Base

GROUND BALL IN THE INFIELD

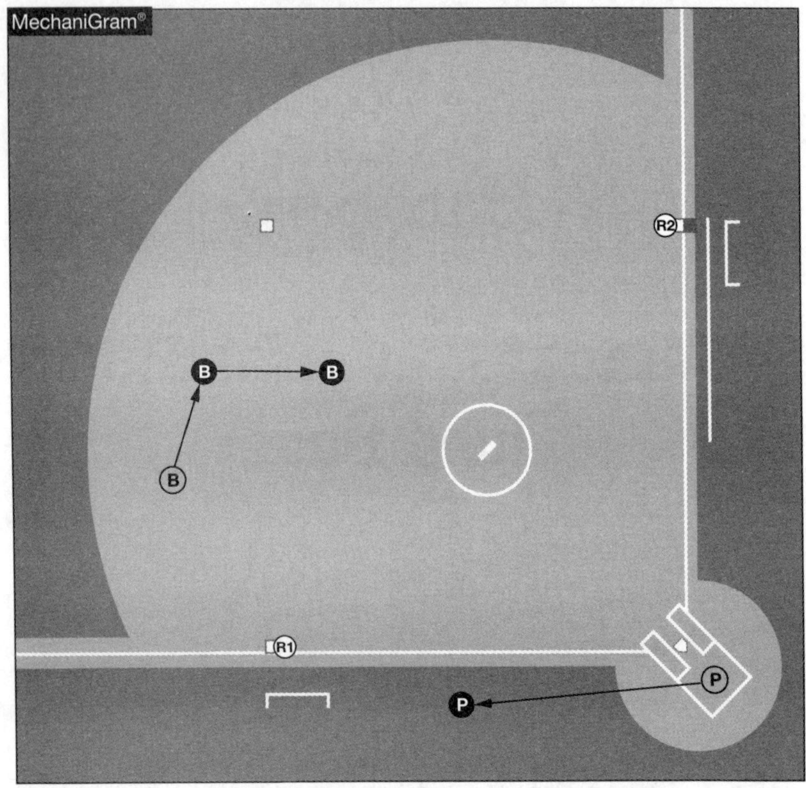

P: Move out from behind the plate toward the holding zone halfway to third base in foul ground to an area where you have an obstructed view of all four elements and read the play. Be prepared to move as the play develops as you are responsible for a subsequent throw to third base on the lead runner (R1 or R2) and any play at the plate.

B: Let the ball take you to the play. Move to get the best angle and distance possible as the play develops. Responsible for the first throw in the infield, any play at first base or second base and the last runner (batter-runner) to third base.

BASE HIT TO THE OUTFIELD, B DOES NOT CHASE

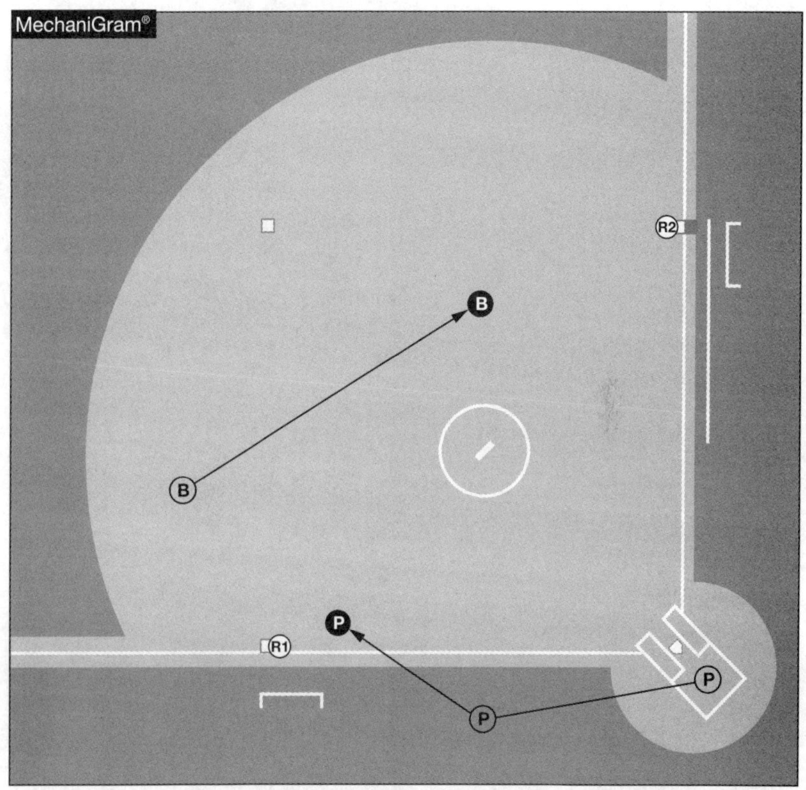

P: Move out from behind the plate toward the holding zone halfway to third base in foul ground to an area where you can see all four elements and read the play. If there is no play developing at home, observe R1 touching home plate from the holding zone and be prepared to cover a play on R2 at third base. Responsible for any play on a lead runner (R1 or R2) at third base and any play at the plate.

B: Pick up the ball and glance at the runner while hustling inside the diamond about halfway between second base and first base. Continue to alternate between the ball and glancing at the runners keeping all four elements in front of you. Be prepared to move parallel to the baseline staying ahead of the runner. Responsible for any play at first base, second base and the last runner (batter-runner) into third base.

FLY BALL TO THE OUTFIELD, BALL IS CAUGHT, B DOES NOT CHASE

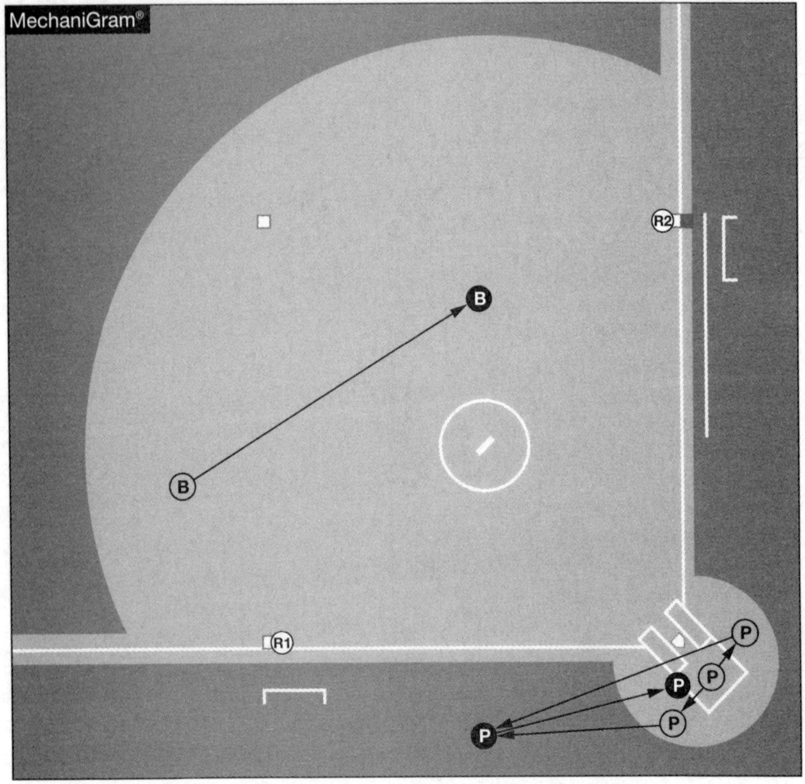

P: Move out from behind the plate to get the best angle and distance possible. Position yourself to observe R1's tag-up at third base as well as the catch. If the ball is near a foul line, position yourself to observe fair/foul, catch/no catch and R1's tag-up at third base, most likely first baseline or third baseline extended. After ruling the catch, move toward the holding zone halfway to third base in foul ground to an area where you have an unobstructed view of all four elements and read the play. Be prepared to move as a play develops, if R1 tags and attempts to score and a play develops, obtain a position at home plate. If there is no play made on R1 at home, remain in the holding zone to watch R1 touch home plate and observe the base umpire bringing R2 to third base. Responsible for fair/foul, catch/no catch, the tag up at third base (R1), any play on the lead runner (R1) at third base and any play at the plate.

B: Pick up the ball and glance at the runner while hustling inside the diamond about halfway between second base and first base. Position yourself to see R2 tag-up and the catch. Continue to alternate between the ball and glancing at R2 keeping all four elements in front of you. Be prepared to move parallel to the baseline staying ahead of R2. Responsible for any play at first base, second base and the last runner (R2) at third base.

FLY BALL TO THE OUTFIELD, BALL IS NOT CAUGHT, B DOES NOT CHASE

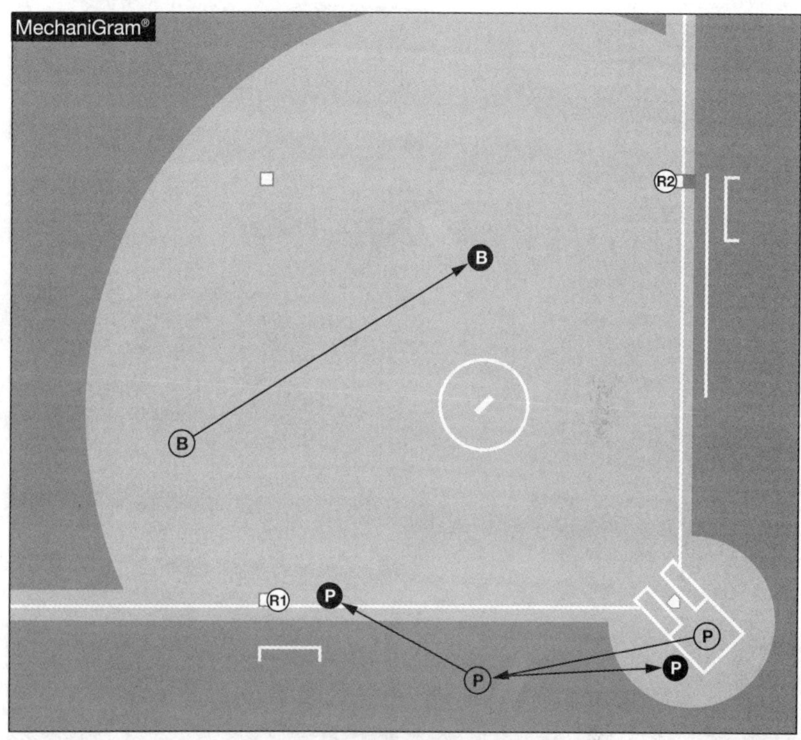

P: Move out from behind the plate to get the best angle and distance possible. Position yourself to observe R1's tag-up at third base as well as the catch. If the ball is near a foul line, position yourself to observe fair/foul, catch/no catch and R1's tag-up at third base, most likely first baseline or third baseline extended. After ruling on the catch, move toward the holding zone halfway to third base in foul ground to an area where you have an unobstructed view of all four elements and read the play. Be prepared to move as a play develops, if R1 attempts to score and a play develops, obtain a position at home plate. If there is no play made on R1 at home, remain in the holding zone to watch R1 touch home plate and be prepared to cover a play on R2 at third base. Responsible for fair/foul, catch/no catch, the tag up at third base (R1), any play on the lead runner (R1 or R2) at third base and any play at the plate.

B: Pick up the ball and glance at the runner while hustling inside the diamond about halfway between second base and first base. Position yourself to see R2 tag-up and the possible catch. Continue to alternate between the ball and glancing at the runners keeping all four elements in front of you. Be prepared to move parallel to the baseline staying ahead of the runners, be prepared for a possible force play at first base or second base or a tag play on the batter-runner at second base. Responsible for any play at first base, second base and the last runner (batter-runner) at third base.

PICKOFF THROW BY CATCHER TO THIRD BASE

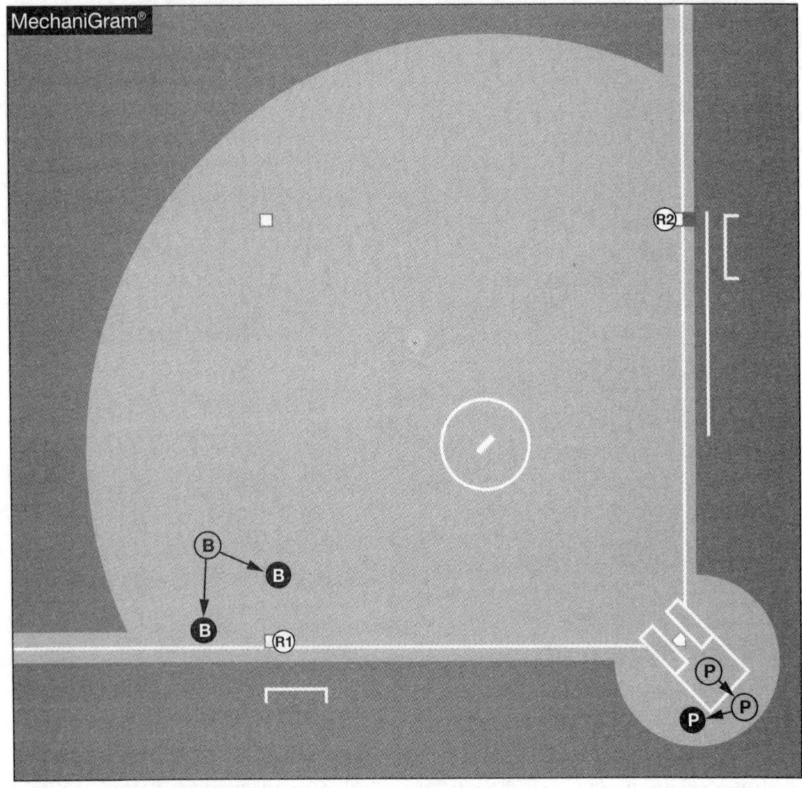

P: When the pitch is delivered, rule it a ball or strike. Step back and observe the action at home plate, watching for batter interference with F2's throw. Adjust your position, if necessary, to observe the play at third base being prepared to rule if an overthrow goes near a dead-ball area or there is a play at the plate.

B: Depending on the player and how they are covering the play either move parallel toward third base line (player at or in front of the base) or forward toward third base (player coming from behind the base) to obtain an unobstructed view of the play. Be prepared for a secondary play on R2 attempting to advance to second base.

Two-Umpire System

Part 6.5

Runners on Second and Third Base

◆ Ground Ball in the Infield

◆ Base Hit to the Outfield

◆ Fly Ball to the Outfield, Ball is Caught, B Does Not Chase

◆ Fly Ball to the Outfield, Ball is Not Caught, B Does Not Chase

◆ Pickoff Throw by Catcher to Third Base

◆ Batter Bunts, Play at First, Second or Third

GROUND BALL IN THE INFIELD

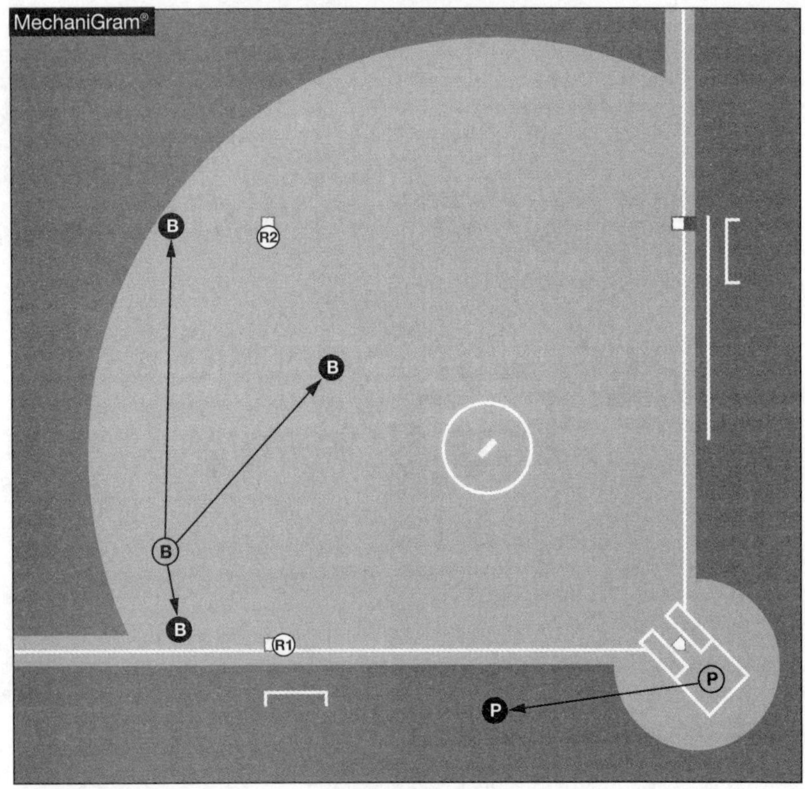

P: Move out from behind the plate toward the holding zone halfway to third base in foul ground to an area where you have an obstructed view of all four elements and read the play. Be prepared to move as the play develops as you are responsible for a subsequent throw to third base on the lead runner (R1 or R2) and any play at the plate.

B: Let the ball take you to the play. Move to get the best angle and distance possible as the play develops. Responsible for the first throw in the infield, any play at first base or second base and the last runner (batter-runner) to third base.

BASE HIT TO THE OUTFIELD

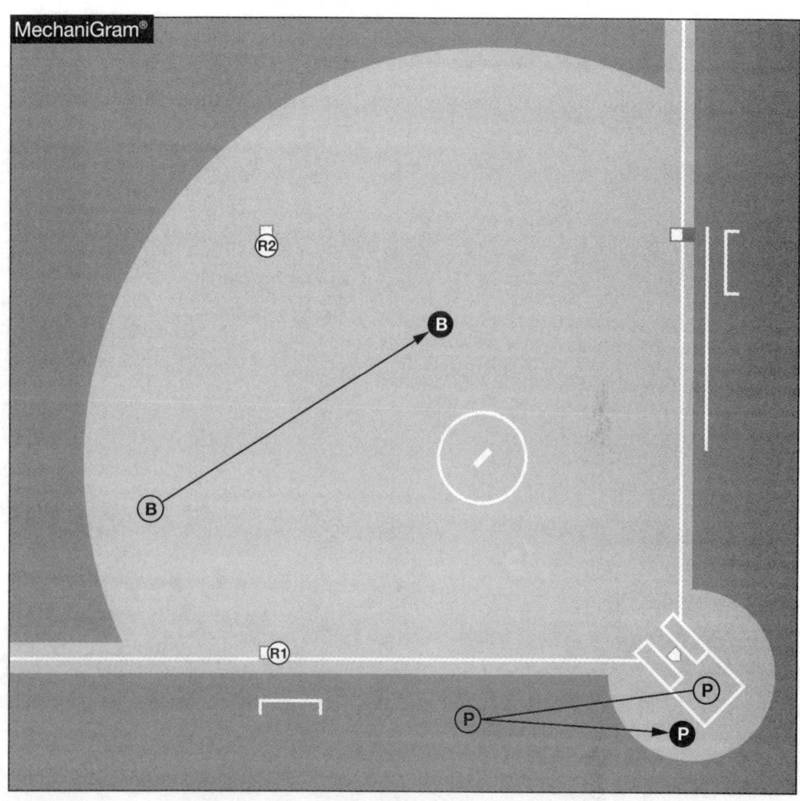

P: Move out from behind the plate toward the holding zone halfway to third base in foul ground to an area where you can see all four elements and read the play. If there is no play developing at home, observe R1 touching home plate from the holding zone and be prepared to cover a play on R2 at third base. Responsible for any play on a lead runner (R1 or R2) at third base and any play at the plate.

B: Pick up the ball and glance at the runner while hustling inside the diamond about halfway between second base and first base. Continue to alternate between the ball and glancing at the runners keeping all four elements in front of you. Be prepared to move parallel to the baseline staying ahead of the runner. Responsible for any play at first base, second base and the last runner (batter-runner) into third base.

FLY BALL TO OUTFIELD, BALL IS CAUGHT, B DOES NOT CHASE

P: Move out from behind the plate to get the best angle and distance possible. Position yourself to observe R1's tag-up at third base as well as the catch. If the ball is near a foul line, position yourself to observe fair/foul, catch/no catch and R1's tag-up at third base, most likely first baseline or third baseline extended. After ruling the catch, move toward the holding zone halfway to third base in foul ground to an area where you have an unobstructed view of all four elements and read the play. Be prepared to move as a play develops, if R1 attempts to score and a play develops, obtain a position at home plate. If there is no play made on R1 at home, remain in the holding zone to watch R1 touch home plate and be prepared to move back toward the plate when the base umpire brings R2 to third base. Responsible for fair/foul, catch/no catch, tag up at third base (R1), any play on a lead runner (R1) at third base and any play at the plate.

B: Pick up the ball and glance at the runner while hustling inside the diamond about halfway between second base and first base. Position yourself to see R2 tag-up and the catch. Continue to alternate between the ball and glancing at the runner keeping all four elements in front of you. Be prepared to move parallel to the baseline staying ahead of R2 if they advance to third base. Responsible for the tag up at second base (R2), any play at second base and the last runner (R2) at third base.

FLY BALL TO OUTFIELD, BALL IS NOT CAUGHT, B DOES NOT CHASE

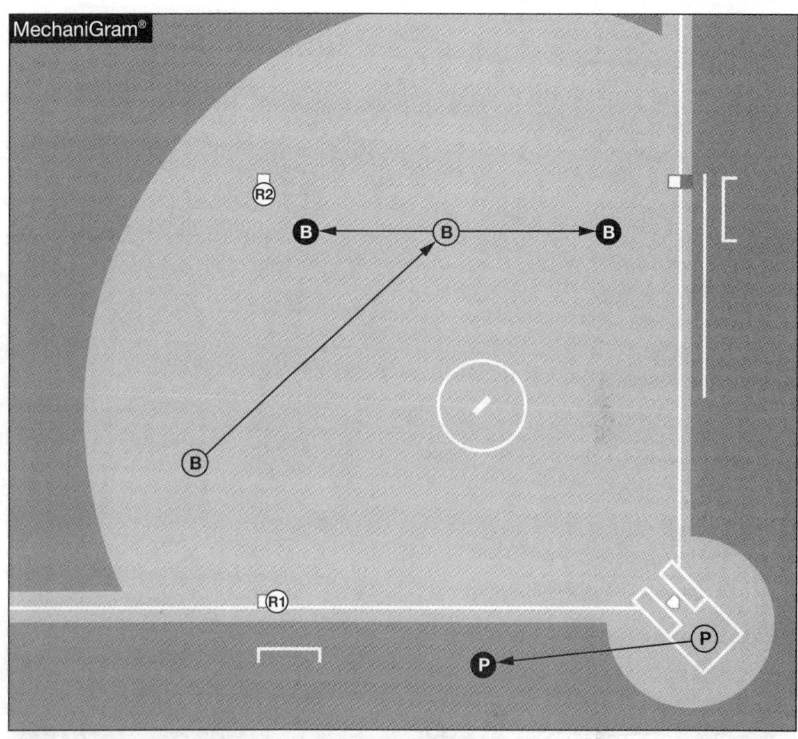

P: Move out from behind the plate to get the best angle and distance possible. Position yourself to observe R1's tag-up at third base as well as the catch. If the ball is near a foul line, position yourself to observe fair/foul, catch/no catch and R1's tag-up at third base, most likely first baseline or third baseline extended. After ruling on the catch, move toward the holding zone halfway to third base in foul ground to an area where you have an unobstructed view of all four elements and read the play. Be prepared to move as a play develops, if R1 attempts to score and a play develops, obtain a position at home plate. If there is no play made on R1 at home, remain in the holding zone to watch R1 touch home plate and be prepared to cover a play on R2 at third base. Responsible for fair/foul, catch/no catch, tag up at third base (R1), any play on a lead runner (R1 or R2) at third base and any play at the plate.

B: Pick up the ball and glance at the runner while hustling inside the diamond about halfway between second base and first base. Position yourself to see R2 tag-up and the possible catch. Continue to alternate between the ball and glancing at the runners keeping all four elements in front of you. Be prepared to move parallel to the baseline staying ahead of the runners, be prepared for a possible force play at first base or a tag play on the batter-runner at second base. Responsible for any play at first base, second base and the last runner (batter-runner) at third base.

PICKOFF THROW BY CATCHER TO THIRD BASE

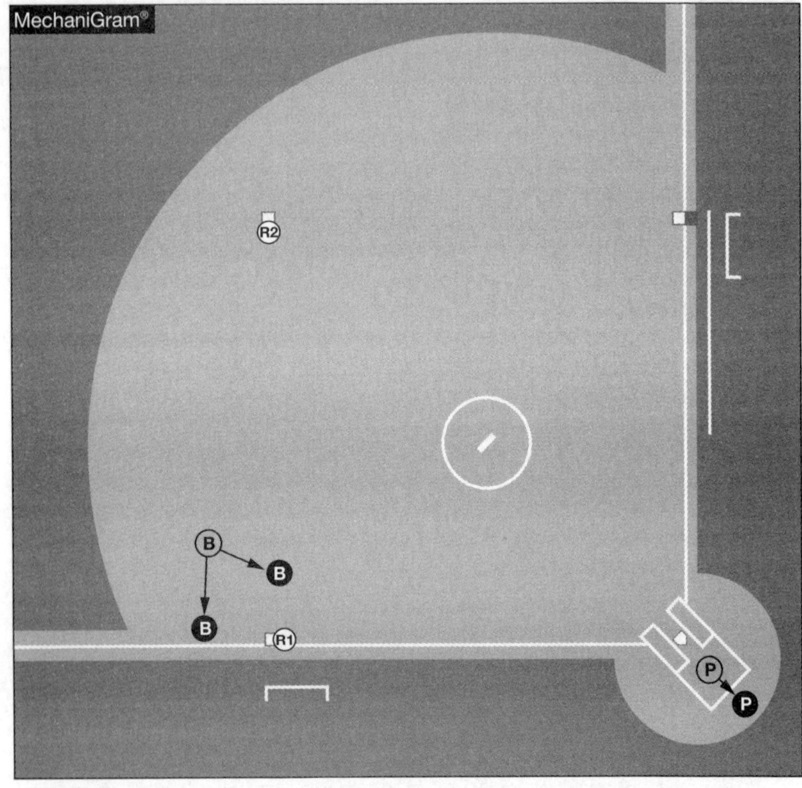

P: When the pitch is delivered, rule it a ball or strike. Step back and observe the action at home plate, watching for batter interference with F2's throw. Adjust your position, if necessary, to observe the play at third base being prepared to rule if an overthrow goes near a dead-ball area or there is a play at the plate.

B: Depending on the player and how they are covering the play either move parallel toward third base line (player at or in front of the base) or forward toward third base (player coming from behind the base) to obtain an unobstructed view of the play.

BATTER BUNTS, PLAY AT FIRST, SECOND OR THIRD

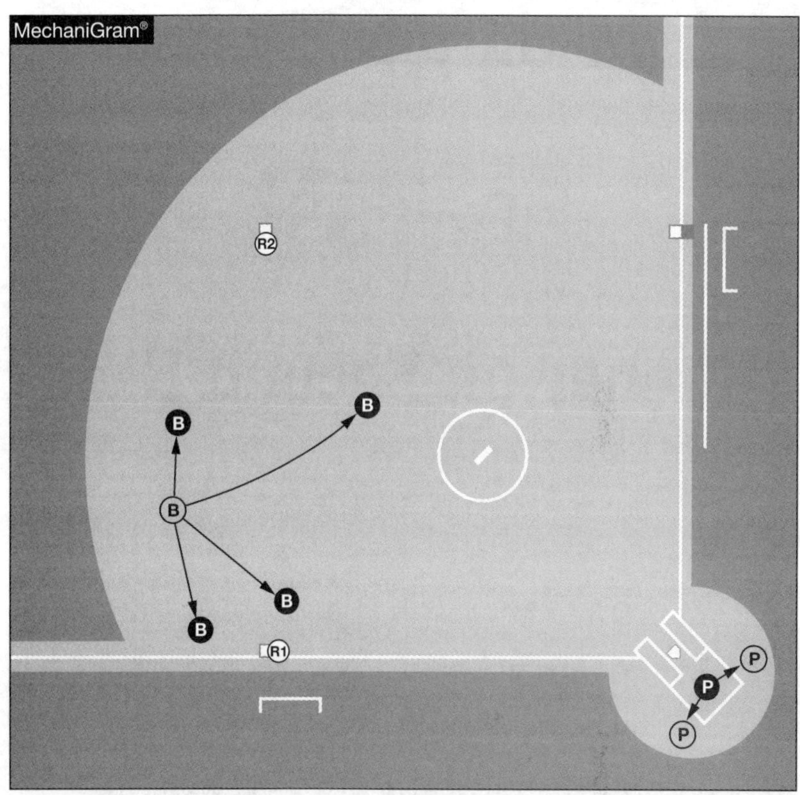

P: Move as necessary to obtain an unobstructed view of the ball to rule fair or foul. If the ball is fair, signal fair then begin moving toward the holding zone halfway to third base keeping all elements in your view. As the play develops, be prepared to offer an opinion on a swipe tag or pulled foot if requested by the base umpire. Be alert for running lane interference and rule immediately if interference occurs. If the initial play is at first base or second base, be prepared to cover third base in the event of a subsequent play on R1 or R2 and any play at the plate. Responsible for fair/foul, a subsequent play on a lead runner (R1 or R2) and any play at the plate.

B: Read the play and determine where the play will develop, first base, second base or third base. Move to obtain the best angle and distance possible to the play, coming to a set position to allow you to focus on the play. If the play breaks down and there is uncertainty of a swipe tag or pulled foot, make a decision on the play based on the information available. After the ball is dead consult with the plate umpire if you have a question about an element of the play. Responsible for the first play in the infield and any play at first base, second base and the last runner (batter-runner) at third base.

Part 6.6

Runner on Second Base

- ◆ Ground Ball in the Infield

- ◆ Base Hit to the Outfield

- ◆ Fly Ball to the Outfield, Ball is Caught, B Does Not Chase

- ◆ Fly Ball to the Outfield, Ball is Not Caught, B Does Not Chase

- ◆ Steal Attempt

- ◆ Batter Bunts, Play at Third or First

GROUND BALL IN THE INFIELD

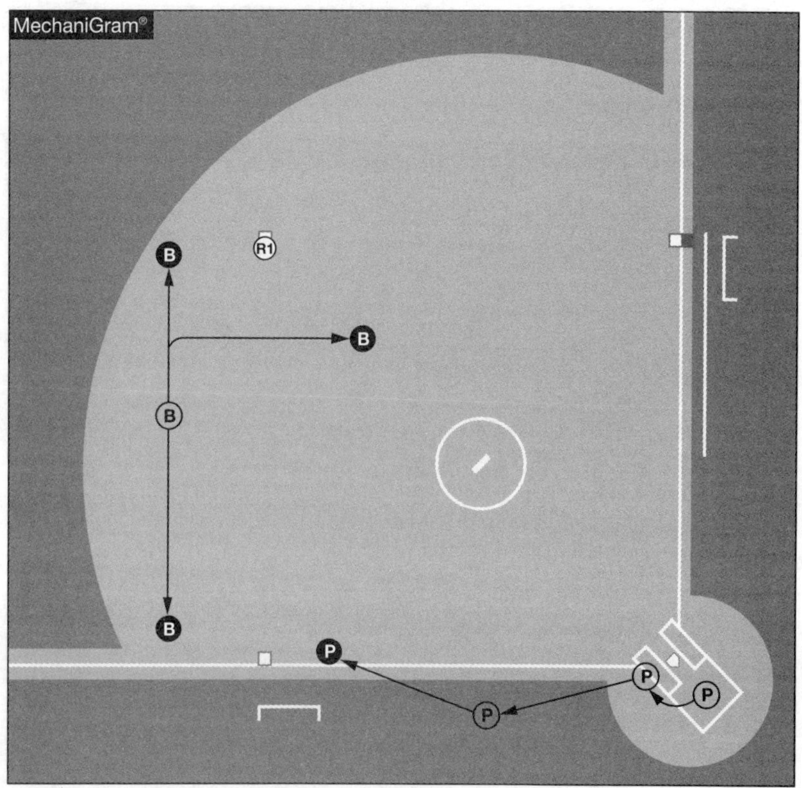

P: Move out from behind the plate toward the holding zone halfway to third base in foul ground to an area where you have an unobstructed view of all four elements and read the play. Be prepared to move as the play develops as you are responsible for a subsequent throw to third base on R1 and any play at the plate.

B: Let the ball take you to the play. Responsible for the first throw in the infield, any play at first base or second base and the last runner to third base.

BASE HIT TO THE OUTFIELD

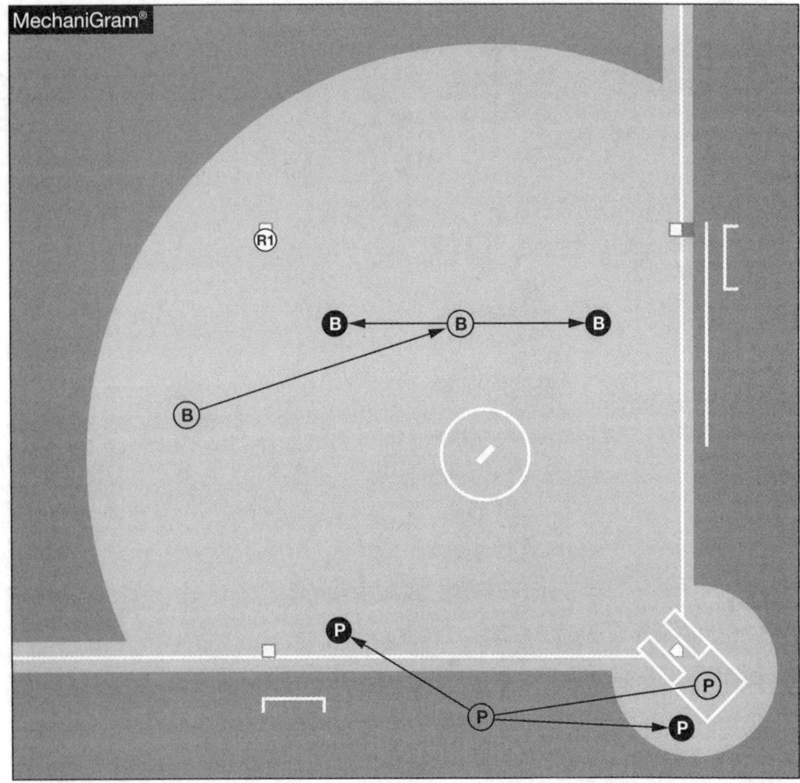

P: Move out from behind the plate toward the holding zone halfway to third base in foul ground to an area where you have an unobstructed view of all four elements and read the play. Be prepared to move as the play develops. Responsible for any play on the lead runner (R1) at third base and any play at the plate.

B: Pick up the ball and glance at the runner while hustling inside the diamond about halfway between second base and first base. Continue to alternate between the ball and glancing at the runners keeping all four elements in front of you. Be prepared to move parallel to the baseline staying ahead of the runner. Responsible for any play at first base, second base and the last runner (batter-runner) into third base.

FLY BALL TO THE OUTFIELD, BALL IS CAUGHT, B DOES NOT CHASE

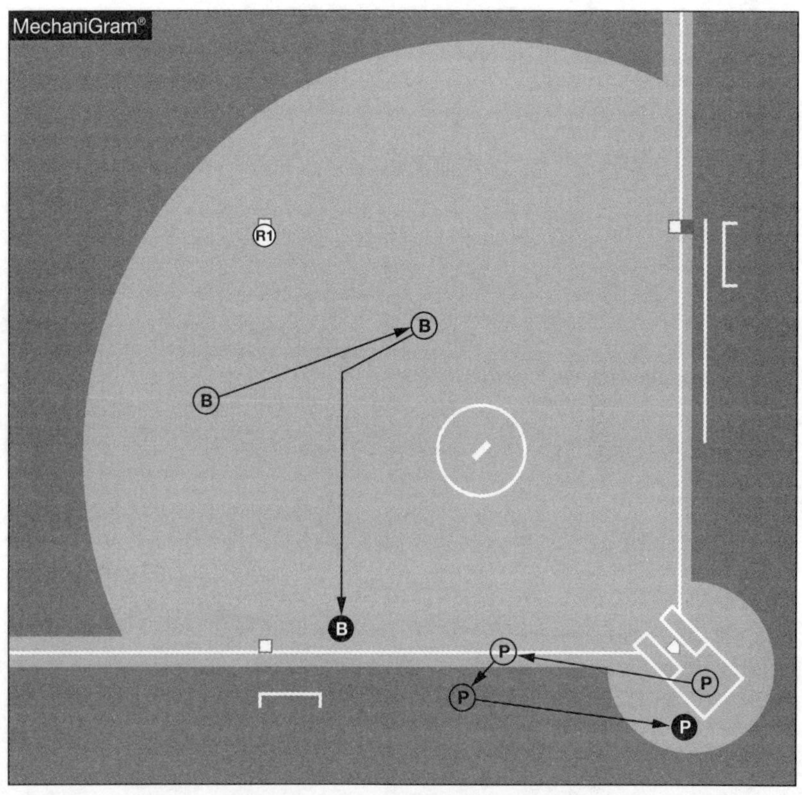

P: Move out from behind the plate to get the best angle and distance possible. Position yourself to call fair/foul, catch/no catch. Once the ball is caught, move toward the holding zone being prepared to cover a rundown at third base if needed. Once BU is covering the play at third base, move back toward the plate for any play at the plate. Responsible for fair/foul, catch/no catch and any play at the plate.

B: Pick up the ball and glance at the runner while hustling inside the diamond about halfway between second base and first base. Continue to alternate between the ball and glancing at the runner keeping all four elements in front of you. Be prepared to move parallel to the baseline staying ahead of the runner. Responsible for R1's tag-up at second base and any play on the last runner (R1) at third base.

FLY BALL TO THE OUTFIELD, BALL IS NOT CAUGHT, B DOES NOT CHASE

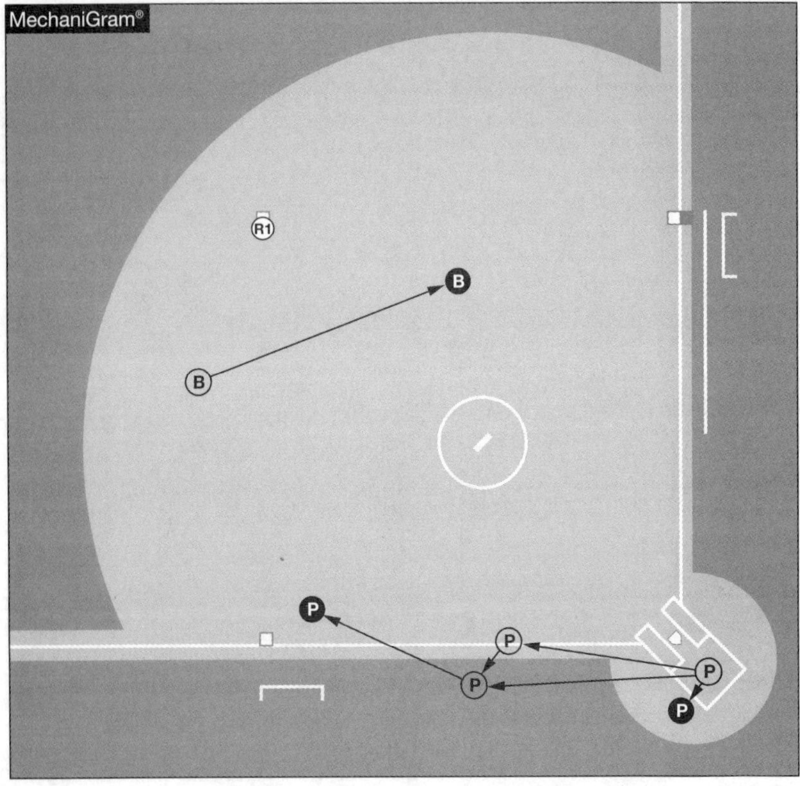

P: Move out from behind the plate to get the best angle and distance possible. Position yourself to call fair/foul, catch/no catch. After the ball is fair and not caught, move to the holding zone about halfway between third base and home plate. Be prepared to move into fair territory if a play develops on R1 at third base or to move back home for any play at the plate. Responsible for fair/foul, catch/no catch, any play on the lead runner (R1) at third base and any play at the plate.

B: Pick up the ball and glance at the runner while hustling inside the diamond about halfway between second base and first base. Continue to alternate between the ball and glancing at the runners keeping all four elements in front of you. Be prepared to move parallel to the baseline staying ahead of the runner. Responsible for R1's tag-up at second base, and any play at first base, second base and the last runner (batter-runner) at third base.

STEAL ATTEMPT

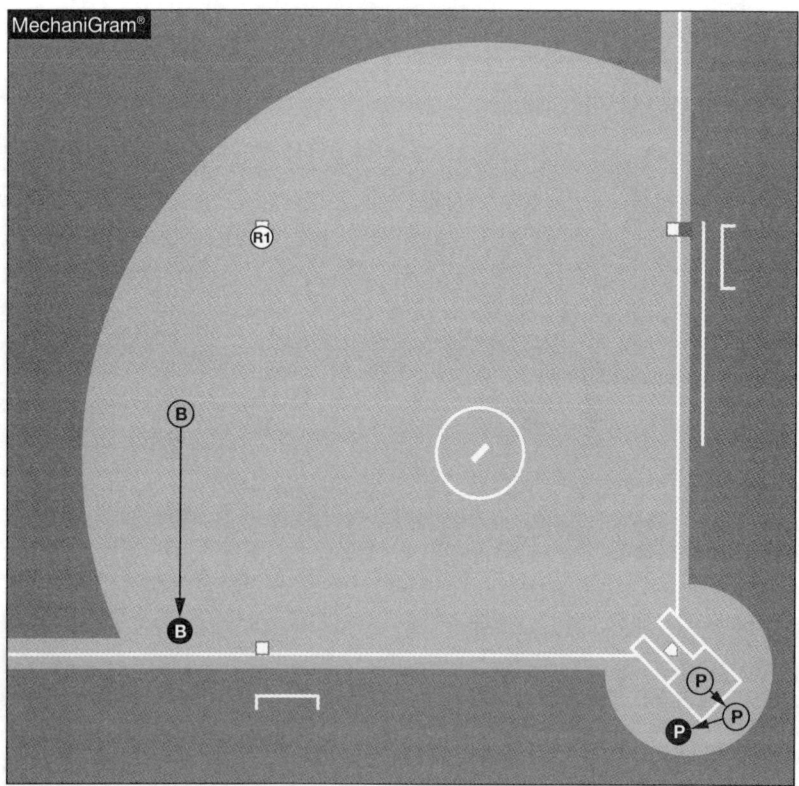

P: When the pitch is delivered, rule it a ball or strike. Step back and observe the action at home plate, watching for batter interference with F2's throw. Adjust your position, if necessary, to observe the play at third base. Move toward the holding zone if there is a potential rundown between second base and third base and be prepared to assist in a rundown covering third base.

B: Move parallel toward third base to obtain an angle 90 degrees to the path of the runner and just short of the base they are trying to reach. Move as necessary to maintain an unobstructed view of the play. If a rundown occurs and the plate umpire is there to help, cover second base.

BATTER BUNTS, PLAY AT THIRD OR FIRST

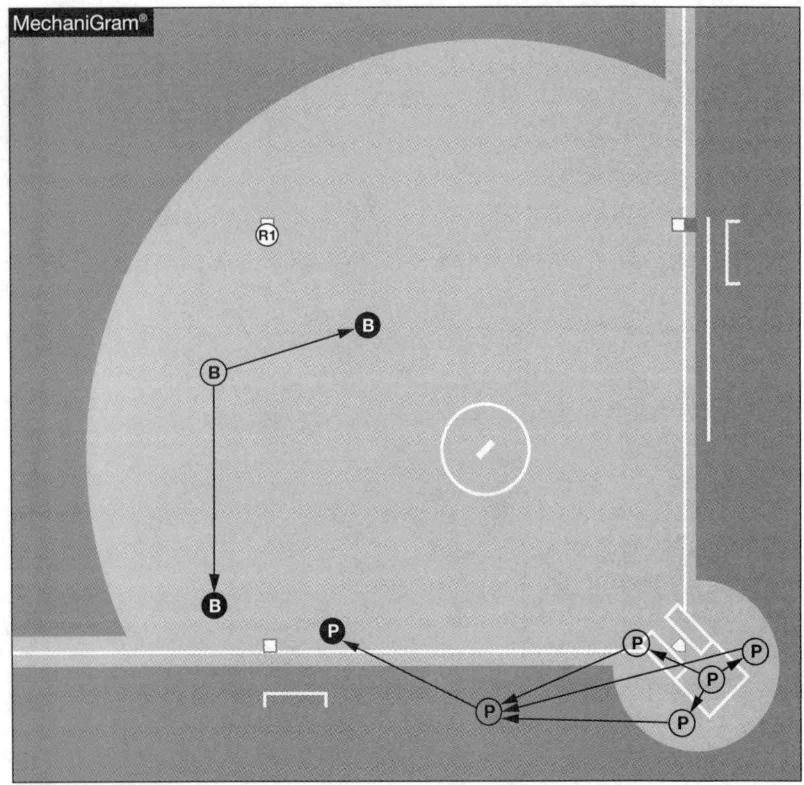

P: Move as necessary to obtain an unobstructed view of the ball to rule fair or foul. If the ball is fair, signal fair then begin moving toward the holding zone halfway to third base keeping all elements in your view. As the play develops, be prepared to offer an opinion on a swipe tag or pulled foot if requested by the base umpire. Be alert for running lane interference and rule immediately if interference occurs. If the initial play is at first base, be prepared to cover third base in the event of a subsequent play on R1 or any play at the plate. Responsible for fair/foul any subsequent play on a lead runner (R1) at third base and any play at the plate.

B: Read the play and determine where the play will develop, first base, second base or third base. Move to obtain the best angle and distance possible to the play, coming to a set position to allow you to focus on the play. If the play breaks down and there is uncertainty of a swipe tag or pulled foot, make a decision on the play based on the information available. After the ball is dead, consult with the plate umpire if you have a question about an element of the play. Responsible for the first throw in the infield, any play at first base or second base and the last runner (batter-runner) at third base.

Two-Umpire System

Part 6.7

Runner on Third Base

◆ Ground Ball in the Infield

◆ Base Hit to the Outfield

◆ Fly Ball to the Outfield, Ball is Caught, B Does Not Chase

◆ Fly Ball to the Outfield, Ball is Not Caught, B Does Not Chase

◆ Pickoff Throw by Catcher to Third Base

◆ Batter Bunts, Play at Third or First

GROUND BALL IN THE INFIELD

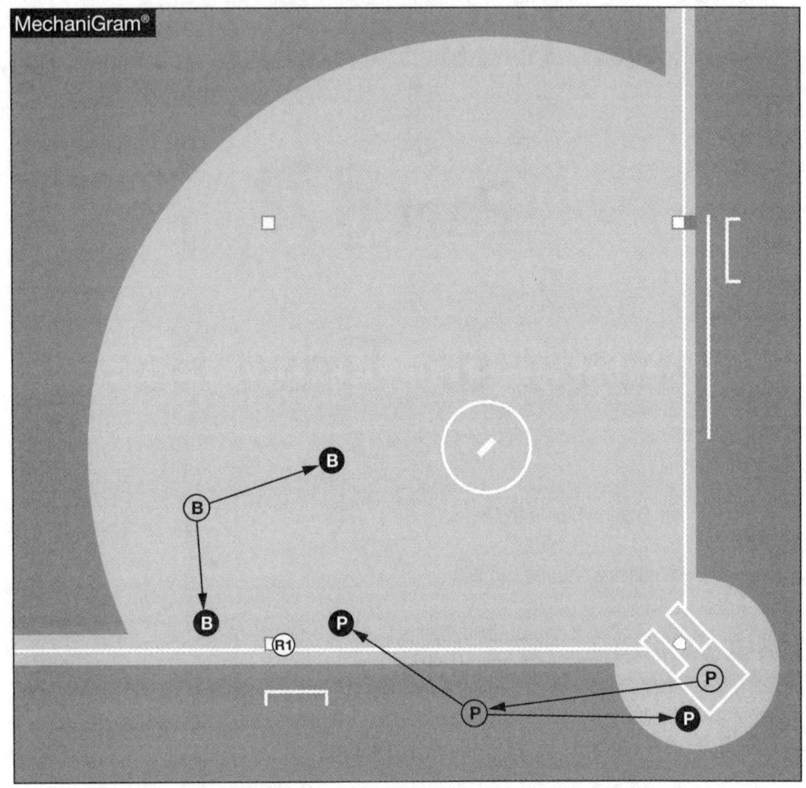

P: Move out from behind the plate toward the holding zone halfway to third base in foul ground to an area where you have an obstructed view of all four elements and read the play. Be prepared to move as the play develops as you are responsible for a subsequent throw to third base on the lead runner (R1) and any play at the plate.

B: Let the ball take you to the play. Move to get the best angle and distance possible as the play develops. Responsible for the first throw in the infield (at any base), any play at first base or second base and the last runner (batter-runner) to third base.

BASE HIT TO THE OUTFIELD

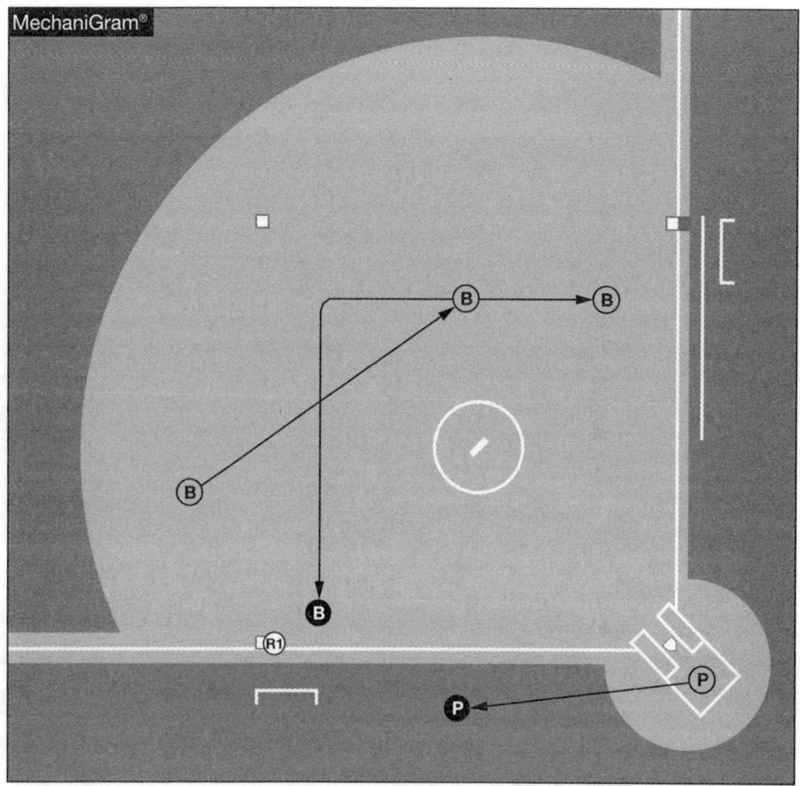

P: Move out from behind the plate toward the holding zone halfway to third base in foul ground to an area where you can see all four elements and read the play. If there is no play developing at home, observe R1 touching home plate from the holding zone and be prepared to move back to the plate area when BU brings the batter-runner to third base. Responsible for any play on a lead runner (R1) at third base and any play at the plate.

B: Pick up the ball and glance at the runner while hustling inside the diamond about halfway between second base and first base. Continue to alternate between the ball and glancing at the runner keeping all four elements in front of you. Be prepared to move parallel to the baseline staying ahead of the runner. Responsible for any play at first base, second base and the last runner (batter-runner) into third base.

FLY BALL TO THE OUTFIELD, BALL IS CAUGHT, B DOES NOT CHASE

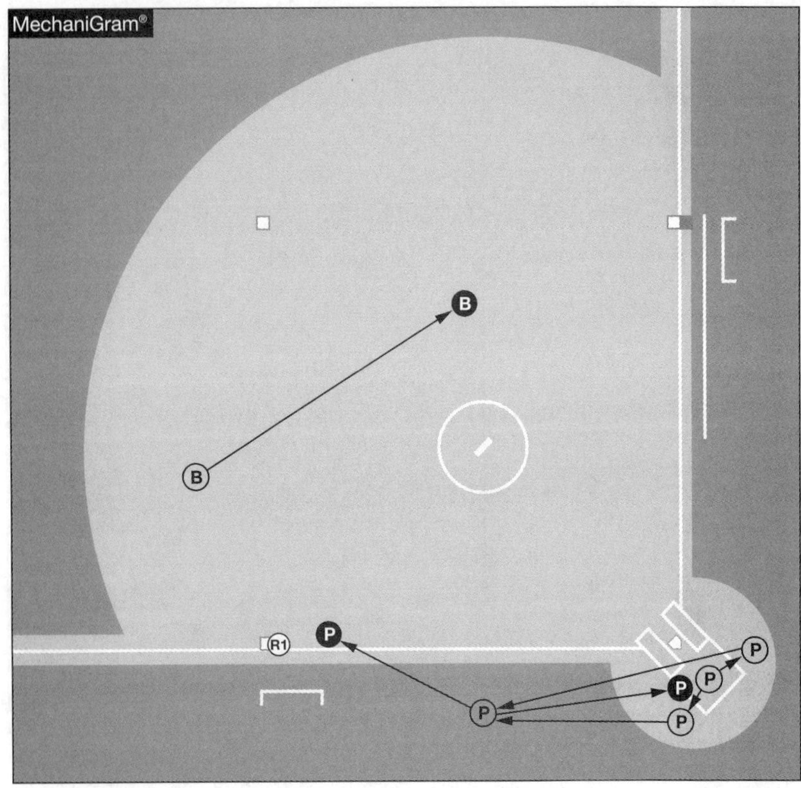

P: Move out from behind the plate to get the best angle and distance possible. Position yourself to observe R1's tag-up at third base as well as the catch. If the ball is near a foul line, position yourself to observe fair/foul, catch/no catch and R1's tag-up at third base, most likely first baseline or third baseline extended. After ruling the catch, move toward the holding zone halfway to third base in foul ground to an area where you have an unobstructed view of all four elements and read the play. Be prepared to move as a play develops. If R1 tags and attempts to score and a play develops, obtain a position at home plate. If there is no play made on R1 at home, remain in the holding zone to watch R1 touch home plate and observe the play. If there is a live ball appeal of R1 at third base position yourself to make that call. Responsible for fair/foul, catch/no catch, tag up at third base (R1), any play on the lead runner (R1) at third base and any play at the plate.

B: Pick up the ball and glance at the runner while hustling inside the diamond about halfway between second base and first base. Continue to alternate between the ball and glancing at the batter-runner keeping all four elements in front of you.

FLY BALL TO THE OUTFIELD, BALL IS NOT CAUGHT, B DOES NOT CHASE

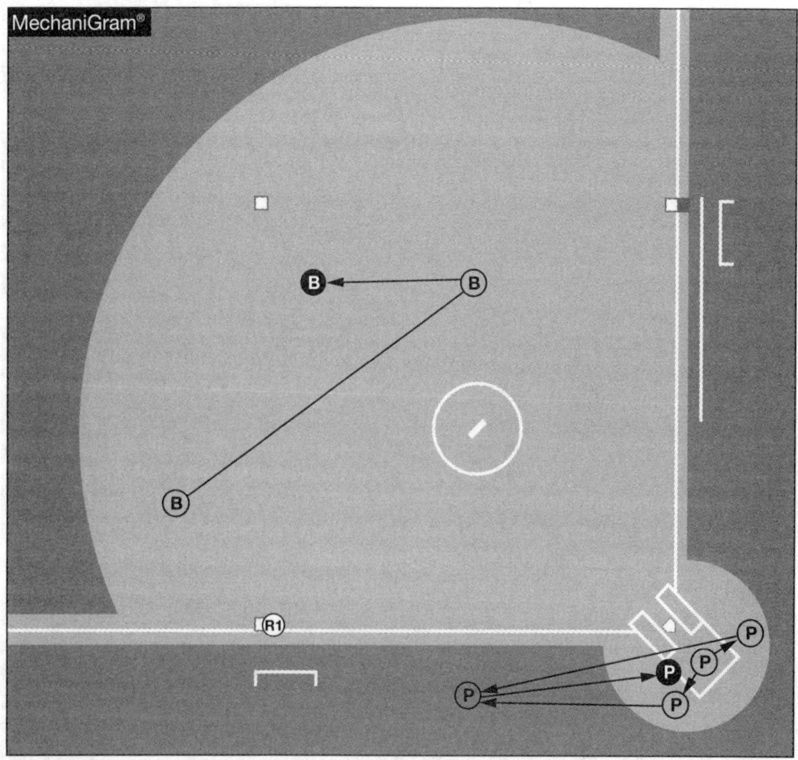

P: Move out from behind the plate to get the best angle and distance possible. Position yourself to observe R1's tag-up at third base as well as the catch. If the ball is near a foul line, position yourself to observe fair/foul, catch/no catch and R1's tag-up at third base, most likely first baseline or third baseline extended. After ruling no catch, move toward the holding zone halfway to third base in foul ground to an area where you have an unobstructed view of all four elements and read the play. Be prepared to move as a play develops. If R1 attempts to score and a play develops, obtain a position at home plate. If there is no play made on R1 at home, remain in the holding zone to watch R1 touch home plate and observe the play. Responsible for fair/foul, catch/no catch, tag up at third base (R1), any play on the lead runner (R1) at third base and any play at the plate.

B: Pick up the ball and glance at the runner while hustling inside the diamond about halfway between second base and first base. Continue to alternate between the ball and glancing at the runner keeping all four elements in front of you. Be prepared to move parallel to the baseline staying ahead of the runner, be prepared for a possible force play at first base or a tag play on the batter-runner at second base. Responsible for any play at first base, second base and the last runner (batter-runner) at third base.

BATTER BUNTS, PLAY AT THIRD OR FIRST

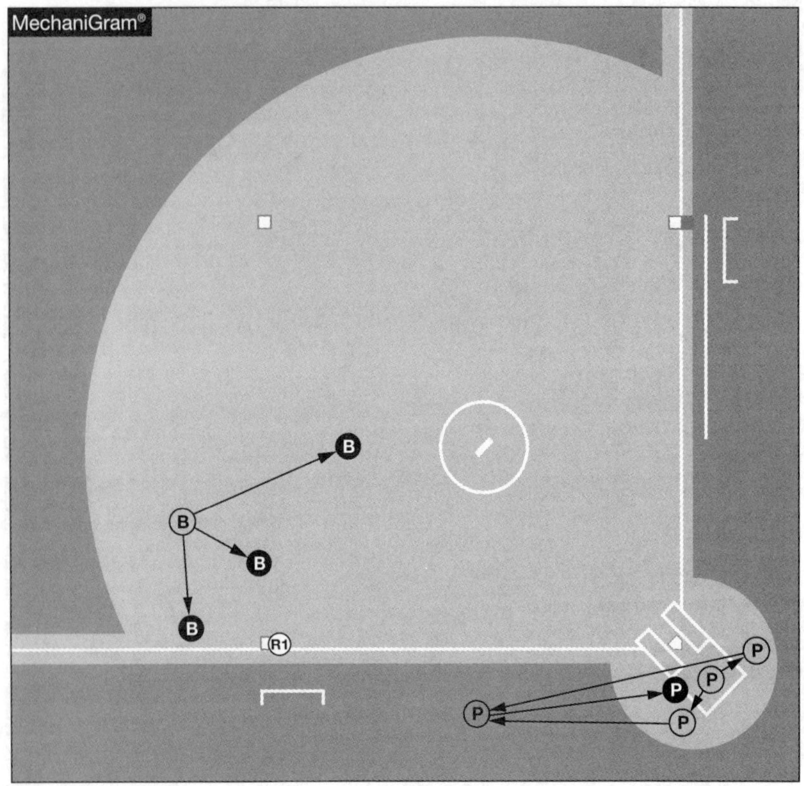

P: Move as necessary to obtain an unobstructed view of the ball to rule fair or foul. If the ball is fair, signal fair then begin moving toward the holding zone reading the play. As the play at first base develops, be prepared to offer an opinion on a swipe tag or pulled foot if requested by the base umpire. Be alert for running lane interference and rule immediately if interference occurs. If the initial play is at first base be prepared to cover any subsequent play on R1 either at third base or at home plate. If the first play is on R1 at home plate, position yourself for this play. Responsible for fair/foul, a subsequent throw to third base on the lead runner (R1) and any play at the plate.

B: Read the play and determine where the play will develop, first base or third base. Move to obtain the best angle and distance possible to the play, coming to a set position to allow you to focus on the play. If the play breaks down and there is uncertainty of a swipe tag or pulled foot, make a decision on the play based on the information available. After the ball is dead, consult with the plate umpire if you have a question about an element of the play. Responsible for the first play in the infield and any play at first base or second base and the last runner (batter-runner) at third base.

Two-Umpire System

Part 6.8

Runners on First, Second and Third Base

◆ Ground Ball in the Infield

◆ Base Hit to the Outfield, B Does Not Chase

◆ Fly Ball to the Outfield, Ball is Caught, B Does Not Chase

◆ Fly Ball to the Outfield, Ball is Not Caught, B Does Not Chase

GROUND BALL IN THE INFIELD

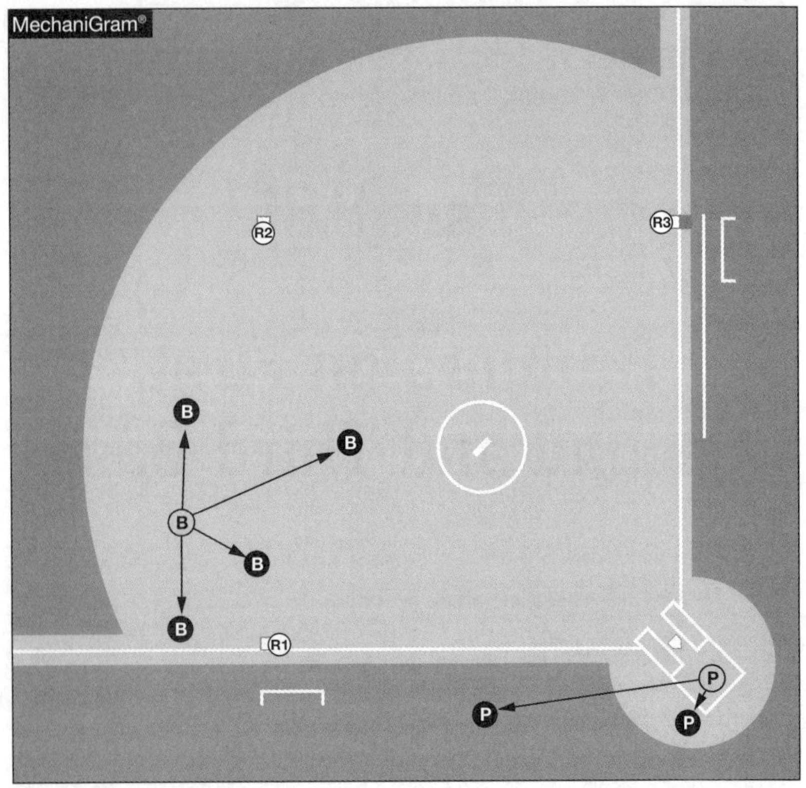

P: Move out from behind the plate and read the play. Be prepared to move as the play develops. Responsible for a subsequent throw to third base on the lead runner (R1, R2 or R3) and any play at the plate.

B: Let the ball take you to the play. Responsible for the first throw in the infield, any play at first base or second base and the last runner (batter-runner) or a return throw from home plate at third base.

BASE HIT TO THE OUTFIELD, B DOES NOT CHASE

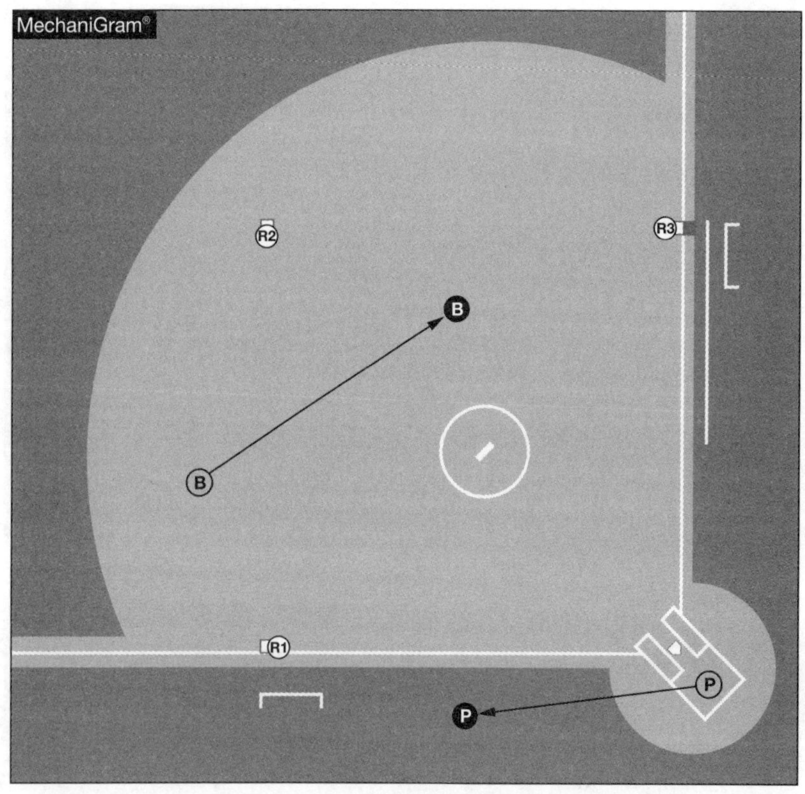

P: Move out from behind the plate toward the holding zone halfway to third base in foul ground to an area where you have an unobstructed view of all four elements and read the play. Be prepared to move as the play develops. Responsible for any play on the lead runner (R1, R2 or R3) at third base and any play at the plate.

B: Pick up the ball and glance at the runner while hustling inside the diamond about halfway between second base and first base. Continue to alternate between the ball and glancing at the runners keeping all four elements in front of you. Be prepared to move parallel to the baseline staying ahead of the runner. Responsible for any play at first base, second base and the last runner (batter-runner) into third base.

FLY BALL TO THE OUTFIELD, BALL IS CAUGHT, B DOES NOT CHASE

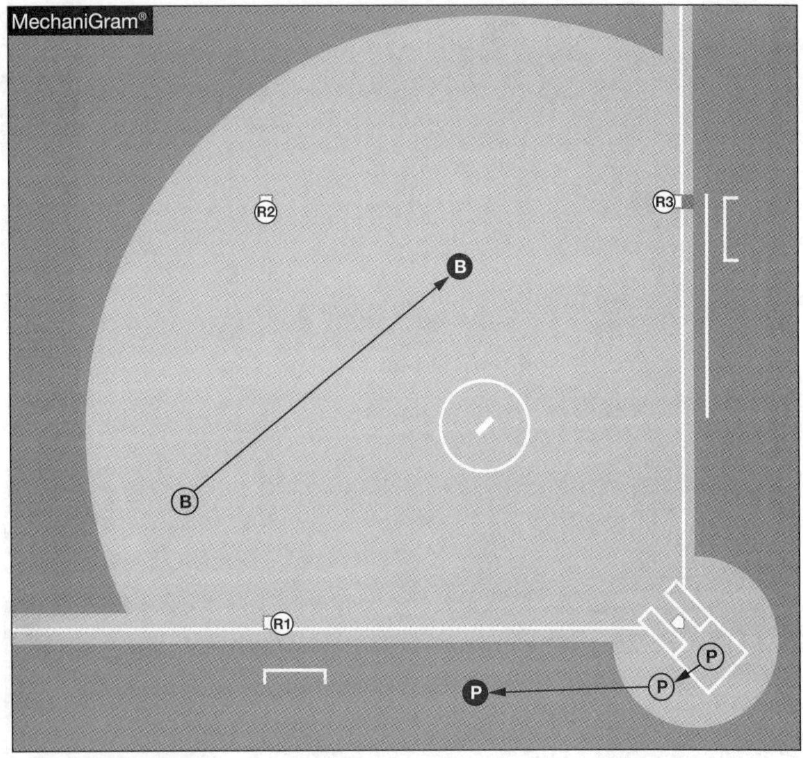

P: Move out from behind the plate to get the best angle and distance possible. Position yourself to observe R1's tag-up at third base as well as the catch. If the ball is near a foul line, position yourself to observe fair/foul, catch/no catch and R1's tag-up at third base, most likely first baseline or third baseline extended. After ruling on the catch, move toward the holding zone halfway to third base in foul ground to an area where you have an unobstructed view of all four elements and read the play. Be prepared to move as a play develops. If R1 attempts to score and a play develops, obtain a position at home plate. If there is no play made on R1 at home, remain in the holding zone to watch R1 touch home plate and be prepared for a play on a lead runner (R2) at third base or any play at the plate. Responsible for fair/foul, catch/no catch, tag up at third base (R1) any play on a lead runner (R1 or R2) at third base and any play at the plate.

B: Pick up the ball and glance at the runner while hustling inside the diamond about halfway between second base and first base. Position yourself to see R2 and R3 tag-up and the catch. Continue to alternate between the ball and glancing at the runners keeping all four elements in front of you. Be prepared to move parallel to the baseline staying ahead of R3 if they advance to second base. Responsible for any play at first base, second base and the last runner (R3) at third base.

FLY BALL TO THE OUTFIELD, BALL IS NOT CAUGHT, B DOES NOT CHASE

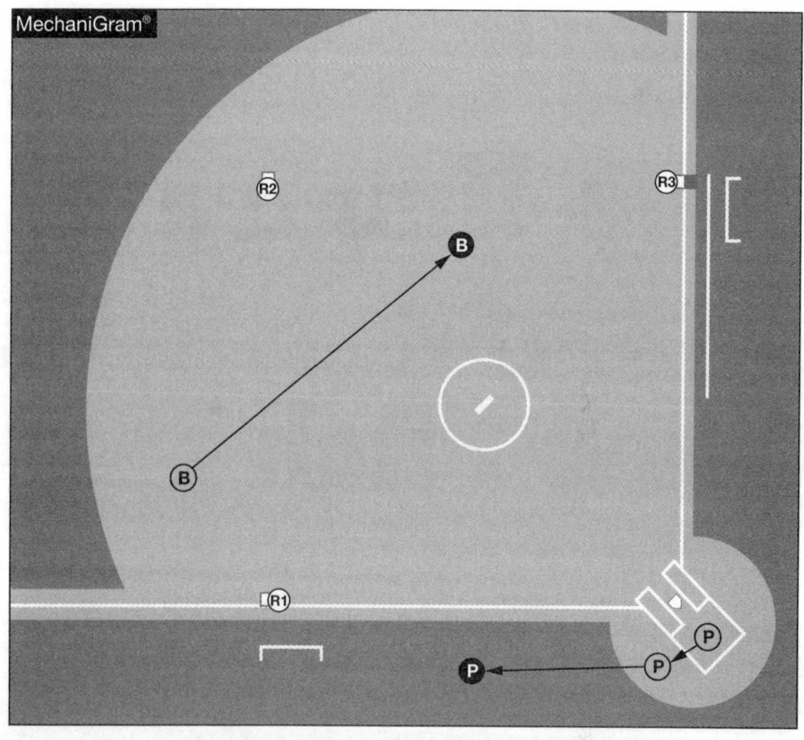

P: Move out from behind the plate to get the best angle and distance possible. Position yourself to observe R1's tag-up at third base as well as the catch. If the ball is near a foul line, position yourself to observe fair/foul, catch/no catch and R1's tag-up at third base, most likely first baseline or third baseline extended. After ruling on the catch, move toward the holding zone halfway to third base in foul ground to an area where you have an unobstructed view of all four elements and read the play. Be prepared to move as a play develops. If a play develops as R1 attempts to score, obtain a position at home plate. If there is no play made on R1 at home, remain in the holding zone to watch R1 touch home plate and be prepared for a play on a lead runner (R2 or R3) at third base or any play at the plate. Responsible for fair/foul, catch/no catch, the tag-up at third base (R1) any play on a lead runner (R1, R2 or R3) at third base and any play at the plate.

B: Pick up the ball and glance at the runner while hustling inside the diamond about halfway between second base and first base. Position yourself to see R2 and R3 tag-up and the catch. Continue to alternate between the ball and glancing at the runners keeping all four elements in front of you. Be prepared to move parallel to the baseline staying ahead of R3 if they advance to second base. Responsible for any play at first base, second base and the last runner (batter-runner) at third base.

Part 7

Two-Umpire System: Slow Pitch

PLATE UMPIRE:

The plate umpire has the same responsibilities as in fast pitch with the following exceptions. In slow pitch, the plate umpire is responsible for:

a. All calls on a pitched ball once it leaves the pitcher's hand.

b. All fair and foul balls.

c. Batter-runner infractions.

d. All calls at third base and home plate with the following exceptions:

- The base umpire is responsible for the batter-runner or the last runner to third base.
- The base umpire is responsible for a lone runner on a tag-up to third base.
- When there is a play at home plate and a subsequent play at third base or a cut off throw, the base umpire is responsible for the subsequent play in the infield regardless of where the play is made.

BASE UMPIRE:

The base umpire is responsible for the following situations:

a. If the base umpire does not go out on a fly ball, the base umpire is responsible for all calls at first and second base.

b. For the batter-runner or the last runner to third base.

c. For a lone runner on a tag-up and advancement on a fly ball to third base.

d. When there is a play at home plate and the throw to home plate is cut off or a subsequent play anywhere in the infield.

e. With a runner on base, the base umpire will normally take a position between first base and second base, off of the second-baseperson, and shading the lead runner. Under no circumstance shall the base umpire take a position inside the base line or on the shortstop side of second base.

NO RUNNERS ON BASE OR THIRD BASE ONLY

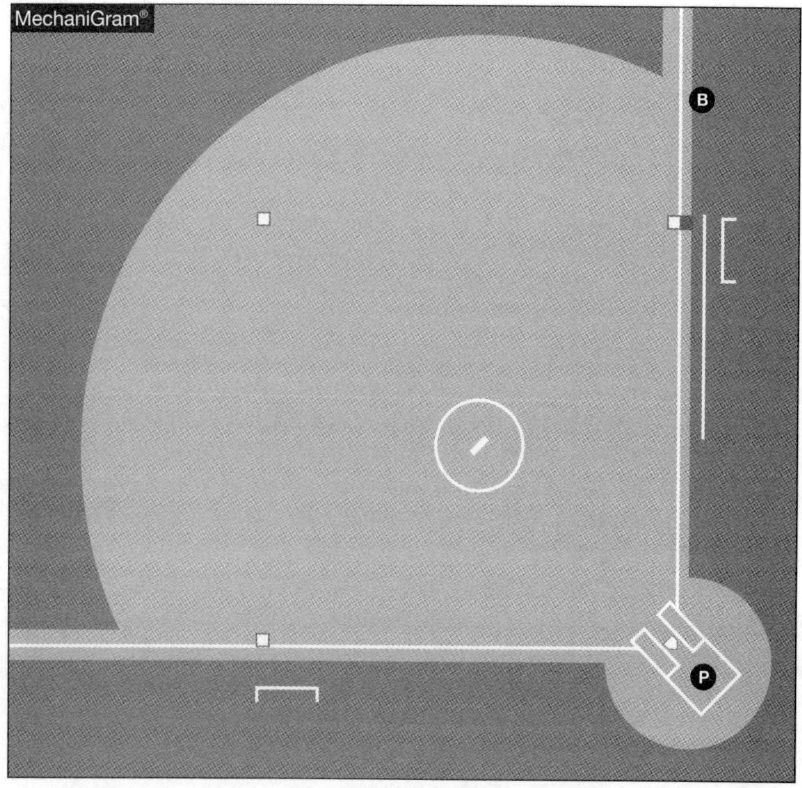

Basic position is 18-21 feet beyond first base in foul territory.

RUNNER ON FIRST BASE ONLY OR FIRST BASE AND THIRD BASE ONLY

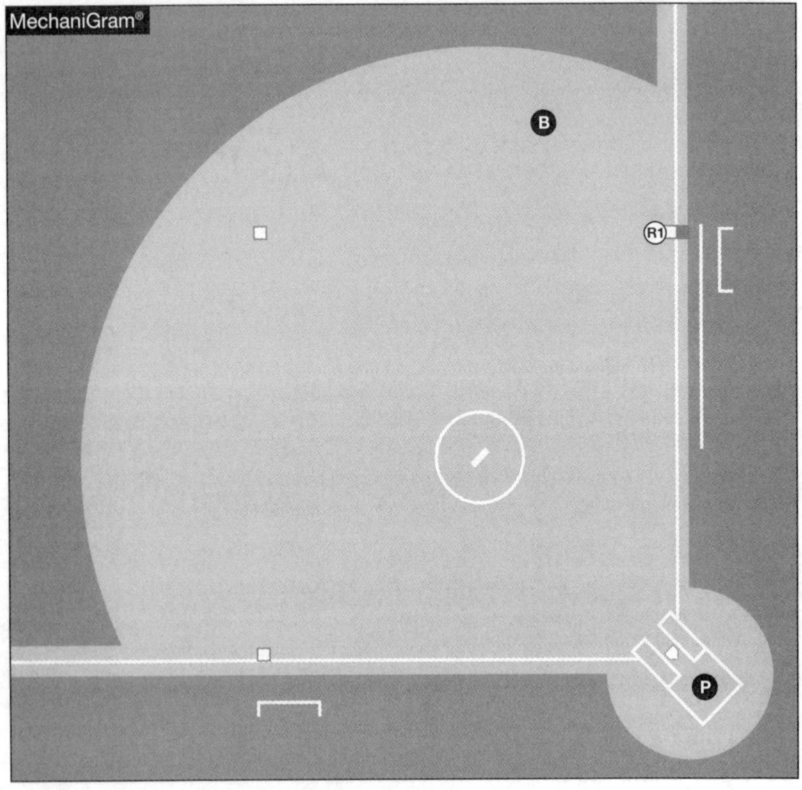

The base umpire should normally shade the runner at first base and take a position off of and to the first-base side of the second-baseperson.

RUNNERS ON FIRST BASE AND SECOND BASE ONLY

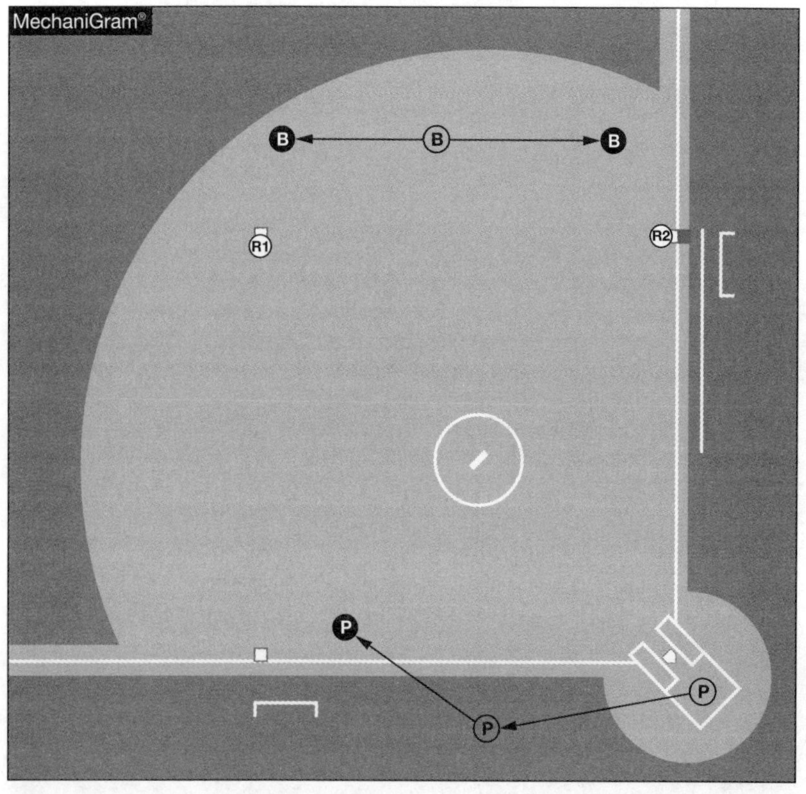

P: Move out from behind the plate toward the holding zone halfway to third base in foul ground to an area where you have an unobstructed view of all four elements and read the play. Be prepared to move as the play develops, as you are responsible for any play on the lead runner at third base and any play at the plate.

B: Let the ball take you to the play. Responsible for any play at first base, second base and the last runner into third base.

RUNNER ON SECOND BASE ONLY, FIRST AND SECOND BASE ONLY, SECOND BASE AND THIRD BASE ONLY OR BASES LOADED

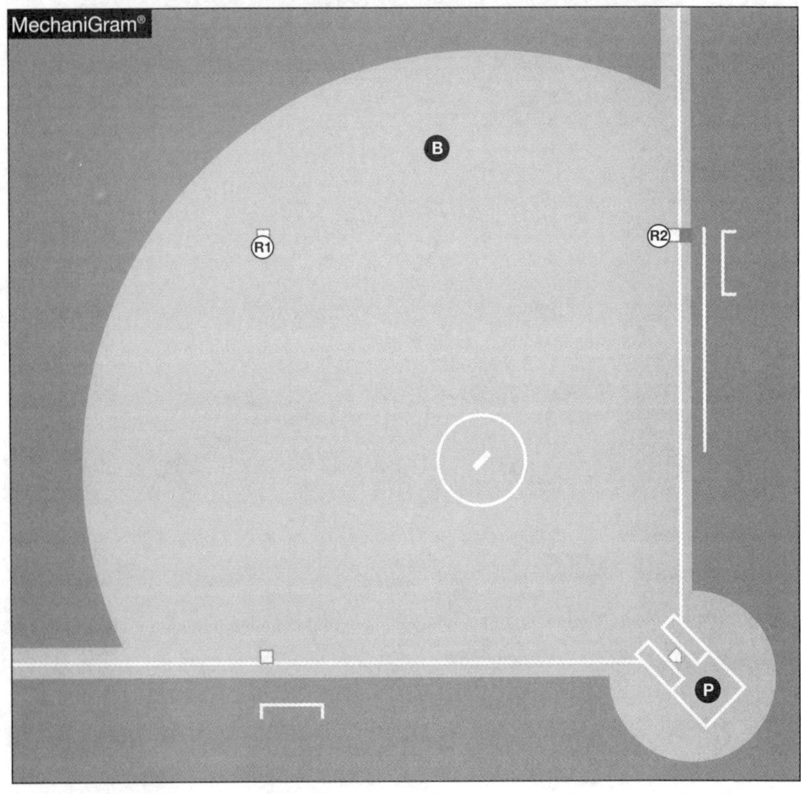

The base umpire should take a position normally off of and to the second-base side of the second-baseperson.

NOTE 1: In some divisions of play, the infielders play very deep making it difficult for the base umpire to button-hook inside ahead of the runner. If the base umpire is positioned off of the second-baseperson when the second-baseperson and shortstop are playing very deep, the base umpire should find a position on an imaginary line directly between the two defenders toward second base. When the ball stays in the infield and there is a play at first base, it is imperative that the umpire move parallel to the baseline to make the call.

NOTE 2: In some divisions of play, teams are bringing an outfielder closer to the infield to play behind second base, referred to as the fifth infielder. If this occurs and all infielders are playing very deep, the imaginary line should be from the second-baseperson to the defensive player positioned behind second base.

Part 8

Three-Umpire System

The three-umpire system, when executed properly, is not only the most enjoyable system of umpiring, but also assures a complete coverage of everything that may occur on the ball field. Because it entails a 50 percent addition to the two-umpire system expense, it may never replace the two-umpire system.

The two-umpire system provides adequate coverage for all but a small proportion of the situations that may arise, but the three-umpire system, when properly executed, insures the undivided attention of one umpire on every play and at each base.

At the start of play, the base umpires assume positions about 18 to 21 feet behind first and third bases. The plate umpire judges batted balls fair/foul and catch/no catch. The base umpires should only help the plate umpire when they turn their back to the infield and go out on a fly ball or a sinking line drive in their coverage area.

Umpires must have a thorough awareness and understanding of the responsibilities, requirements and expectations of not only their position, but the other positions as well.

Umpires should use the standard starting positions, areas of coverage, and rotations, and to employ, at all times, the core philosophy of general mechanics when working this system. Any deviation or adjustment from the standard must be dictated by the action on the field and communicated among umpires.

The Basics
- Rotation for the three-umpire system is always clockwise.
- Once a base umpire turns their back to the infield to go to the outfield on a play, that umpire should remain outside until the play has been completed.
- Once an umpire goes to the outfield, revert to a two-umpire system.
- When the umpires start counter-rotated, there is no rotation.

• With an enclosed field, a base umpire should go to the outfield on any fly ball hit that goes beyond the infield when there is an opportunity for the ball to be caught and the ball is in that umpire's coverage area.

• With an open field, a base umpire should go out on any ball hit beyond the infield where there is an opportunity for the ball to go into dead-ball territory.

Guides

Before every pitch each umpire should pre-pitch plan by running through a mental checklist on such things as:

- Could I be involved in a rotation?
- What's my fly-ball coverage area?
- Where are the fielders playing? Are they shifted or playing normal position?
- How deep are the fielders playing?
- Where do I go if my partner chases?
- Where do I go on a ball hit to the infield?
- Where do I go on a ball hit to the outfield that no umpire chases?
- What are my tag-up responsibilities — no chase, partner chases?
- How many outs?
- What is the count?
- What is the score?
- What type of play is most likely?
- What type of batted ball presents high potential for interference?
- Where would obstruction likely occur?

Starting Positions

There are only three positions umpires will take at the start of the pitch.

- Standard
- Rotated
- Counter-Rotated
  1. Shading first base with R2 on first base.
  2. Shading second base with R1 or R2 on second base.

Runner configurations when umpires start in the standard starting position.

- No runners on base.
- Runner on third base only.

Runner configuration when umpires start in the rotated starting position.

- Runner on first base.

Umpires will start in the counter-rotated position when the first-base umpire is positioned between first and second base. There will be no umpire rotation in these situations.

- Runners on first and third base.
- Runners on first and second base.
- Runner on second base.
- Runners on second and third base.
- Runners on first, second and third base.

Leaving a Base Too Soon and Tag-Up Responsibilities

Runner(s) Location(s)	Runner Leaving Early on the Pitch		Fly Ball Tag-Up No Umpire Chases		Fly Ball Tag-Up Base Umpire Chases	
	U1	U3	U1	U3	Base Umpire*	Plate Umpire
Runner at 1B Only	R1 at 1B	N/A	R1 at 1B	N/A	R1 at 1B	N/A
Runner at 2B Only	R1 at 2B	N/A	R1 at 2B	N/A	R1 at 2B	N/A
Runner at 3B Only	N/A	R1 at 3B	N/A	R1 at 3B	N/A	R1 at 3B
Runner at 1B & 2B Only	R1 at 2B	R2 at 1B	R2 at 1B	R1 at 2B	R2 at 1B	R1 at 2B
Runner at 2B & 3B Only	R2 at 2B	R1 at 3B	R2 at 2B	R1 at 3B	R2 at 2B	R1 at 3B
Runner at 1B & 3B Only	R2 at 1B	R1 at 3B	R2 at 1B	R1 at 3B	R2 at 1B	R1 at 3B
Bases Loaded	R2 at 2B	R1 at 3B & R3 at 1B	R2 at 2B & R3 at 1B	R1 at 3B	R2 at 2B & R3 at 1B	R1 at 3B

* Base umpire that did not chase (U1 or U3).

BETWEEN INNING MECHANICS

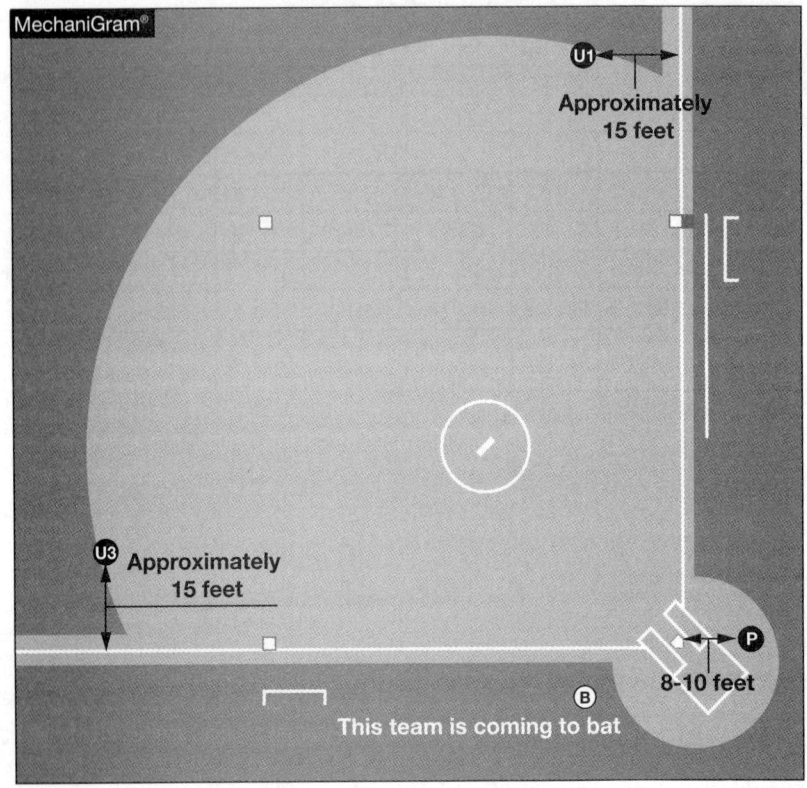

P: Facing the team that is coming to bat. About 8-10 feet from the line on a perpendicular line from where the foul line meets the plate. This is called first base/third baseline extended.

U1: Facing the plate no more than 15 feet off the foul line at approximately where the grass starts.

U3: Facing the plate no more than 15 feet off the foul line at approximately where the grass starts.

STANDARD STARTING POSITION WITH NO RUNNERS ON BASE

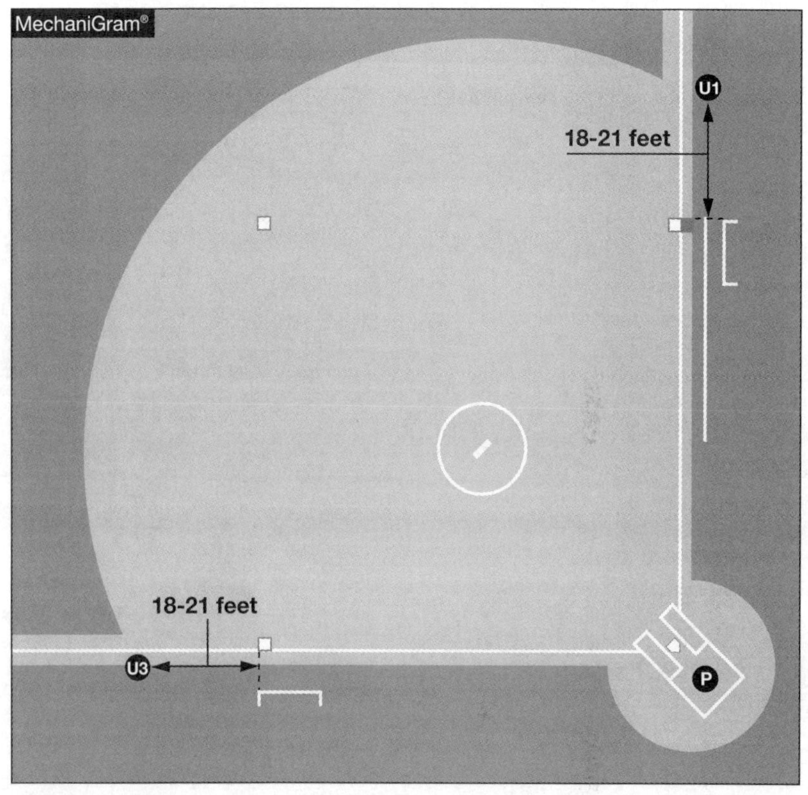

P: Behind the plate.

U1 and U3: 18-21 feet down and close to the line, completely in foul territory in an upright, standing position and squared to the plate. As the pitch is delivered, U1 and U3 walk the line taking no more than two steps forward, ending on the outer foot allowing them to push off and move into the diamond when the ball is hit.

STANDARD STARTING POSITION WITH A RUNNER ON THIRD

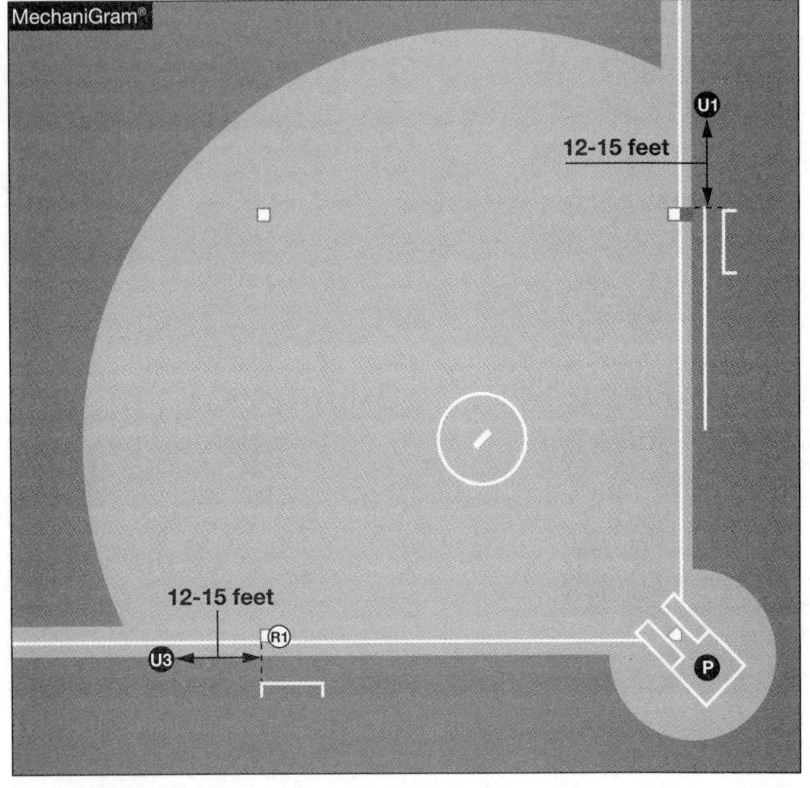

P: Behind the plate.

U1: 12-15 feet down the line square to the plate, completely in foul territory going to the set or ready position at the start of the pitch.

U3: 12-15 feet down the line square to the plate, completely in foul territory going to the set or ready position at the start of the pitch. If necessary to maintain an unobstructed view of the plate move slightly off the line, especially for left handed batters.

ROTATED STARTING POSITION WITH A RUNNER ON FIRST

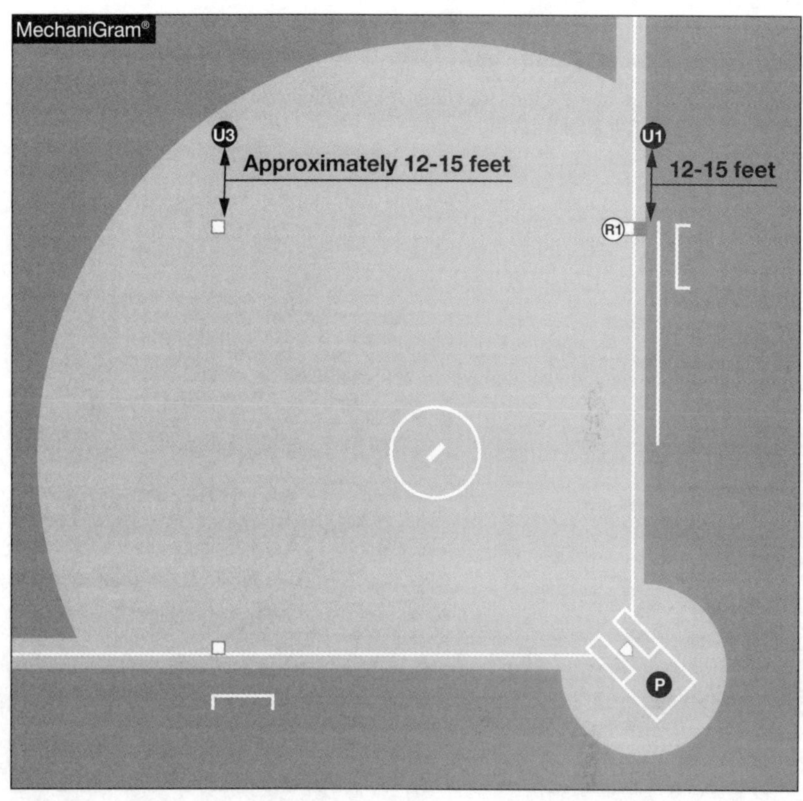

P: Behind the plate.

U1: 12-15 feet down the line square to the plate, completely in foul territory going to the set or ready position at the start of the pitch.

U3: Square to the plate, 12-15 feet beyond second base on an imaginary line extending straight from the home plate side of third base in line with the first base side of second base, going to the set or ready position at the start of the pitch.

COUNTER-ROTATED STARTING POSITION, RUNNERS ON FIRST AND SECOND

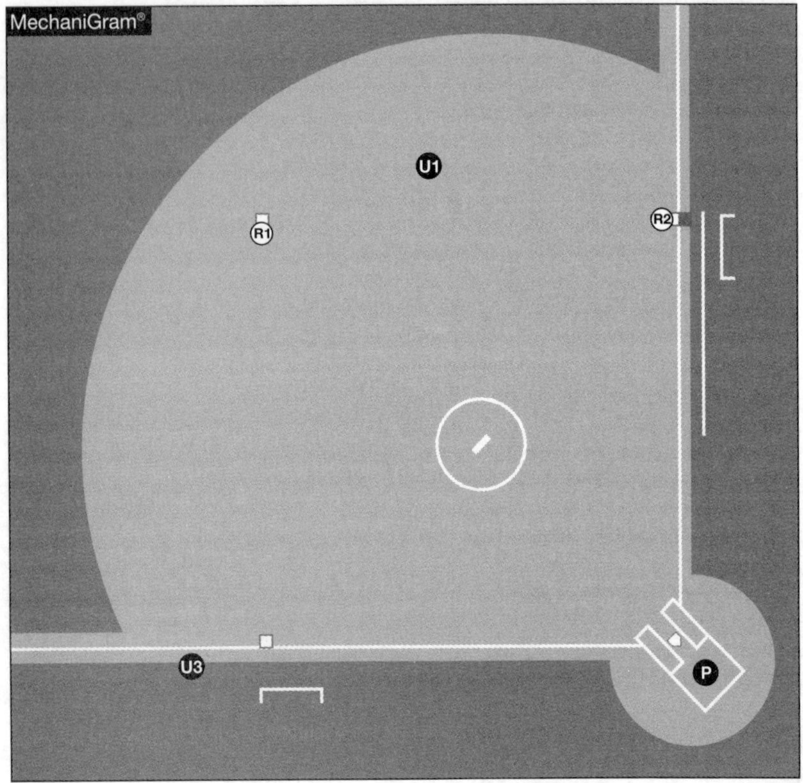

P: Behind the plate

U1: Shade the lead runner at second base being behind or off of F4, square to the plate, going to the set or ready position at the start of the pitch.

U3: 12-15 feet down the line square to the plate, completely in foul territory near the foul line going to the set or ready position at the start of the pitch.

COUNTER-ROTATED STARTING POSITION, RUNNERS ON FIRST AND THIRD

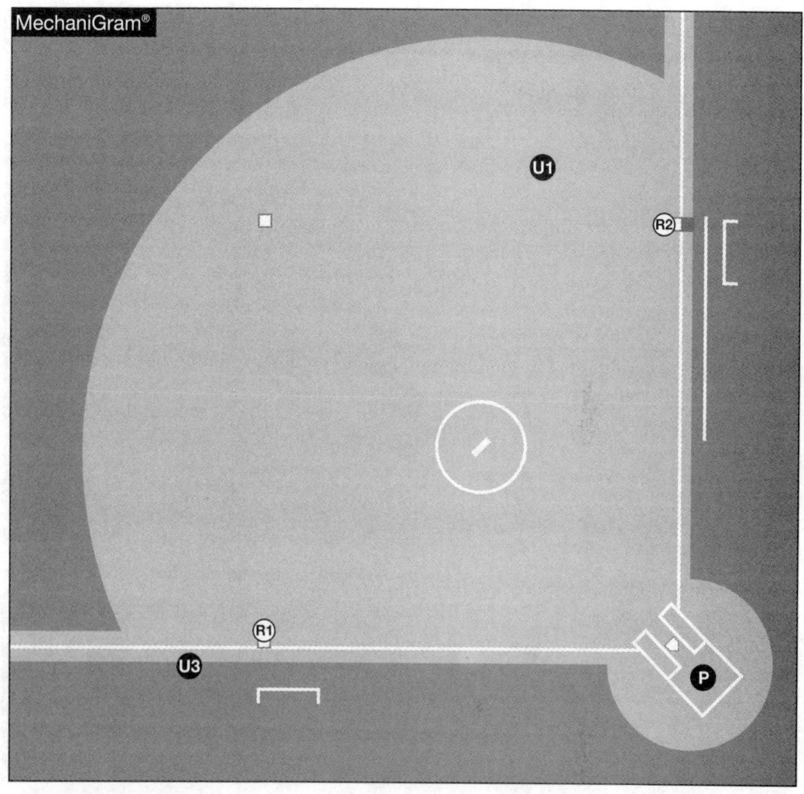

P: Behind the plate

U1: Shade the runner at first base being behind or off of F4, square to the plate, going to the set or ready position at the start of the pitch.

U3: 12-15 feet down the line square to the plate, completely in foul territory going to the set or ready position at the start of the pitch. If necessary to maintain an unobstructed view of the plate move slightly off the line, especially for left handed batters.

COUNTER-ROTATED STARTING POSITION, RUNNER ON SECOND

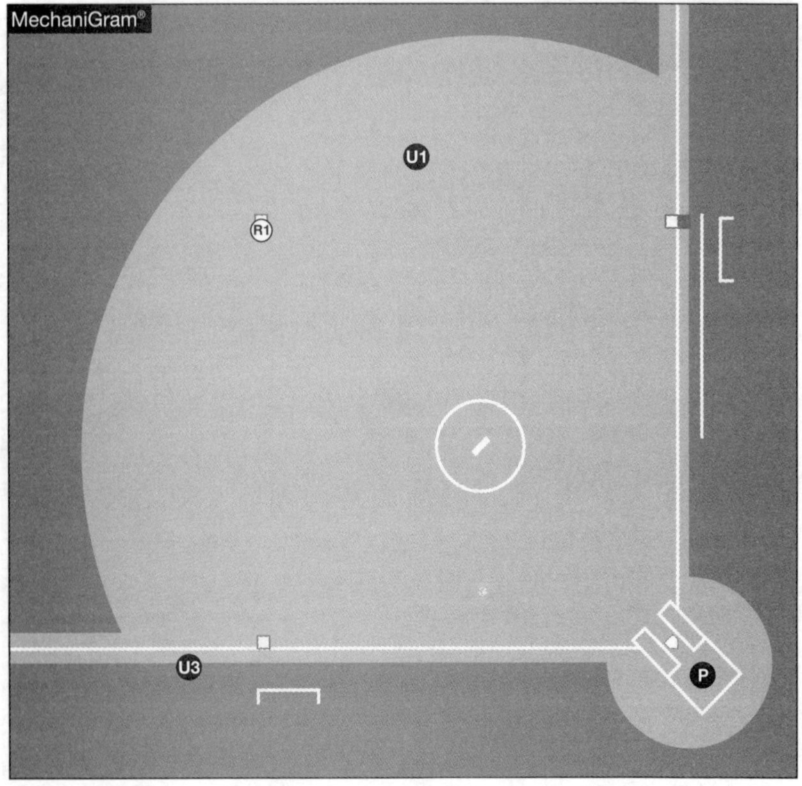

P: Behind the plate

U1: Shade the lead runner at second base being behind or off of F4, square to the plate, going to the set or ready position at the start of the pitch.

U3: 12-15 feet down the line square to the plate, completely in foul territory near the foul line going to the set or ready position at the start of the pitch.

STANDARD STARTING POSITION, CHASE RESPONSIBILITIES

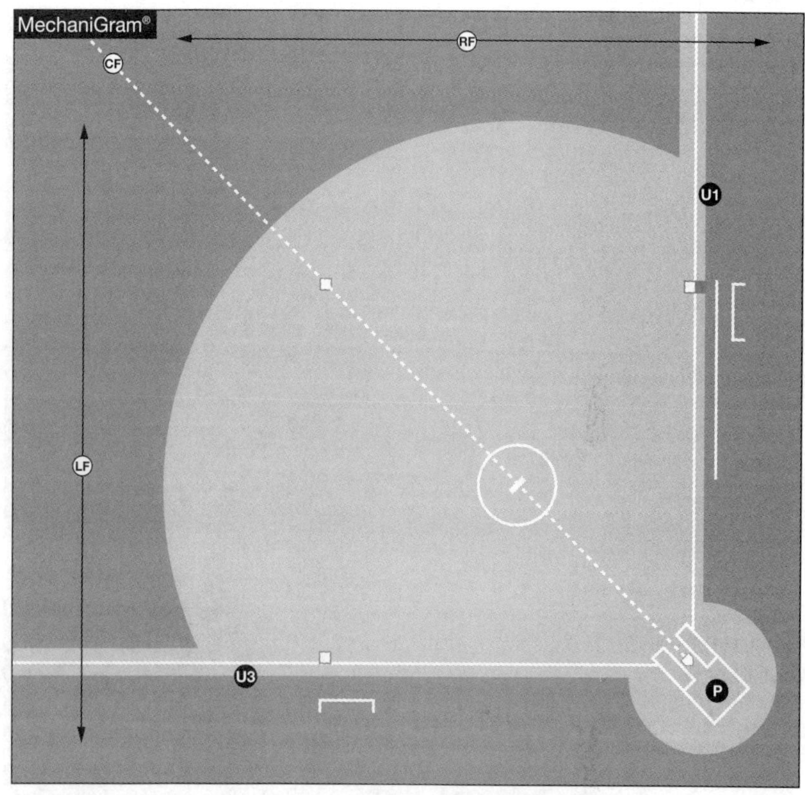

P: No fly ball responsibility, unless a base umpire does not chase.

U1: Responsible for fly balls from the center fielder to the right field dead-ball line. U1 has the "right of first refusal" on balls hit to center field since the impending play is coming at U1. Also, it is easier for U3 to adjust after having started or not started to chase.

U3: Responsible for fly balls from the center fielder to the left field dead-ball line. Key off U1.

ROTATED STARTING POSITION, CHASE RESPONSIBILITIES

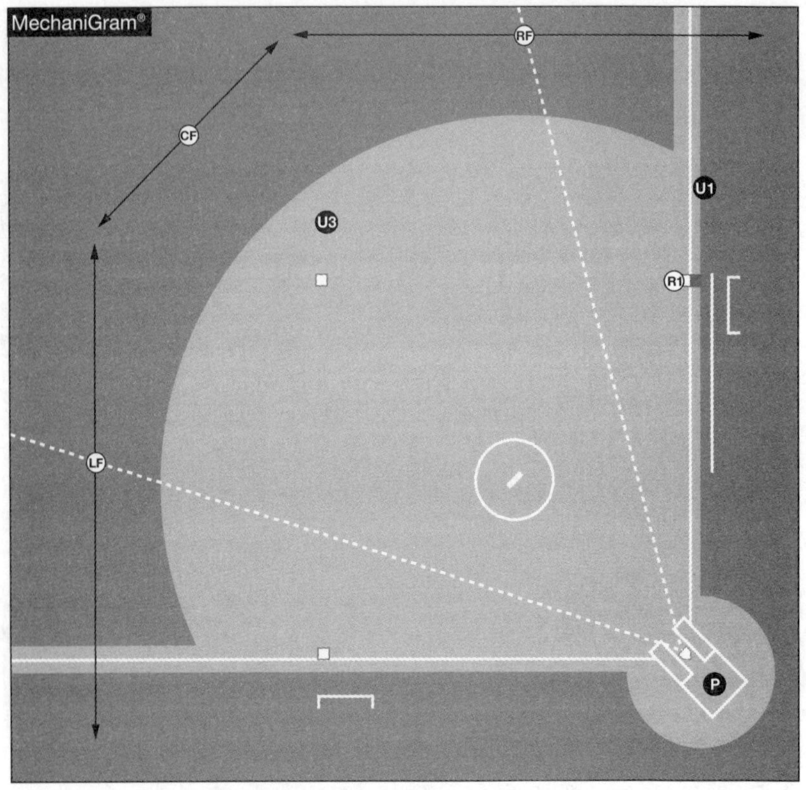

P: Responsible for fly balls from the left fielder to the left field dead-ball line.

U1: Responsible for fly balls from the right fielder to the right field dead-ball line.

U3: Responsible for fly balls from the left fielder to the right fielder (in the "V"). No fair/foul responsibilities.

COUNTER-ROTATED STARTING POSITION, CHASE RESPONSIBILITIES

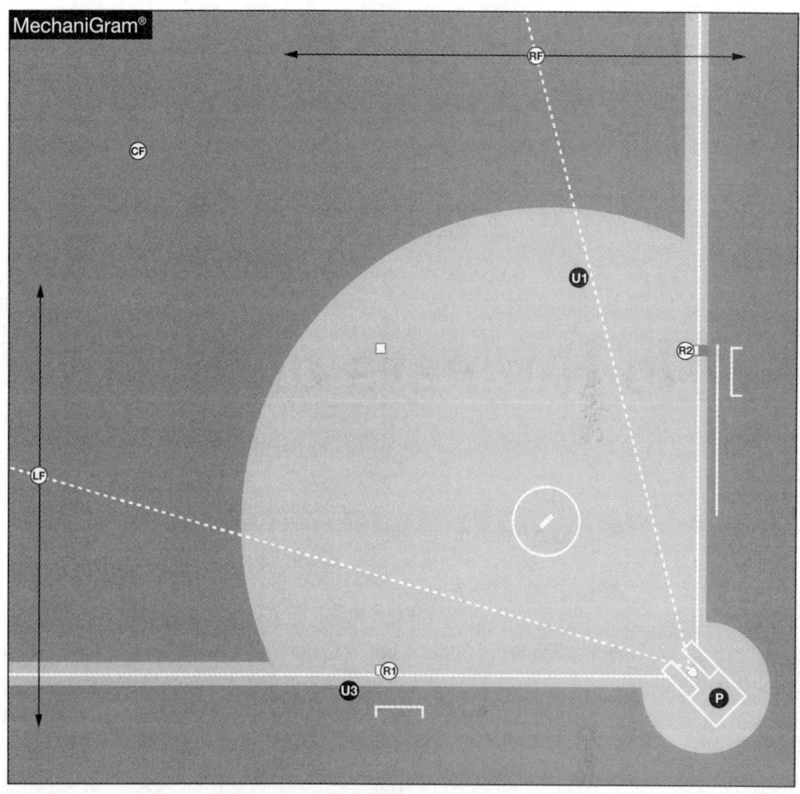

P: Responsible for fly balls from the right fielder to the right-field dead-ball line.

U1: Responsible for fly balls from the left fielder, coming in or going back, to the right fielder (in the V). No fair/foul responsibilities.

U3: Responsible for fly balls from the left fielder to the left-field dead-ball line.

Three-Umpire System

Part 8.1

No Runners on Base

◆ Ground Ball in the Infield

◆ Base Hit to the Outfield

◆ Fly Ball to the Outfield, Ball is Caught, U1 Chases

◆ Fly Ball to the Outfield, Ball is Not Caught, U1 Chases

◆ Fly Ball to the Outfield, Ball is Caught, U3 Chases

◆ Fly Ball to the Outfield, Ball is Not Caught, U3 Chases

GROUND BALL IN THE INFIELD

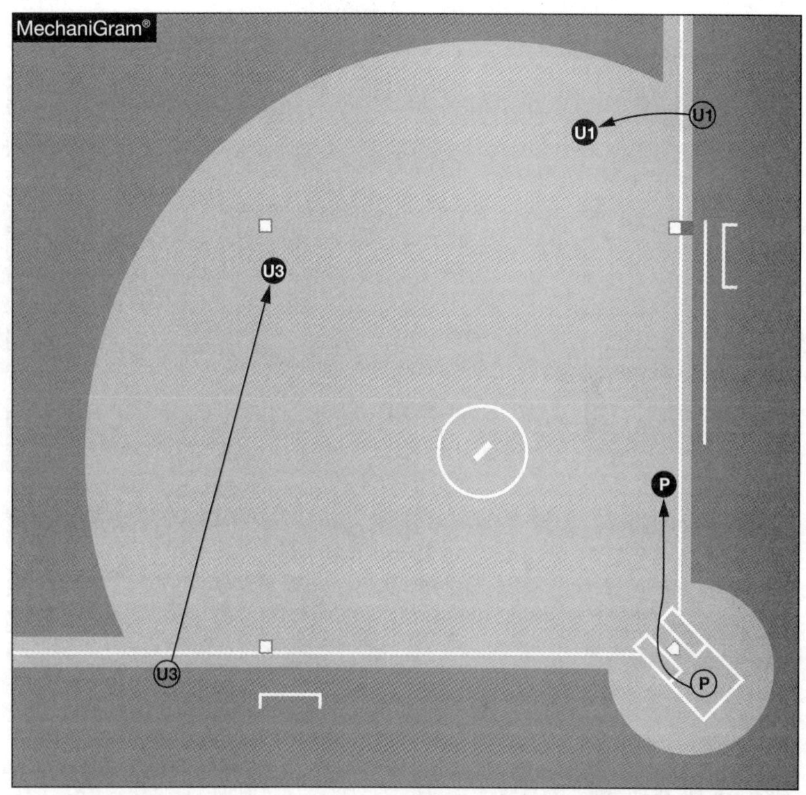

P: Trail the batter-runner no more than one-third of the way to first base in fair territory, stop to see the play at first base. If a subsequent play occurs, then read the play and move to third base as the batter-runner approaches second base. First, obtain the proper angle, then close your distance as the play develops working to get an unobstructed view of the play and to obtain a minimum distance of 10-12 feet from the play. Remember as the four elements come together; stop, read the play and make the call. Responsible for fair/foul and any play at third base.

U1: Step into fair territory, at an angle 90 degrees to the path of the throw, but no more than a 45-degree angle from the foul line and let the ball take you to the play. Responsible for any play at first base.

U3: Hustle into the diamond to a 90-degree angle and a minimum of 10-12 feet from second base. Responsible for any play at second base.

BASE HIT TO THE OUTFIELD

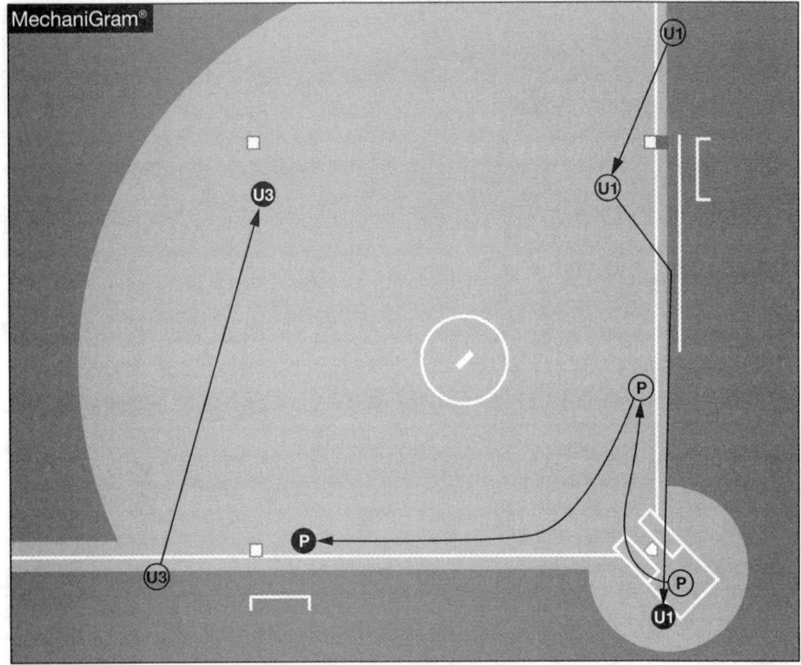

P: Trail the batter-runner no more than one-third of the way to first base in fair territory and read the play. As the runner approaches second base, move across the diamond in front of the pitcher's plate to first obtain the proper angle, then close your distance as the play develops working to get an unobstructed view of the play and to obtain a minimum distance of 10-12 feet from the play. Remember, as the four elements come together, stop, read the play and make the call. As the runner reaches third base, visually confirm that U1 has rotated into position at home. Responsible for fair/foul and any play at third base.

U1: Pick up the ball and glance at the runner while hustling inside the diamond to button hook at a minimum depth of 10-12 feet. Continue to alternate between the ball and glancing at the runner keeping all four elements in front of you. If the runner continues on to second base, visually confirm U3 has rotated to second base. As the runner commits to second base, rotate to home in foul ground to the farthest back corner of no right-hand batter's box, a minimum of 10-12 feet from the plate, for any possible play at home plate. Responsible for any play at first base when at first base and any play at the plate when rotated to the plate.

U3: While picking up the ball and glancing at the runner, rotate to a position a minimum of 10-12 feet from second base at a 90-degree angle. Continue to alternate between the ball and the runner keeping all four elements in front of you. As the runner reaches second base, visually confirm that the plate umpire has rotated into position at third base. Responsible for any play at second base and any play at first base when U1 has rotated to the plate.

FLY BALL TO THE OUTFIELD, BALL IS CAUGHT, U1 CHASES

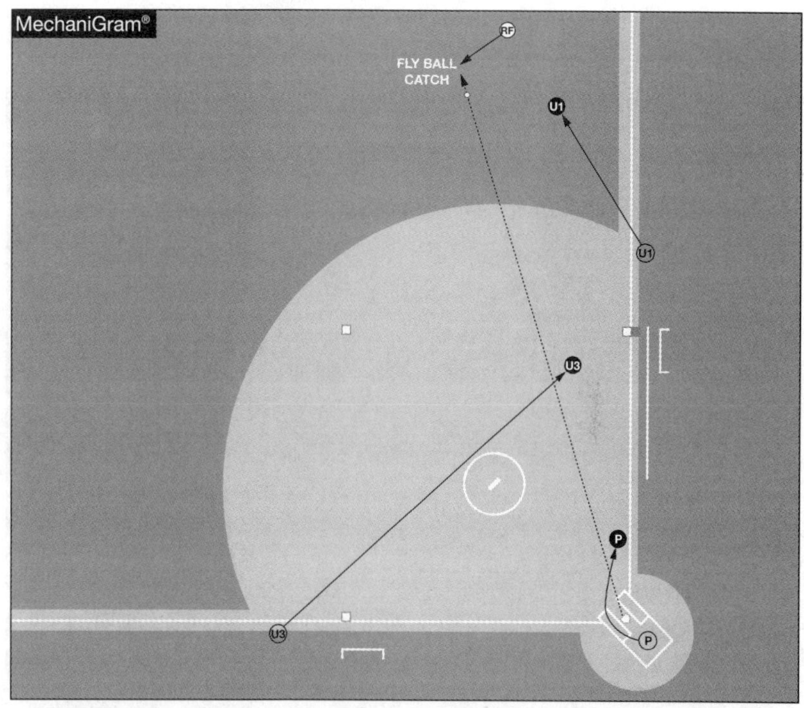

P: Trail the batter-runner no more than one-third of the way to first base in fair territory and read the play. When the batter-runner rounds first base and advances to second base, move toward the holding zone about halfway to third base in foul ground to an area where you have an unobstructed view of all four elements. Be prepared to move as the play develops. Responsible for any play at the plate.

U1: Pick up the flight of the ball and glance at your partner. Responsible for any fly ball from the center fielder to the right fielder and up to dead-ball territory. When chasing the fly ball communicate with the crew you are chasing. Move parallel to the flight of the ball, or if necessary to gain a better angle, move away from the fielder being stopped facing the player when the play happens. If caught, give the out signal and verbal facing the play. If the ball is dropped and it is not obvious, give the safe/no catch signal. Responsible for fair/foul, catch/no catch.

U3: When a fly ball is hit and U1 goes out, pick up the ball and glance at the runner while hustling inside the diamond toward first base. Continue to alternate between the ball and the runner keeping all four elements in front of you. Be prepared to move parallel to the baseline staying ahead of the runner. Responsible for any play at first base, second base and third base.

FLY BALL TO THE OUTFIELD, BALL IS NOT CAUGHT, U1 CHASES

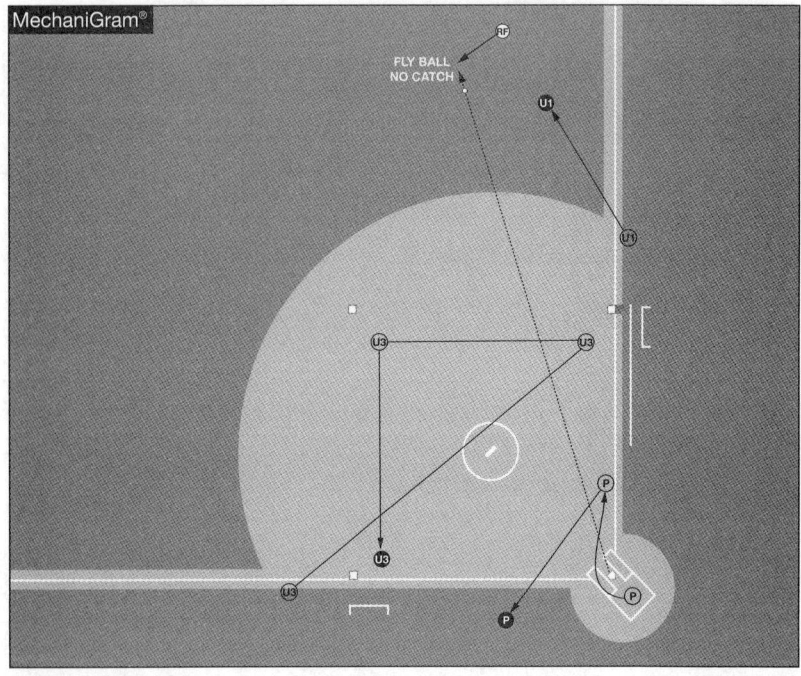

P: Trail the batter-runner no more than one-third of the way to first base in fair territory and read the play. When the batter-runner rounds first base and advances to second base, move toward the holding zone about halfway to third base in foul ground to an area where you have an unobstructed view of all four elements. Be prepared to move as the play develops. Responsible for any play at the plate.

U1: Pick up the flight of the ball and glance at your partner. Responsible for any fly ball from the center fielder to the right fielder and up to dead-ball territory. When chasing the fly ball communicate with the crew you are chasing. Move parallel to the flight of the ball, or if necessary to gain a better angle, move away from the fielder stop facing the player when the play happens. If caught, give the out signal and verbal facing the play. If the ball is dropped and it is not obvious, give the safe/no catch signal. Let the ball turn you back toward the infield and observe the rest of the play from there. Responsible for fair/foul, catch/no catch.

U3: When a fly ball is hit and U1 goes out, pick up the ball and glance at the runner while hustling inside the diamond toward first base. Continue to alternate between the ball and the runner keeping all four elements in front of you. Be prepared to move parallel to the baseline staying ahead of the runner. Responsible for any play at first base, second base and third base.

FLY BALL TO THE OUTFIELD, BALL IS CAUGHT, U3 CHASES

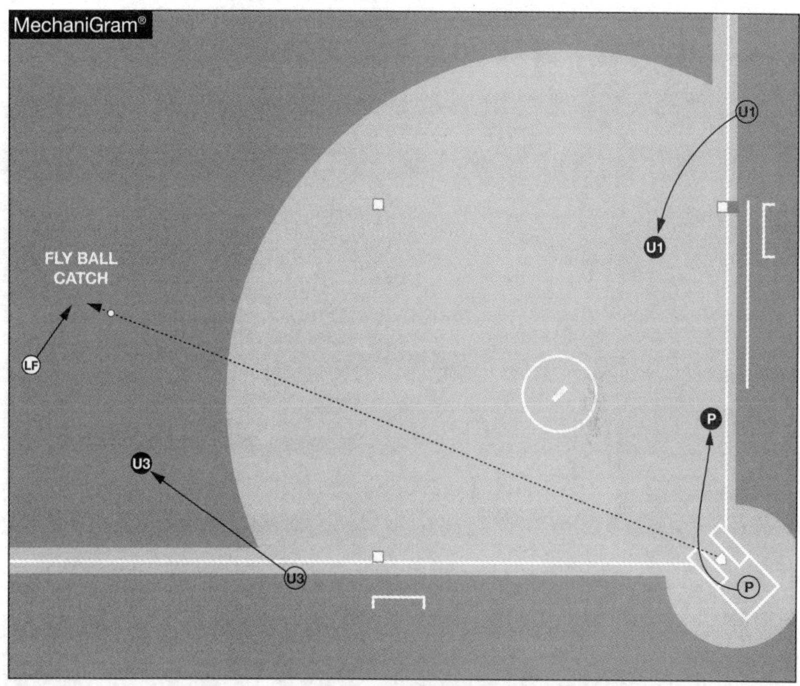

P: Trail the batter-runner no more than one-third of the way to first base in fair territory and read the play. When the batter-runner rounds first base and advances to second base, move toward the holding zone about halfway to third base in foul ground to an area where you have an unobstructed view of all four elements. Be prepared to move as the play develops. Responsible for any play at the plate.

U1: When a fly ball is hit and U3 goes out, pick up the ball and glance at the runner while hustling inside the diamond to button hook at a minimum depth of 10-12 feet. Continue to alternate between the ball and the runner keeping all four elements in front of you. Be prepared to move parallel to the baseline staying ahead of the runner. Responsible for any play at first base, second base and third base.

U3: Pick up the flight of the ball and glance at your partner. Responsible for any fly ball from the center fielder to the left fielder and up to dead-ball territory. When chasing the fly ball communicate with the crew you are chasing. Move parallel to the flight of the ball, or if necessary to gain a better angle, move away from the fielder; stop facing the player when the play happens. If caught, give the out signal and verbal facing the play. If the ball is dropped and it is not obvious, give the safe/no catch signal. Responsible for fair/foul, catch/no catch.

FLY BALL TO THE OUTFIELD, BALL IS NOT CAUGHT, U3 CHASES

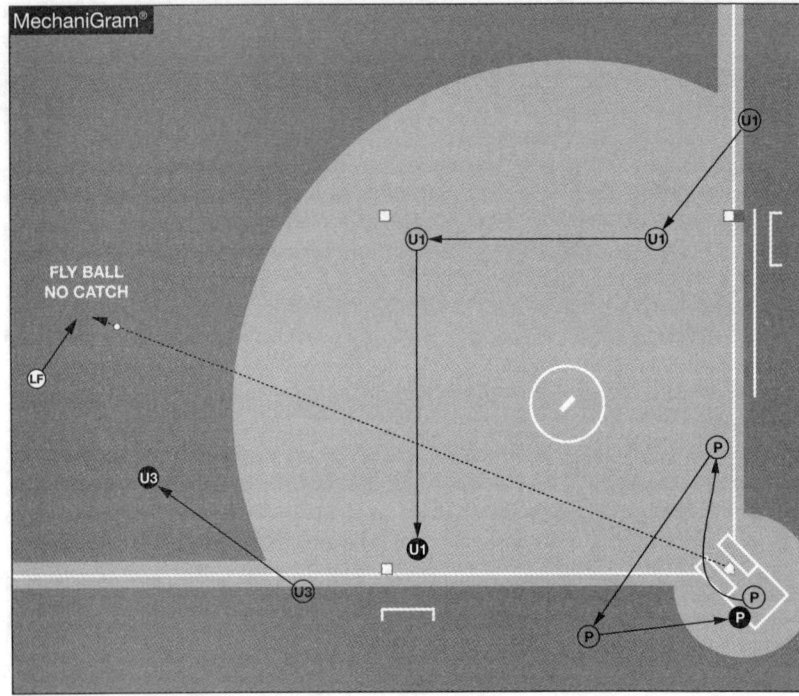

P: Trail the batter-runner no more than one-third of the way to first base in fair territory and read the play. When the batter-runner rounds first base and advances to second base, move toward the holding zone about halfway to third base in foul ground to an area where you have an unobstructed view of all four elements. Be prepared to move as the play develops. Responsible for any play at the plate.

U1: When a fly ball is hit and U3 goes out, pick up the ball and glance at the runner while hustling inside the diamond to button hook at a minimum depth of 10-12 feet. Continue to alternate between the ball and the runner keeping all four elements in front of you. Be prepared to move parallel to the baseline staying ahead of the runner. Responsible for any play at first base, second base and third base.

U3: Pick up the flight of the ball and glance at your partner. Responsible for any fly ball from the center fielder to the left fielder and up to dead-ball territory. When chasing the fly ball communicate with the crew you are chasing. Move parallel to the flight of the ball, or if necessary to gain a better angle, move away from the fielder; stop facing the player when the play happens. If caught, give the out signal and verbal facing the play. If the ball is dropped and it is not obvious, give the safe/no catch signal. Responsible for fair/foul, catch/ no catch.

Three-Umpire System

Part 8.2

Runner on First Base

- Ground Ball in the Infield

- Base Hit to the Outfield

- Fly Ball to the Outfield, Ball is Caught, No Umpire Chases

- Fly Ball to the Outfield, Ball is Not Caught, No Umpire Chases

- Fly Ball to the Outfield, Ball is Caught, U1 Chases

- Fly Ball to the Outfield, Ball is Not Caught, U1 Chases

- Fly Ball to the Outfield, Ball is Caught, U3 Chases

- Fly Ball to the Outfield, Ball is Not Caught, U3 Chases

GROUND BALL IN THE INFIELD

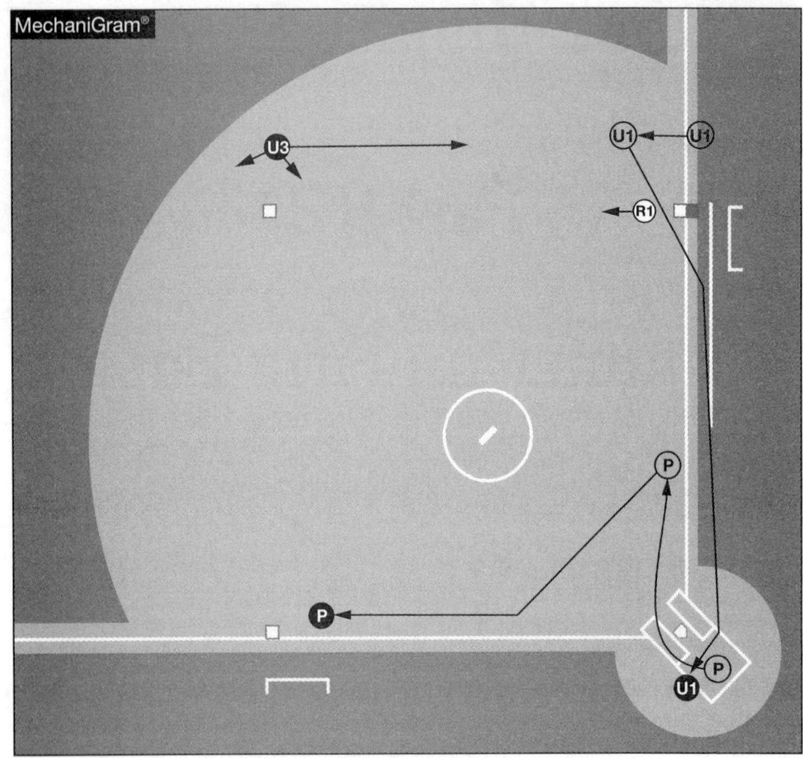

P: Trail the batter-runner no more than one-third of the way to first base in fair territory, read the play. As the lead runner (R1) approaches second base, move directly to third base in fair territory. First obtain the proper angle, then close your distance as the play develops working to get an unobstructed view of the play and to obtain a minimum distance of 10-12 feet from the play. Remember, as the four elements come together, stop, read the play and make the call. As the runner reaches third base, visually confirm that U1 has rotated into position at home. Responsible for fair/foul and any play at third base.

U1: Step into fair territory, at an angle 90 degrees to the path of the throw, but no more than a 45-degree angle from the foul line and let the ball take you to the play. As the runner (R1) commits to second base, rotate to home in foul ground to the farthest back corner of the right-hand batter's box, a minimum of 10-12 feet from the plate, for any possible play at home plate. Responsible for the runner at first base (R1) leaving before the pitch, any play at first base when at first base and any play at the plate when rotated to the plate.

U3: Read the play. Responsible for any play at second base and any play at first base when U1 has rotated to the plate.

BASE HIT TO THE OUTFIELD

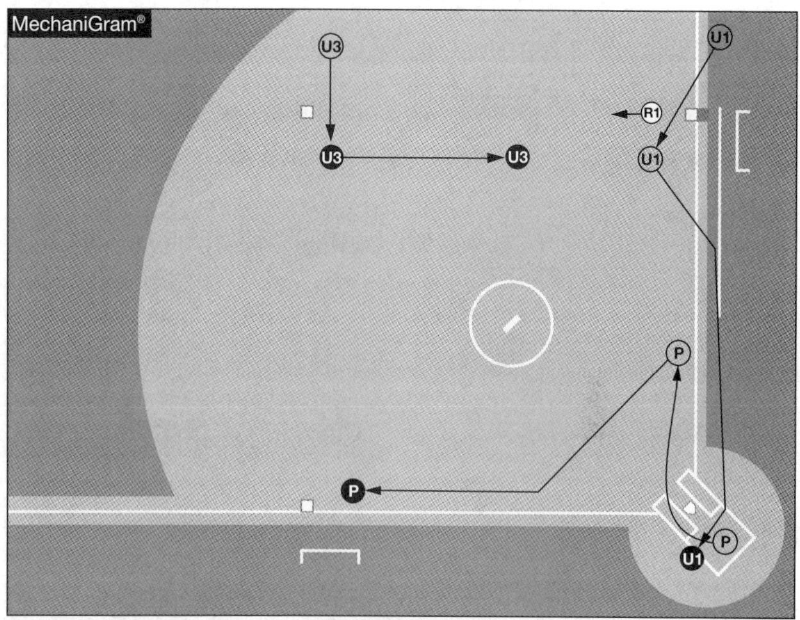

P: Trail the batter-runner no more than one-third of the way to first base in fair territory and read the play. As the lead runner (R1) approaches second base, move directly to third base. First, obtain the proper angle, then close your distance as the play develops working to get an unobstructed view of the play and to obtain a minimum distance of 10-12 feet from the play. Remember, as the four elements come together, stop, read the play and make the call. As the runner reaches third base visually confirm that U1 has rotated into position at home. Responsible for fair/foul and any play at third base.

U1: Pick up the ball and glance at the runner while hustling inside the diamond to button hook at a minimum depth of 10-12 feet. Continue to alternate between the ball and glancing at the runners keeping all four elements in front of you. As the runner from first base (R1) approaches second base, rotate to home in foul ground to the farthest back corner of the right-hand batter's box at a minimum of 10-12 feet from the plate, for any possible play at home plate. Responsible for the runner at first base (R1) leaving early on the pitch, any play at first base when at first base and any play at the plate when rotated to the plate.

U3: Pick up the ball and glance at the runner while hustling inside the diamond to button hook at a minimum depth of 10-12 feet. Continue to alternate between the ball and the runner keeping all four elements in front of you. As the runner (R1) reaches second base, visually confirm that the plate umpire has rotated into position at third base. Responsible for any play at second base and any play at first base when U1 has rotated to the plate.

FLY BALL TO THE OUTFIELD, BALL IS CAUGHT, NO UMPIRE CHASES

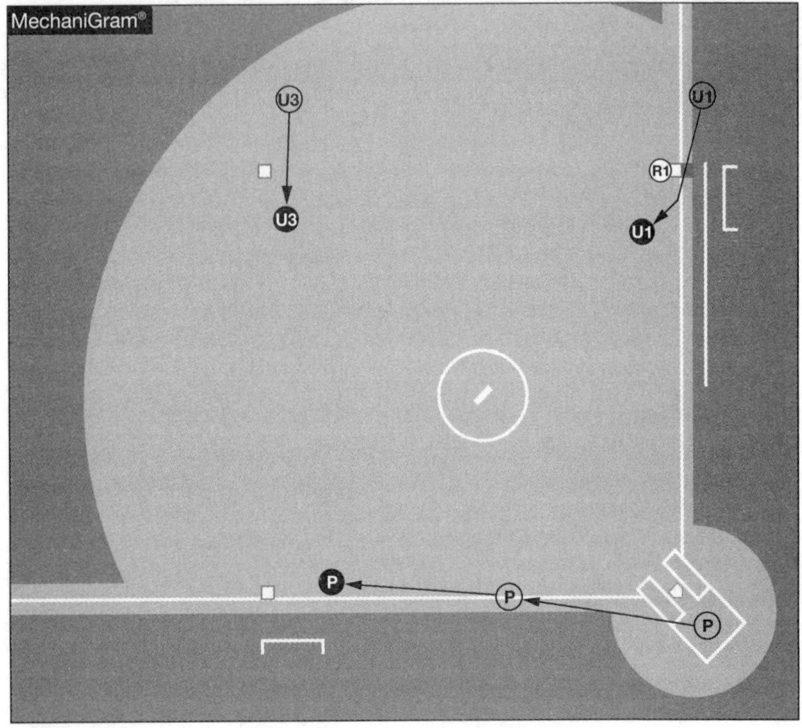

P: When a fly ball is hit from the left fielder up to dead-ball territory move up the third-base line to get an unobstructed view of the play. Responsible for fair/foul, catch/no catch and any play at third base.

U1: Pick up the ball and glance at the runner while hustling inside the diamond to button hook at a minimum depth of 10-12 feet. Continue to alternate between the ball and glancing at the runners keeping all four elements in front of you. As the runner from first base (R1) approaches second base, rotate to home in foul ground to the farthest back corner of the right-hand batter's box at a minimum of 10-12 feet from the plate, for any possible play at home plate. Responsible for the runner at first base (R1) leaving early on the pitch, the tag up at first base (R1), any play at first base when at first base and any play at the plate when rotated to the plate.

U3: Pick up the ball and glance at the runner while hustling inside the diamond to button hook at a minimum depth of 10-12 feet. Continue to alternate between the ball and the runner keeping all four elements in front of you. As the runner (R1) reaches second base, visually confirm that the plate umpire has rotated into position at third base. Responsible for any play at second base and any play at first base when U1 has rotated to the plate.

FLY BALL TO THE OUTFIELD, BALL IS NOT CAUGHT, NO UMPIRE CHASES

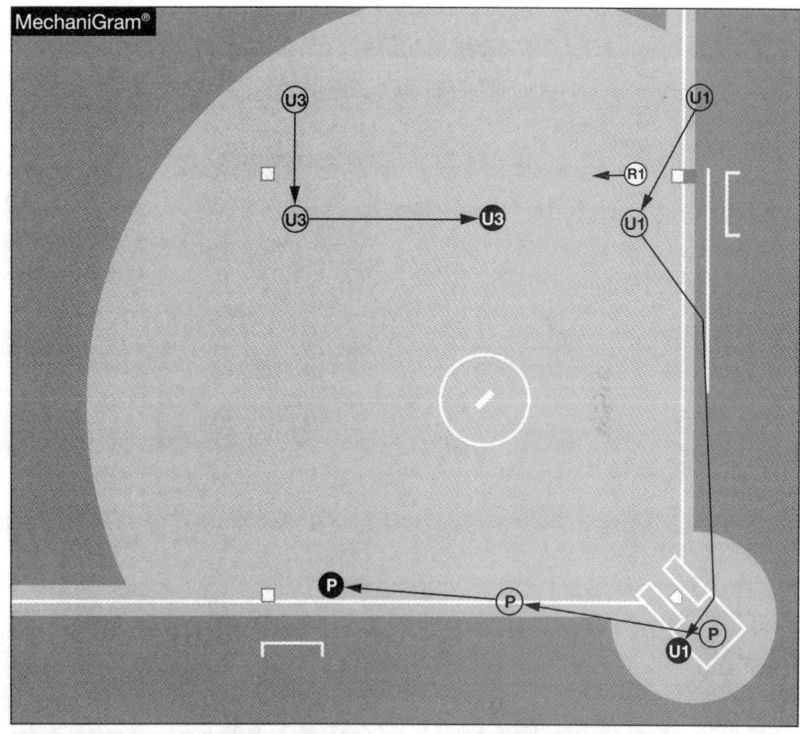

P: When a fly ball is hit from the left fielder up to dead-ball territory move up the third-base line to get an unobstructed view of the play. Responsible for fair/foul, catch/no catch and any play at third base.

U1: Pick up the ball and glance at the runner while hustling inside the diamond to button hook at a minimum depth of 10-12 feet. Continue to alternate between the ball and glancing at the runners keeping all four elements in front of you. As the runner from first base (R1) approaches second base, rotate to home in foul ground to the farthest back corner of the right-hand batter's box at a minimum of 10-12 feet from the plate, for any possible play at home plate. Responsible for the runner at first base (R1) leaving early on the pitch, the tag up at first base (R1), any play at first base when at first base and any play at the plate when rotated to the plate.

U3: Pick up the ball and glance at the runner while hustling inside the diamond to button hook at a minimum depth of 10-12 feet. Continue to alternate between the ball and the runner keeping all four elements in front of you. As the runner (R1) reaches second base, visually confirm that the plate umpire has rotated into position at third base. Responsible for any play at second base and any play at first base when U1 has rotated to the plate.

FLY BALL TO THE OUTFIELD, BALL IS CAUGHT, U1 CHASES

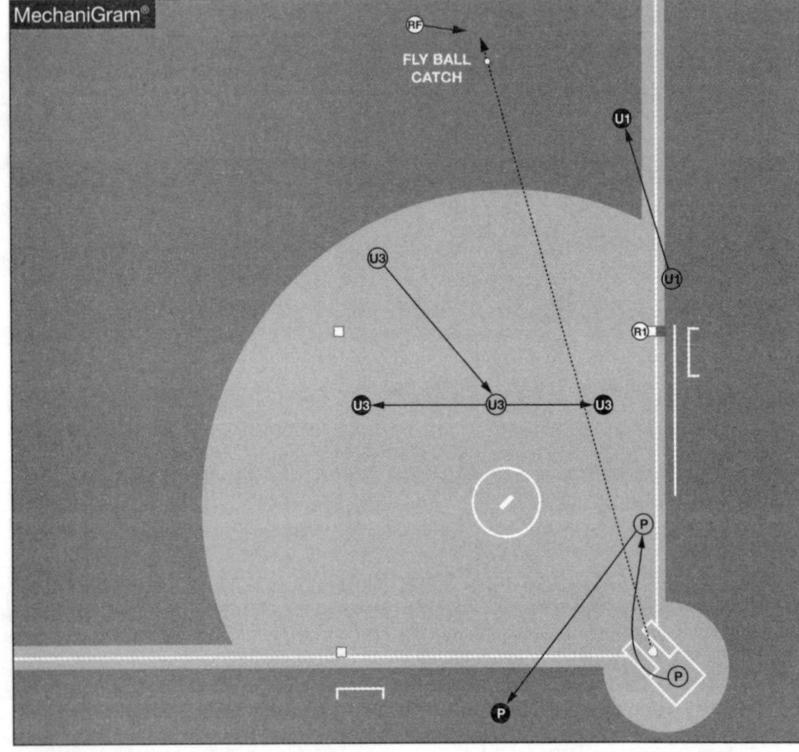

P: When a fly ball is hit and a base umpire goes out, trail the batter-runner no more than one-third of the way to first base in fair territory and read the play. As the runner (R1) approaches second base, move toward the holding zone about halfway to third base in foul ground to an area where you have an unobstructed view of all four elements. Be prepared to move as the play develops. Responsible for any play at the plate.

U1: Pick up the flight of the ball and glance at your partner. Responsible for any fly ball from the right fielder up to dead-ball territory. When chasing the fly ball communicate with the crew you are chasing. Move parallel to the flight of the ball, or if necessary to gain a better angle, move away from the fielder; stop facing the player when the play happens. If caught, give the out signal and verbal facing the play. If the ball is dropped and it is not obvious, give the safe/no catch signal. Let the ball turn you back toward the infield and observe the rest of the play from there. Responsible for the runner at first base (R1) leaving early on the pitch, fair/foul, catch/no catch.

U3: When a fly ball is hit and U1 goes out, pick up the ball and glance at the runner while hustling inside the diamond to button hook at a minimum depth of 10-12 feet. Continue to alternate between the ball and the runner keeping all four elements in front of you. Be prepared to move parallel to the baseline staying ahead of the runner. Responsible for the tag-up at first base (R1), any play at first base or second base and the last runner (R1) at third base.

FLY BALL TO THE OUTFIELD, BALL IS NOT CAUGHT, U1 CHASES

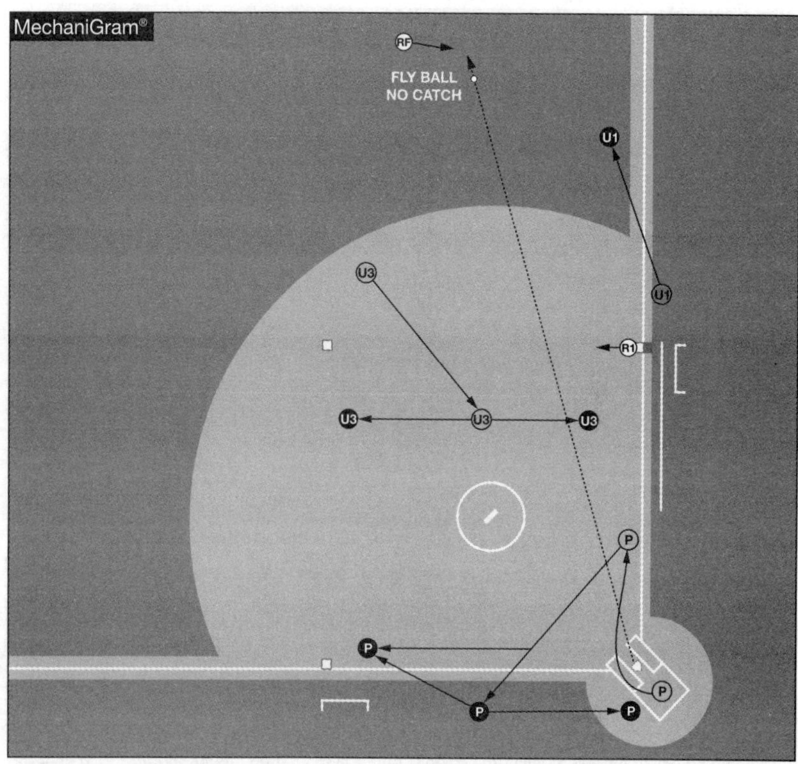

P: When a fly ball is hit and a base umpire goes out, trail the batter-runner no more than one-third of the way to first base in fair territory and read the play. As the lead runner (R1) approaches second base, move toward the holding zone about halfway to third base in foul ground to an area where you have an unobstructed view of all four elements. Be prepared to move as the play develops. Responsible for any play on the lead runner (R1) at third base and any play at the plate.

U1: Pick up the flight of the ball and glance at your partner. Responsible for any fly ball from the right fielder up to dead-ball territory. When chasing the fly ball communicate with the crew you are chasing. Move parallel to the flight of the ball, or if necessary to gain a better angle, move away from the fielder; stop facing the player when the play happens. If caught, give the out signal and verbal facing the play. If the ball is dropped and it is not obvious, give the safe/no catch signal. Let the ball turn you back toward the infield and observe the rest of the play from there. Responsible for the runner at first base (R1) leaving early on the pitch, fair/foul, catch/no catch.

U3: When a fly ball is hit and U1 goes out, pick up the ball and glance at the runner while hustling inside the diamond to button hook at a minimum depth of 10-12 feet. Continue to alternate between the ball and the runner keeping all four elements in front of you. Be prepared to move parallel to the baseline staying ahead of the runner. Responsible for the tag-up at first base (R1), any play at first base or second base and the last runner (batter-runner) at third base.

FLY BALL TO THE OUTFIELD, BALL IS CAUGHT, U3 CHASES

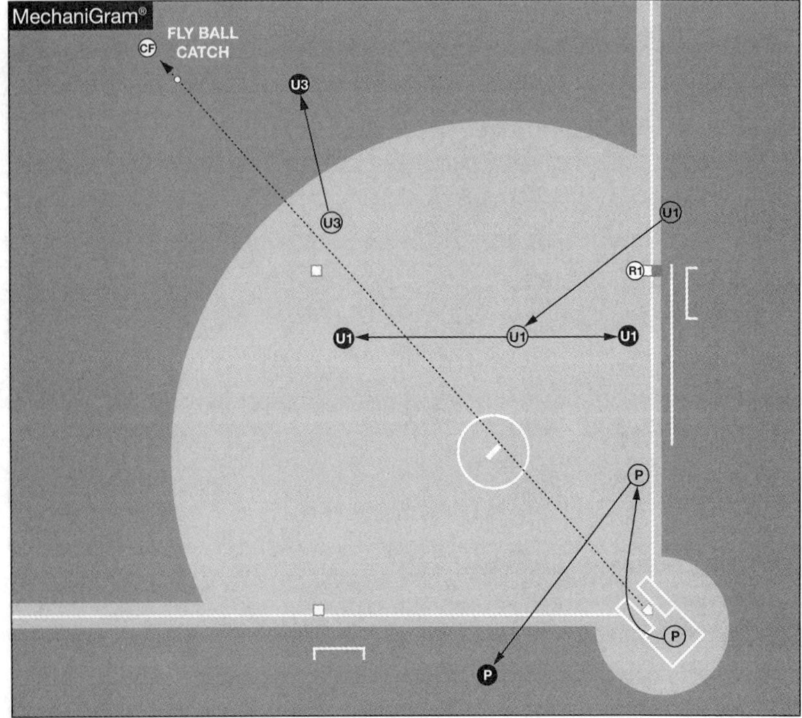

P: When a fly ball is hit and a base umpire goes out, trail the batter-runner no more than one-third of the way to first base in fair territory and read the play. As the runner (R1) approaches second base, move toward the holding zone about halfway to third base in foul ground to an area where you have an unobstructed view of all four elements. Be prepared to move as the play develops. Responsible for any play at the plate.

U1: When a fly ball is hit and U3 goes out, pick up the ball and glance at the runner while hustling inside the diamond to button hook at a minimum depth of 10-12 feet. Continue to alternate between the ball and the runner (R1) keeping all four elements in front of you. Be prepared to move parallel to the baseline staying ahead of the runner. Responsible for the runner at first base (R1) leaving early on the pitch, the tag-up at first base (R1), any play at first base or second base and the last runner (R1) at third base.

U3: Pick up the flight of the ball and glance at your partner. Responsible for any fly ball hit from the right fielder up to left fielder. When chasing the fly ball communicate with the crew you are chasing. Move parallel to the flight of the ball, or if necessary to gain a better angle, move away from the fielder; stop facing the player when the play happens. If caught, give the out signal and verbal facing the play. If the ball is dropped and it is not obvious, give the safe/no catch signal. Let the ball turn you back toward the infield and observe the rest of the play from there. Responsible for catch/no catch.

FLY BALL TO THE OUTFIELD, BALL IS NOT CAUGHT, U3 CHASES

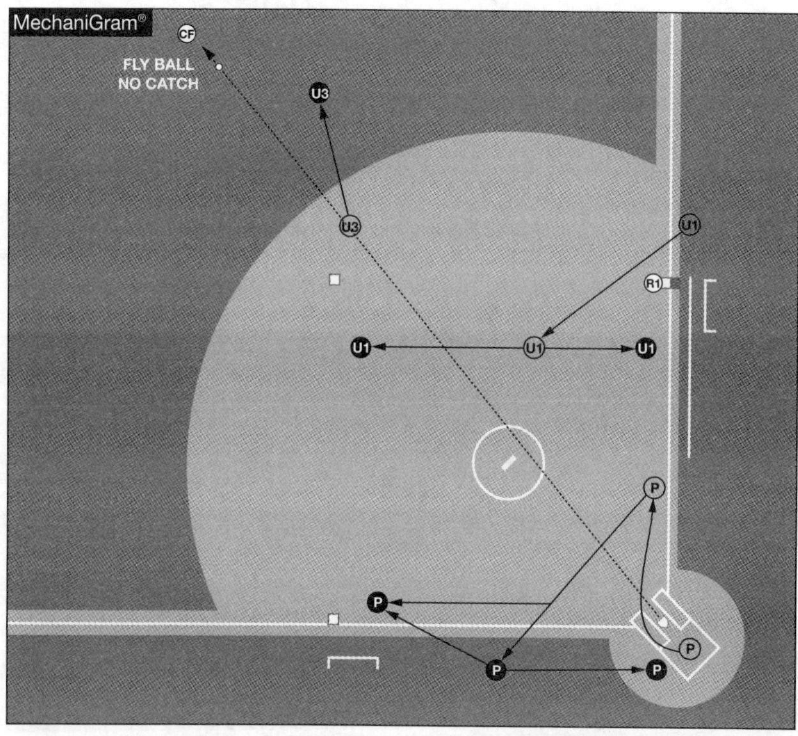

P: When a fly ball is hit and a base umpire goes out, trail the batter-runner no more than one-third of the way to first base in fair territory and read the play. As the lead runner (R1) approaches second base, move toward the holding zone about halfway to third base in foul ground to an area where you have an unobstructed view of all four elements. Be prepared to move as the play develops. Responsible for any play on lead runner (R1) at third base and any play at the plate.

U1: When a fly ball is hit and U3 goes out, pick up the ball and glance at the runner while hustling inside the diamond to button hook at a minimum depth of 10-12 feet. Continue to alternate between the ball and the runners keeping all four elements in front of you. Be prepared to move parallel to the baseline staying ahead of the runner. Responsible for the runner at first base (R1) leaving early on the pitch, the tag-up at first base (R1), any play at first base or second base and the last runner (batter-runner) at third base.

U3: Pick up the flight of the ball and glance at your partner. Responsible for any fly ball hit from the right fielder up to left fielder. When chasing the fly ball communicate with the crew you are chasing. Move parallel to the flight of the ball, or if necessary to gain a better angle, move away from the fielder; stop facing the player when the play happens. If caught, give the out signal and verbal facing the play. If the ball is dropped and it is not obvious, give the safe/no catch signal. Let the ball turn you back toward the infield and observe the rest of the play from there. Responsible for catch/no catch.

Part 8.3

Runners on First and Second Base

◆ Ground Ball in the Infield

◆ Base Hit to the Outfield

◆ Fly Ball to the Outfield, Ball is Caught, No Umpire Chases

◆ Fly Ball to the Outfield, Ball is Not Caught, No Umpire Chases

◆ Fly Ball to the Outfield, Ball is Caught, U1 Chases

◆ Fly Ball to the Outfield, Ball is Not Caught, U1 Chases

◆ Fly Ball to the Outfield, Ball is Caught, U3 Chases

◆ Fly Ball to the Outfield, Ball is Not Caught, U3 Chases

GROUND BALL IN THE INFIELD

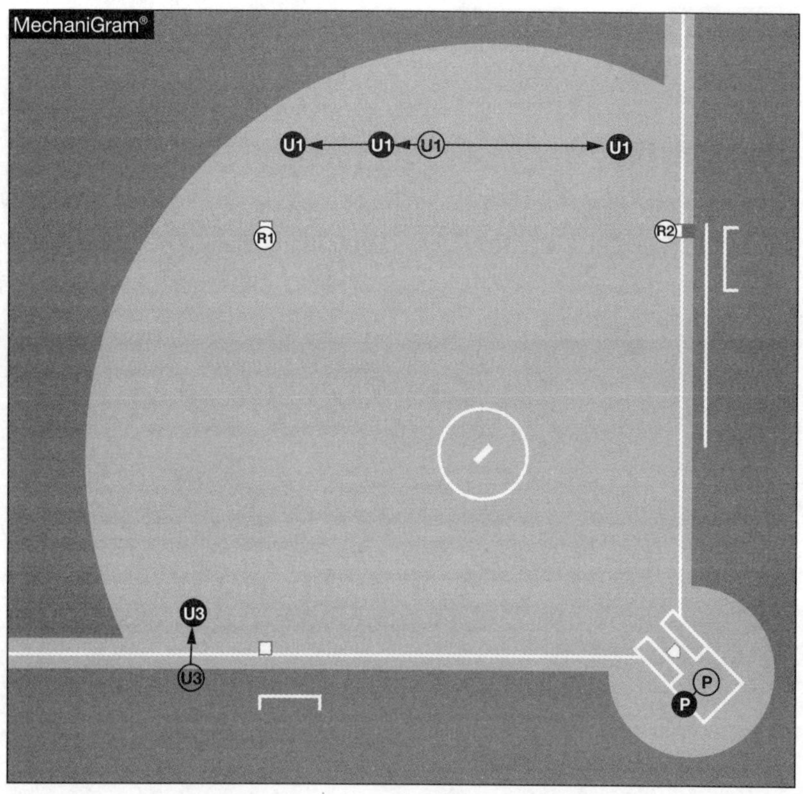

P: Move out from behind the plate and read the play. Responsible for fair/foul and any play at the plate.

U1: Let the ball take you to the play. Responsible for the runner leaving early on the pitch at second base (R1) and any play at first base or second base.

U3: Step into fair territory and read the play. Responsible for the runner leaving early on the pitch at first base (R2) and any play at third base.

BASE HIT TO THE OUTFIELD

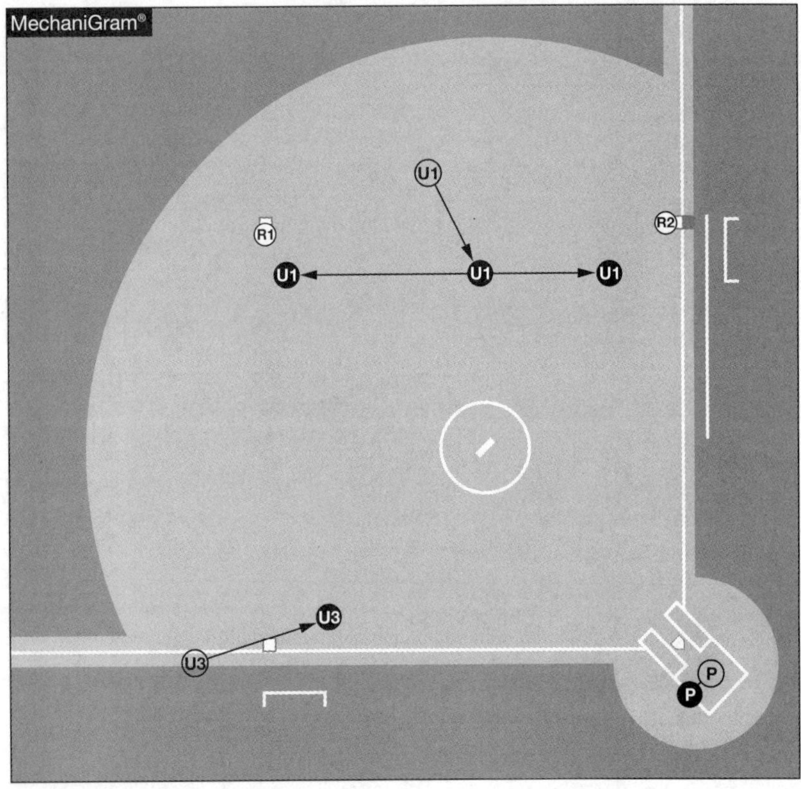

P: Move out from behind the plate and read the play. Responsible for fair/foul and any play at the plate.

U1: Pick up the ball and glance at the runner while hustling inside the diamond to button hook at a minimum depth of 10-12 feet. Continue to alternate between the ball and the runners (R2 and batter-runner) keeping all four elements in front of you. Be prepared to move parallel to the baseline staying ahead of the runner. Responsible for any play at first base or second base.

U3: Pick up the ball and glance at the runner while hustling inside the diamond to button hook at a minimum depth of 10-12 feet. Continue to alternate between the ball and the runners keeping all four elements in front of you. Responsible for any play at third base.

FLY BALL TO THE OUTFIELD, BALL IS CAUGHT, NO UMPIRE CHASES

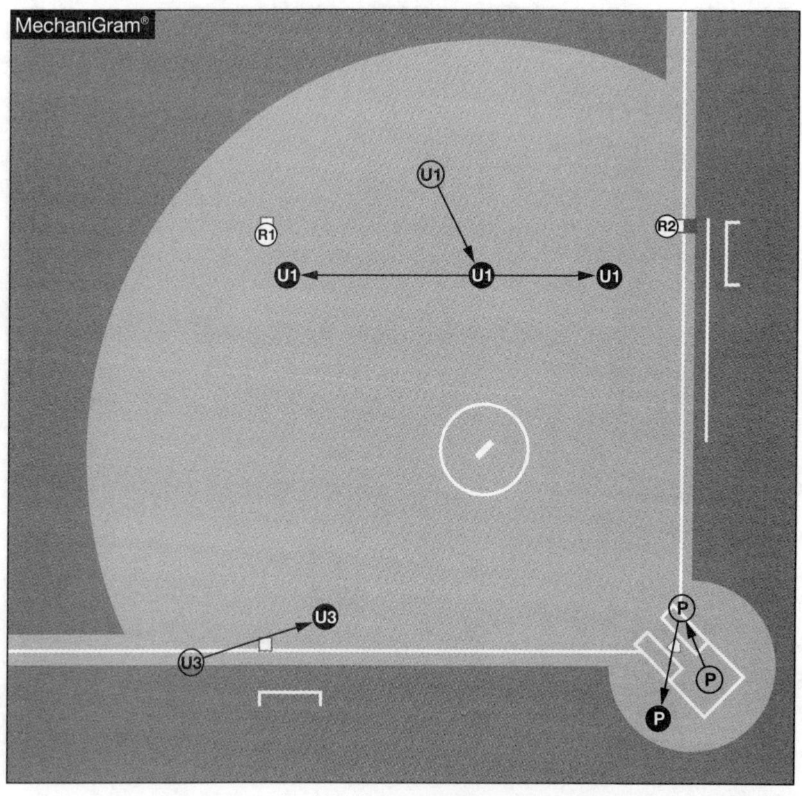

P: When a fly ball is hit from the right fielder up to dead-ball territory, step out from behind the plate and move up the first-base line one or two steps to get an unobstructed view of the play. Responsible for fair/foul, catch/no catch and any play at the plate.

U1: Pick up the ball and glance at the runner while hustling inside the diamond to button hook at a minimum depth of 10-12 feet. Continue to alternate between the ball and the runner keeping all four elements in front of you. Be prepared to move parallel to the baseline staying ahead of the runner (R2). Responsible for the runner leaving early on the pitch at second base (R1), the tag up at first base (R2) and any play at first base or second base.

U3: Pick up the ball and glance at the runner while hustling inside the diamond to button hook at a minimum depth of 10-12 feet. Continue to alternate between the ball and the runner keeping all four elements in front of you. Responsible for the runner leaving early on the pitch at first base (R2), the tag up at second base (R1) and any play at third base.

FLY BALL TO THE OUTFIELD, BALL IS NOT CAUGHT, NO UMPIRE CHASES

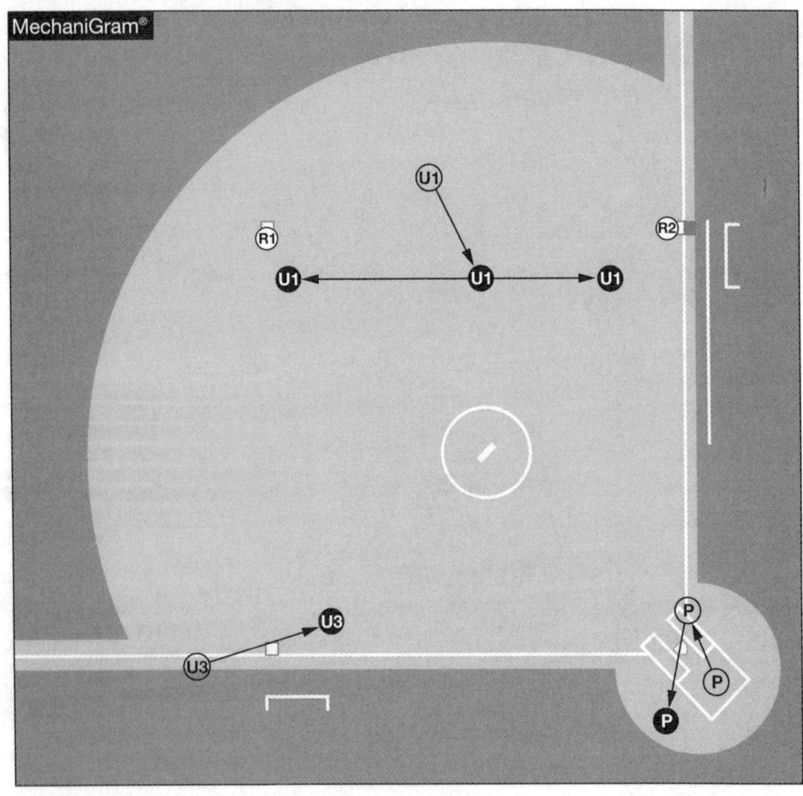

P: When a fly ball is hit from the right fielder up to dead-ball territory, step out from behind the plate and move up the first-base line one or two steps to get an unobstructed view of the play. Responsible for fair/foul, catch/no catch and any play at the plate.

U1: Pick up the ball and glance at the runner while hustling inside the diamond to button hook at a minimum depth of 10-12 feet. Continue to alternate between the ball and the runner keeping all four elements in front of you. Be prepared to move parallel to the baseline staying ahead of the runners (R2 and batter-runner). Responsible for the runner leaving early on the pitch at second base (R1), the tag up at first base (R2) and any play at first base and second base.

U3: Pick up the ball and glance at the runner while hustling inside the diamond to button hook at a minimum depth of 10-12 feet. Continue to alternate between the ball and the runner keeping all four elements in front of you. Responsible for the runner leaving early on the pitch at first base (R2), the tag up at second base (R1) and any play at third base.

FLY BALL TO THE OUTFIELD, BALL IS CAUGHT, U1 CHASES

P: When a fly ball is hit and a base umpire goes out, move toward the holding zone about halfway to third base in foul ground to an area where you have an unobstructed view of all four elements. Be prepared to move as the play develops. Responsible for the tag up at second base (R1), any play on the lead runner (R1) at third base and any play at the plate.

U1: Pick up the flight of the ball and glance at your partner. Responsible for any fly ball from the right fielder up to the left fielder. When chasing the fly ball communicate with the crew you are chasing. Move parallel to the flight of the ball, or if necessary to gain a better angle, move away from the fielder; stop facing the player when the play happens. If caught, give the out signal and verbal facing the play. If the ball is dropped and it is not obvious, give the safe/no catch signal. Let the ball turn you back toward the infield and observe the rest of the play from there. Responsible for the runner leaving early on the pitch at second base (R1) and catch/no catch.

U3: When a fly ball is hit and U1 goes out, pick up the ball and glance at the runner while hustling across the diamond toward first base to a position about halfway between second base and first base. Continue to alternate between the ball and the runner keeping all four elements in front of you. Be prepared to move parallel to the baseline staying ahead of the runner. Responsible for the runner leaving early on the pitch at first base (R2), the tag up at first base (R2) and any play at first base or second base and the last runner to third base (R2).

FLY BALL TO THE OUTFIELD, BALL IS NOT CAUGHT, U1 CHASES

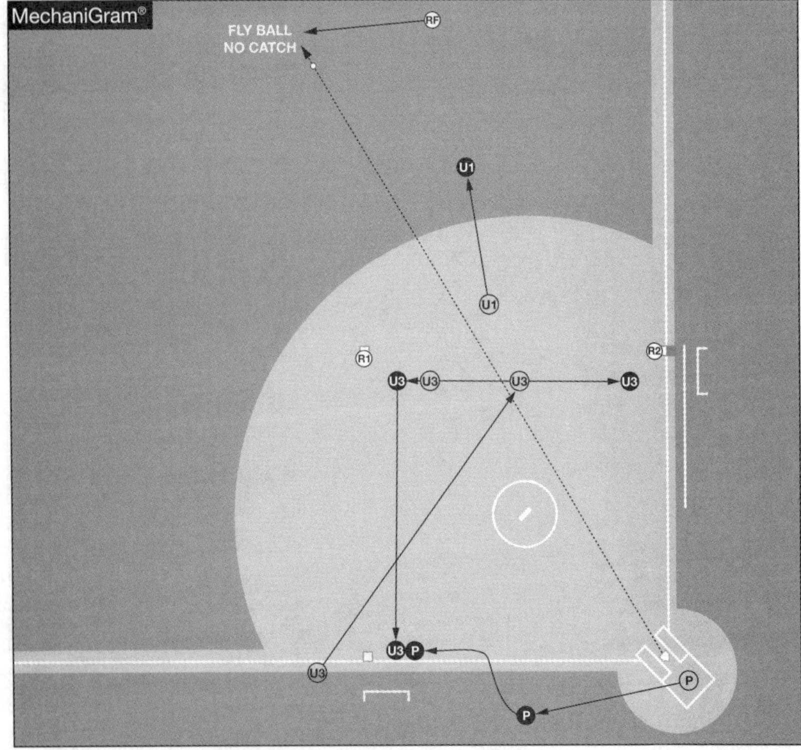

P: When a fly ball is hit and a base umpire goes out, move toward the holding zone about halfway to third base in foul ground to an area where you have an unobstructed view of all four elements. Be prepared to move as the play develops. Responsible for the tag up at second base (R1), any play on a lead runner (R1 and R2) at third base and any play at the plate.

U1: Pick up the flight of the ball and glance at your partner. Responsible for any fly ball from the right fielder up to the left fielder. When chasing the fly ball communicate with the crew you are chasing. Move parallel to the flight of the ball, or if necessary to gain a better angle, move away from the fielder; stop facing the player when the play happens. If caught, give the out signal and verbal facing the play. If the ball is dropped and it is not obvious, give the safe/no catch signal. Let the ball turn you back toward the infield and observe the rest of the play from there. Responsible for the runner leaving early on the pitch at second base (R1) and catch/no catch.

U3: When a fly ball is hit and U1 goes out, pick up the ball and glance at the runner while hustling across the diamond toward first base to a position about halfway between second base and first base. Continue to alternate between the ball and the runners keeping all four elements in front of you. Be prepared to move parallel to the baseline staying ahead of the runner. Responsible for the runner leaving early on the pitch at first base (R2) and the tag up at first base (R2), any play at first base or second base and the last runner (batter-runner) at third base.

FLY BALL TO THE OUTFIELD, BALL IS CAUGHT, U3 CHASES

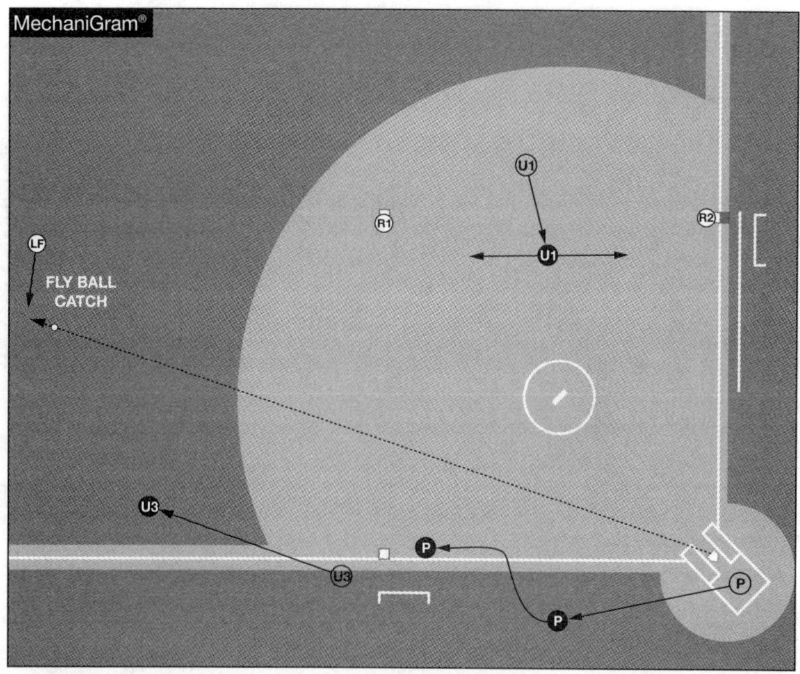

P: When a fly ball is hit and a base umpire goes out, move toward the holding zone about halfway to third base in foul ground to an area where you have an unobstructed view of all four elements. Be prepared to move as the play develops. Responsible for the tag up at second base (R1), any play on the lead runner (R1) at third base and any play at the plate.

U1: When a fly ball is hit and U3 goes out, pick up the ball and glance at the runner while hustling inside the diamond to button hook at a minimum depth of 10-12 feet. Continue to alternate between the ball and the runner (R2) keeping all four elements in front of you. Be prepared to move parallel to the baseline staying ahead of the runner. Responsible for the runner leaving early on the pitch at second base (R1) the tag-up at first base (R2), any play at first base or second base and the last runner (R2) at third base.

U3: Pick up the flight of the ball and glance at your partner. Responsible for any fly ball hit from the left fielder up to dead-ball territory. When chasing the fly ball communicate with the crew you are chasing. Move parallel to the flight of the ball, or if necessary to gain a better angle, move away from the fielder; stop facing the player when the play happens. If caught, give the out signal and verbal facing the play. If the ball is dropped and it is not obvious, give the safe/no catch signal. Let the ball turn you back toward the infield and observe the rest of the play from there. Responsible for the runner leaving early on the pitch at first base (R2), fair/foul, catch/no catch.

FLY BALL TO THE OUTFIELD, BALL IS NOT CAUGHT, U3 CHASES

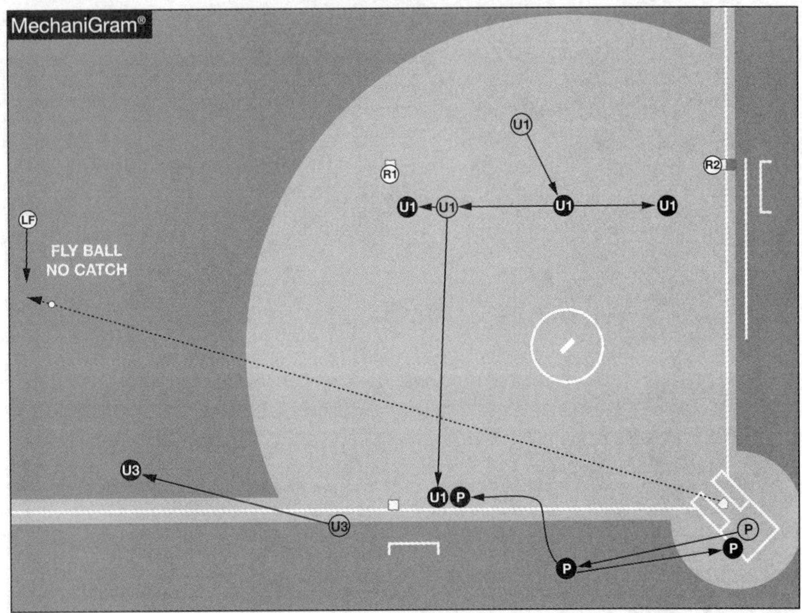

P: When a fly ball is hit and a base umpire goes out, move toward the holding zone about halfway to third base in foul ground to an area where you have an unobstructed view of all four elements. Be prepared to move as the play develops. Responsible for the tag up at second base (R1), any play on a lead runner (R1 and R2) at third base and any play at the plate.

U1: When a fly ball is hit and U3 goes out, pick up the ball and glance at the runner while hustling inside the diamond to button hook at a minimum depth of 10-12 feet. Continue to alternate between the ball and the runners (R2 and batter-runner) keeping all four elements in front of you. Be prepared to move parallel to the baseline staying ahead of the runner. Responsible for the runner leaving early on the pitch at second base (R1), the tag-up at first base (R2), any play at first base or second base and the last runner (batter-runner) at third base.

U3: Pick up the flight of the ball and glance at your partner. Responsible for any fly ball hit from the left fielder up to dead-ball territory. When chasing the fly ball communicate with the crew you are chasing. Move parallel to the flight of the ball, or if necessary to gain a better angle, move away from the fielder; stop facing the player when the play happens. If caught, give the out signal and verbal facing the play. If the ball is dropped and it is not obvious, give the safe/no catch signal. Let the ball turn you back toward the infield and observe the rest of the play from there. Responsible for the runner leaving early on the pitch at first base (R2), fair/foul, catch/no catch.

Three-Umpire System

Part 8.4

Runners on First and Third Base

◆ Ground Ball in the Infield

◆ Base Hit to the Outfield

◆ Fly Ball to the Outfield, Ball is Caught, No Umpire Chases

◆ Fly Ball to the Outfield, Ball is Not Caught, No Umpire Chases

◆ Fly Ball to the Outfield, Ball is Caught, U1 Chases

◆ Fly Ball to the Outfield, Ball is Not Caught, U1 Chases

◆ Fly Ball to the Outfield, Ball is Caught, U3 Chases

◆ Fly Ball to the Outfield, Ball is Not Caught, U3 Chases

GROUND BALL IN THE INFIELD

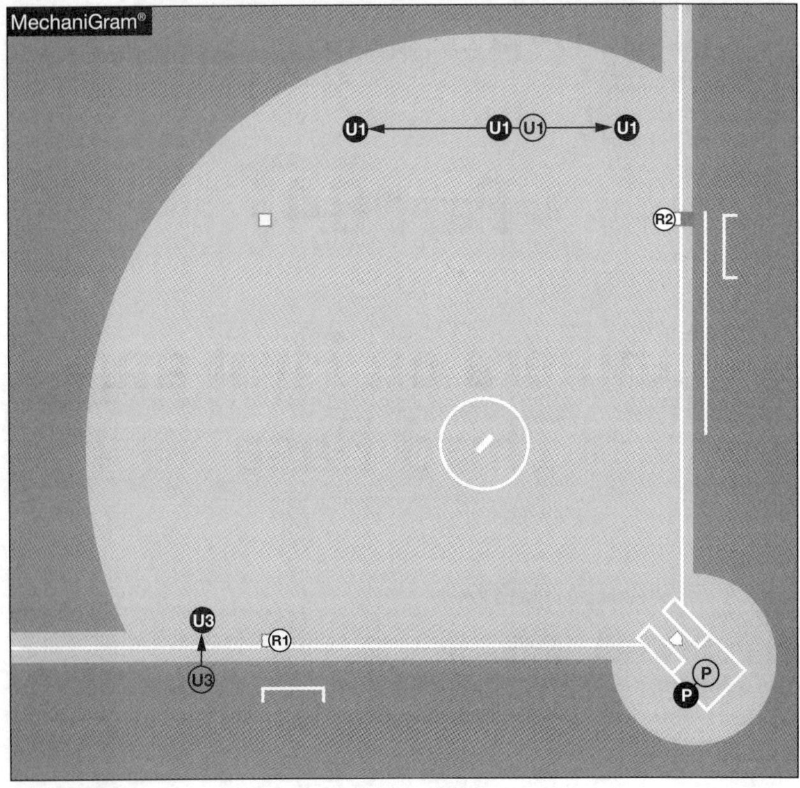

P: Move out from behind the plate and read the play. Responsible for fair/foul and any play at the plate.

U1: Let the ball take you to the play. Responsible for the runner leaving early on the pitch at first base (R2) and any play at first base or second base.

U3: Step into fair territory and read the play. Responsible for the runner leaving early on the pitch at third base (R1) and any play at third base.

BASE HIT TO THE OUTFIELD

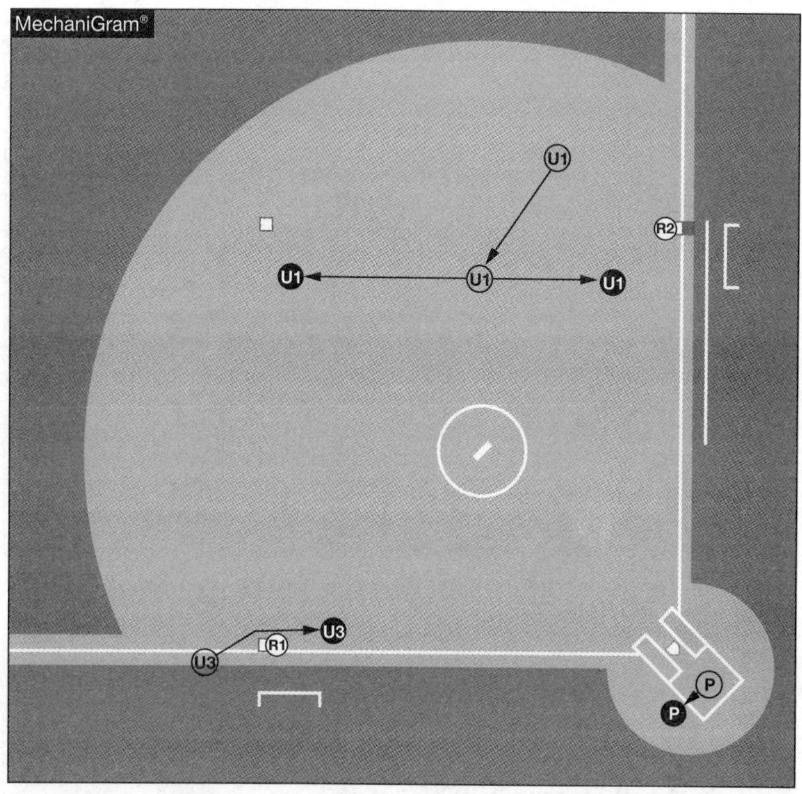

P: Move out from behind the plate and read the play. Responsible for fair/foul and any play at the plate.

U1: Pick up the ball and glance at the runner while hustling inside the diamond to button hook at a minimum depth of 10-12 feet. Continue to alternate between the ball and the runners (R2 and batter-runner) keeping all four elements in front of you. Be prepared to move parallel to the baseline staying ahead of the runner. Responsible for the runner leaving early on the pitch at first base (R2) and any play at first base or second base.

U3: Pick up the ball and glance at the runner while hustling inside the diamond to button hook at a minimum depth of 10-12 feet. Continue to alternate between the ball and the runners keeping all four elements in front of you. Responsible for the runner leaving early on the pitch at third base (R1) and any play at third base.

FLY BALL TO OUTFIELD, BALL IS CAUGHT, NO UMPIRE CHASES

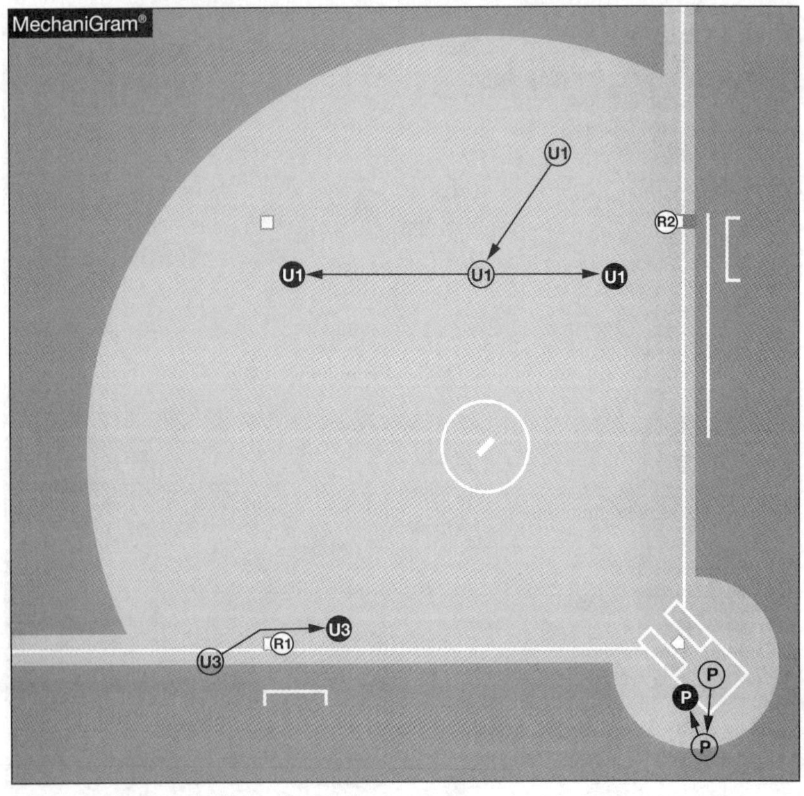

P: When a fly ball is hit from the right fielder up to dead-ball territory, move to the first-base line extended to get the best view and angle of the play. Responsible for fair/foul, catch/no catch and any play at the plate.

U1: Pick up the ball and glance at the runner while hustling inside the diamond to button hook at a minimum depth of 10-12 feet. Continue to alternate between the ball and the runner keeping all four elements in front of you. Be prepared to move parallel to the baseline staying ahead of the runner (R2). Responsible for the runner leaving early on the pitch at first base (R2), the tag up at first base (R2) and any play at first base or second base.

U3: Pick up the ball and glance at the runner while hustling inside the diamond to button hook at a minimum depth of 10-12 feet. Continue to alternate between the ball and the runner keeping all four elements in front of you. Responsible for the runner leaving early on the pitch at third base (R1), the tag up at third base (R1) and any play at third base.

FLY BALL TO THE OUTFIELD, BALL IS NOT CAUGHT, NO UMPIRE CHASES

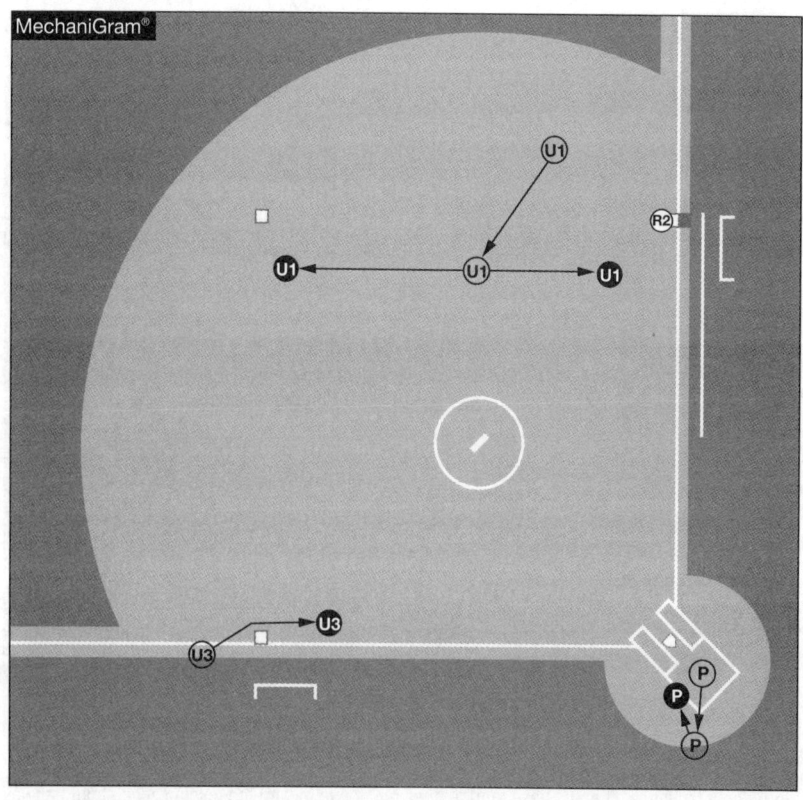

P: When a fly ball is hit from the right fielder up to dead-ball territory, move to the first-base line extended to get the best view and angle of the play. Responsible for fair/foul, catch/no catch and any play at the plate.

U1: Pick up the ball and glance at the runner while hustling inside the diamond to button hook at a minimum depth of 10-12 feet. Continue to alternate between the ball and the runner keeping all four elements in front of you. Be prepared to move parallel to the baseline staying ahead of the runners (R2 and batter-runner). Responsible for the runner leaving early on the pitch at first base (R2), the tag up at first base (R2) and any play at first base or second base.

U3: Pick up the ball and glance at the runner while hustling inside the diamond to button hook at a minimum depth of 10-12 feet. Continue to alternate between the ball and the runner keeping all four elements in front of you. Responsible for the runner leaving early on the pitch at third base (R1), the tag up at third base (R1) and any play at third base.

FLY BALL TO THE OUTFIELD, BALL IS CAUGHT, U1 CHASES

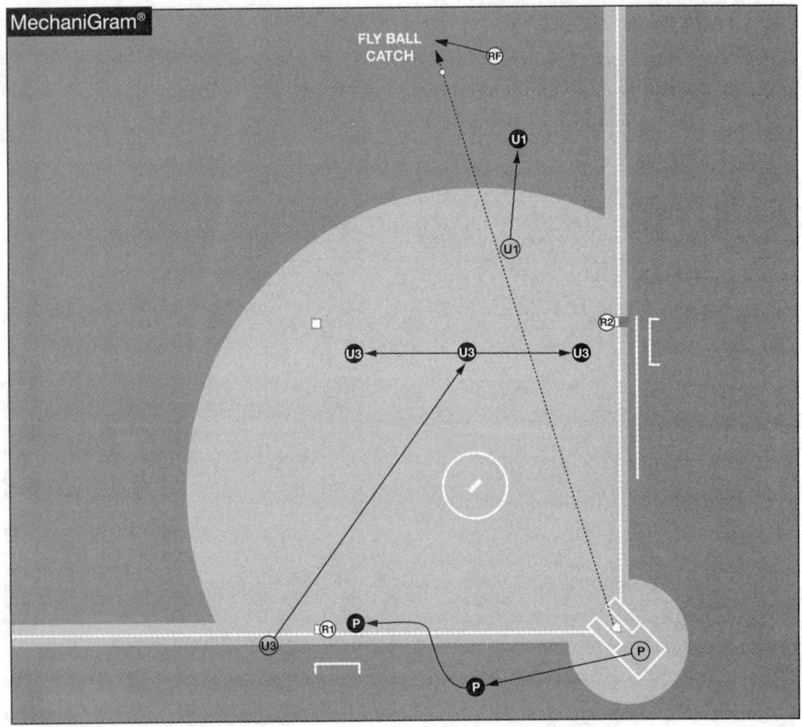

P: When a fly ball is hit and a base umpire goes out, move toward the holding zone about halfway to third base in foul ground to an area where you have an unobstructed view of all four elements. Be prepared to move as the play develops. Responsible for the tag up at third base (R1), any play on the lead runner (R1) at third base and any play at the plate.

U1: Pick up the flight of the ball and glance at your partner. Responsible for any fly ball from the right fielder up to the left fielder. When chasing the fly ball communicate with the crew you are chasing. Move parallel to the flight of the ball, or if necessary to gain a better angle, move away from the fielder; stop facing the player when the play happens. If caught, give the out signal and verbal facing the play. If the ball is dropped and it is not obvious, give the safe/no catch signal. Let the ball turn you back toward the infield and observe the rest of the play from there. Responsible for the runner leaving early on the pitch at first base (R2) and catch/no catch.

U3: When a fly ball is hit and U1 goes out, pick up the ball and glance at the runner while hustling across the diamond toward first base to a position about halfway between second base and first base. Continue to alternate between the ball and the runner keeping all four elements in front of you. Be prepared to move parallel to the baseline staying ahead of the runner (R2). Responsible for the runner leaving early on the pitch at third base (R1), the tag up at first base (R2) and any play at first base or second base and the last runner to third base (R2).

FLY BALL TO THE OUTFIELD, BALL IS NOT CAUGHT, U1 CHASES

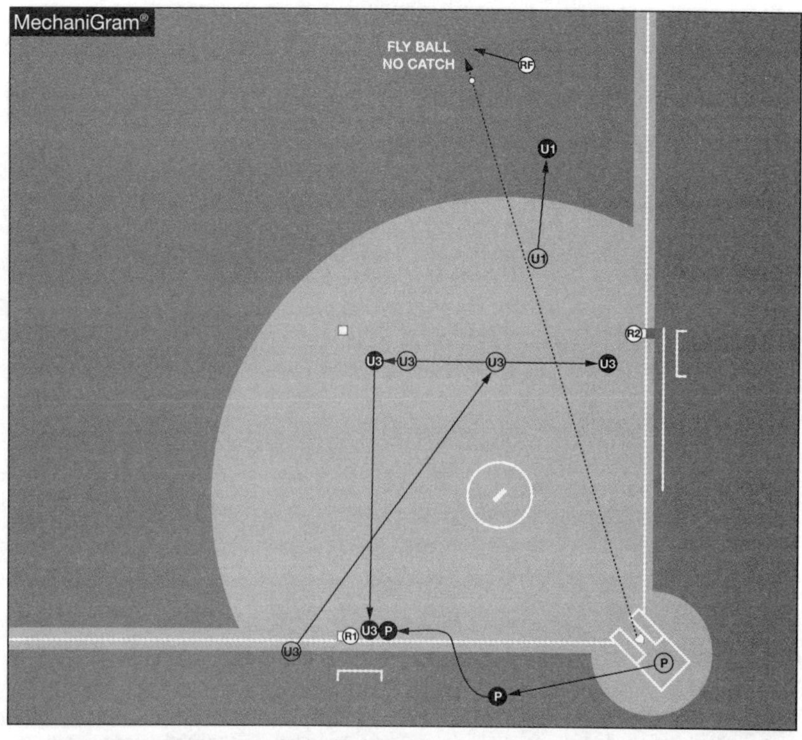

P: When a fly ball is hit and a base umpire goes out, move toward the holding zone about halfway to third base in foul ground to an area where you have an unobstructed view of all four elements. Be prepared to move as the play develops. Responsible for the tag up at third base (R1), any play on the lead runner (R1) at third base and any play at the plate.

U1: Pick up the flight of the ball and glance at your partner. Responsible for any fly ball from the right fielder up to the left fielder. When chasing the fly ball communicate with the crew you are chasing. Move parallel to the flight of the ball, or if necessary to gain a better angle, move away from the fielder; stop facing the player when the play happens. If caught, give the out signal and verbal facing the play. If the ball is dropped and it is not obvious, give the safe/no catch signal. Let the ball turn you back toward the infield and observe the rest of the play from there. Responsible for the runner leaving early on the pitch at first base (R2) and catch/no catch.

U3: When a fly ball is hit and U1 goes out, pick up the ball and glance at the runner while hustling across the diamond toward first base to a position about halfway between second base and first base. Continue to alternate between the ball and the runner keeping all four elements in front of you. Be prepared to move parallel to the baseline staying ahead of the runner. Responsible for the runner leaving early on the pitch at third base (R1), the tag up at first base (R2) and any play at first base or second base and the last runner to third base (batter-runner).

FLY BALL TO THE OUTFIELD, BALL IS CAUGHT, U3 CHASES

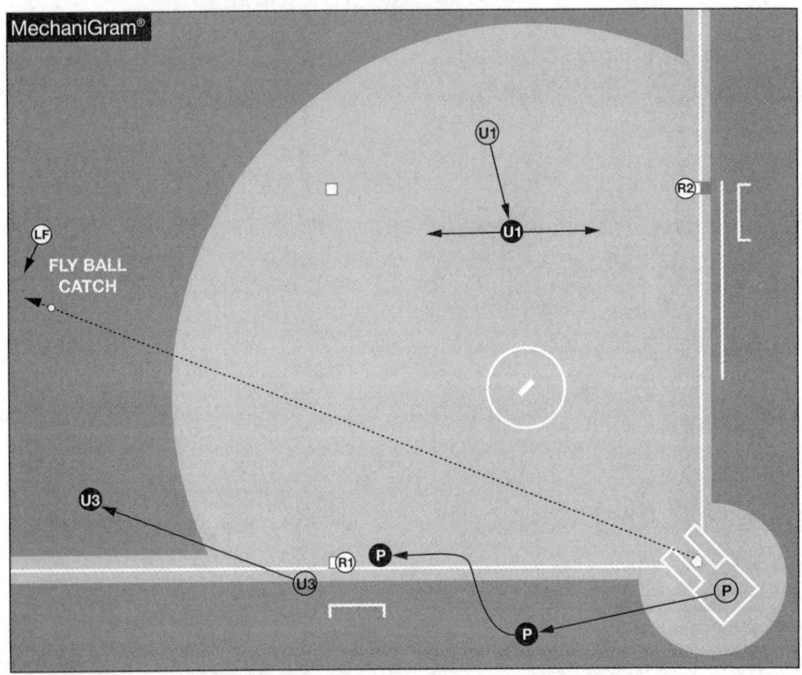

P: When a fly ball is hit and a base umpire goes out, move toward the holding zone about halfway to third base in foul ground to an area where you have an unobstructed view of all four elements. Be prepared to move as the play develops. Responsible for the tag up at third base (R1), any play on the lead runner (R1) at third base and any play at the plate.

U1: When a fly ball is hit and U3 goes out, pick up the ball and glance at the runner while hustling inside the diamond to button hook at a minimum depth of 10-12 feet. Continue to alternate between the ball and the runner (R2) keeping all four elements in front of you. Be prepared to move parallel to the baseline staying ahead of the runner. Responsible for the runner leaving early on the pitch at first base (R2) the tag-up at first base (R2), any play at first base or second base and the last runner (R2) at third base.

U3: Pick up the flight of the ball and glance at your partner. Responsible for any fly ball hit from the left fielder up to dead-ball territory. When chasing the fly ball communicate with the crew you are chasing. Move parallel to the flight of the ball, or if necessary to gain a better angle, move away from the fielder; stop facing the player when the play happens. If caught, give the out signal and verbal facing the play. If the ball is dropped and it is not obvious, give the safe/no catch signal. Let the ball turn you back toward the infield and observe the rest of the play from there. Responsible for the runner leaving early on the pitch at third base (R1), fair/foul, catch/no catch.

FLY BALL TO THE OUTFIELD, BALL IS NOT CAUGHT, B3 CHASES

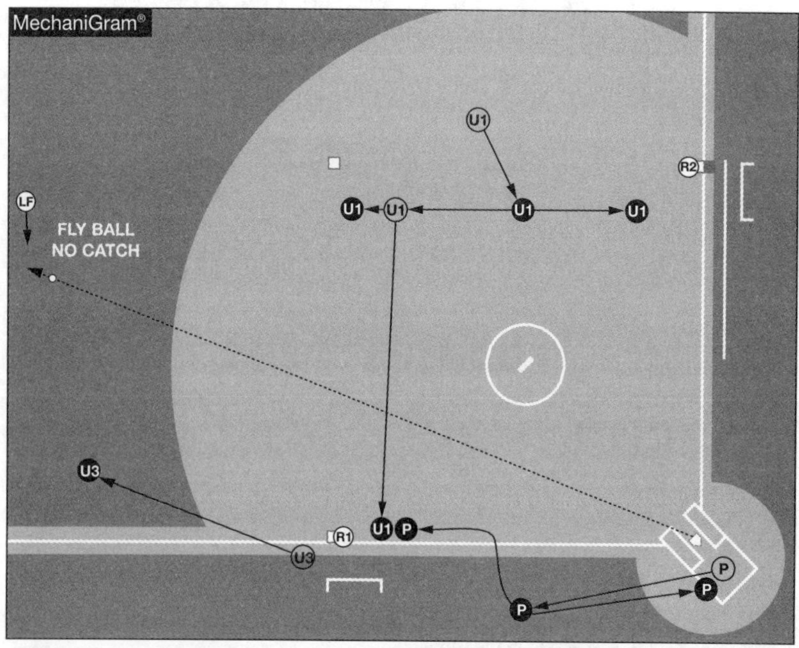

P: When a fly ball is hit and a base umpire goes out, move toward the holding zone about halfway to third base in foul ground to an area where you have an unobstructed view of all four elements. Be prepared to move as the play develops. Responsible for the tag up at third base (R1), any play on a lead runner (R1 and R2) at third base and any play at the plate.

U1: When a fly ball is hit and U3 goes out, pick up the ball and glance at the runner while hustling inside the diamond to button hook at a minimum depth of 10-12 feet. Continue to alternate between the ball and the runners (R2 and batter-runner) keeping all four elements in front of you. Be prepared to move parallel to the baseline staying ahead of the runner. Responsible for the runner leaving early on the pitch at first base (R2), the tag-up at first base (R2), any play at first base or second base and the last runner (batter-runner) at third base.

U3: Pick up the flight of the ball and glance at your partner. Responsible for any fly ball hit from the left fielder up to dead-ball territory. When chasing the fly ball communicate with the crew you are chasing. Move parallel to the flight of the ball, or if necessary to gain a better angle, move away from the fielder; stop facing the player when the play happens. If caught, give the out signal and verbal facing the play. If the ball is dropped and it is not obvious, give the safe/no catch signal. Let the ball turn you back toward the infield and observe the rest of the play from there. Responsible for the runner leaving early on the pitch at third base (R1), fair/foul, catch/no catch.

Part 8.5

Runners on Second and Third Base

- Ground Ball in the Infield

- Base Hit to the Outfield

- Fly Ball to the Outfield, Ball is Caught, No Umpire Chases

- Fly Ball to the Outfield, Ball is Not Caught, No Umpire Chases

- Fly Ball to the Outfield, Ball is Caught, U1 Chases

- Fly Ball to the Outfield, Ball is Not Caught, U1 Chases

- Fly Ball to the Outfield, Ball is Caught, U3 Chases

- Fly Ball to the Outfield, Ball is Not Caught, U3 Chases

GROUND BALL IN THE INFIELD

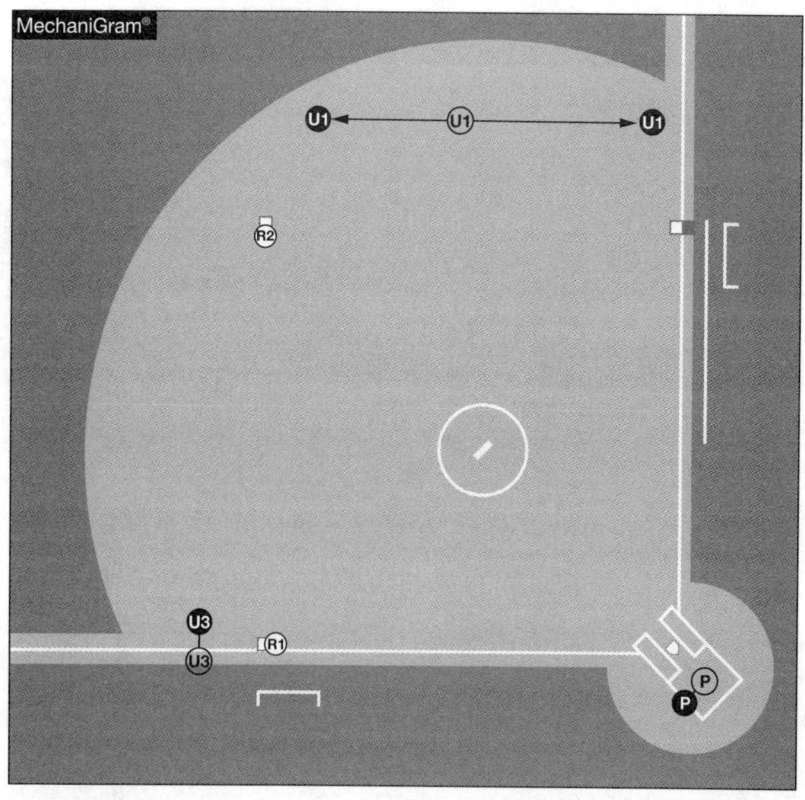

P: Move out from behind the plate and read the play. Responsible for fair/foul and any play at the plate.

U1: Let the ball take you to the play. Responsible for the runner leaving early on the pitch at second base (R2) and any play at first base or second base.

U3: Step into fair territory and read the play. Responsible for the runner leaving early on the pitch at third base (R1) and any play at third base.

BASE HIT TO THE OUTFIELD

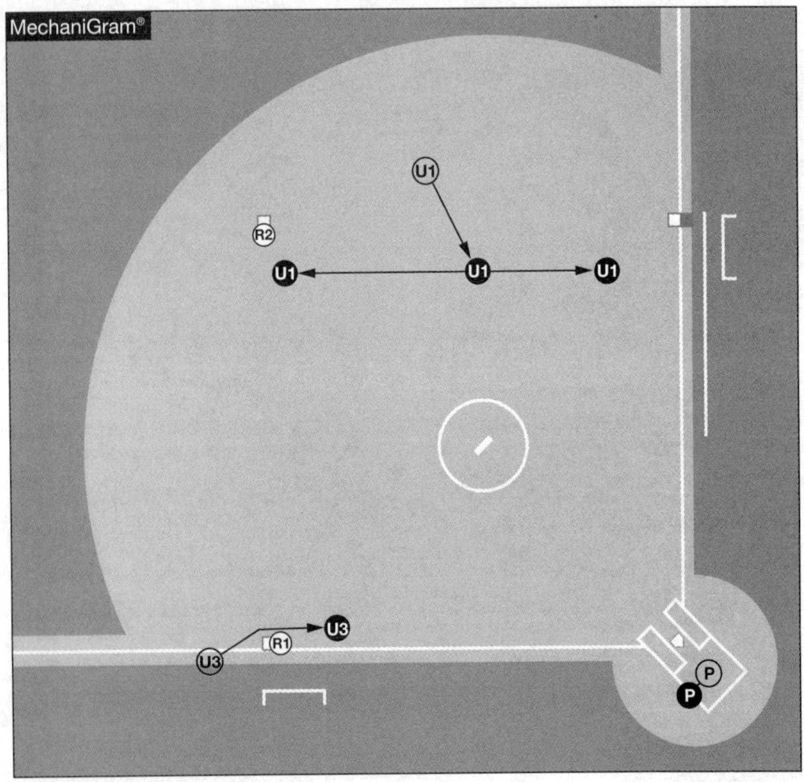

P: Move out from behind the plate and read the play. Responsible for fair/foul and any play at the plate.

U1: Pick up the ball and glance at the runner while hustling inside the diamond to button hook at a minimum depth of 10-12 feet. Continue to alternate between the ball and the runner (batter-runner) keeping all four elements in front of you. Be prepared to move parallel to the baseline staying ahead of the runner. Responsible for the runner leaving early on the pitch at second base (R2) and any play at first base or second base.

U3: Pick up the ball and glance at the runner while hustling inside the diamond to button hook at a minimum depth of 10-12 feet. Continue to alternate between the ball and the runners keeping all four elements in front of you. Responsible for the runner leaving early on the pitch at third base (R1) and any play at third base.

FLY BALL TO THE OUTFIELD, BALL IS CAUGHT, NO UMPIRE CHASES

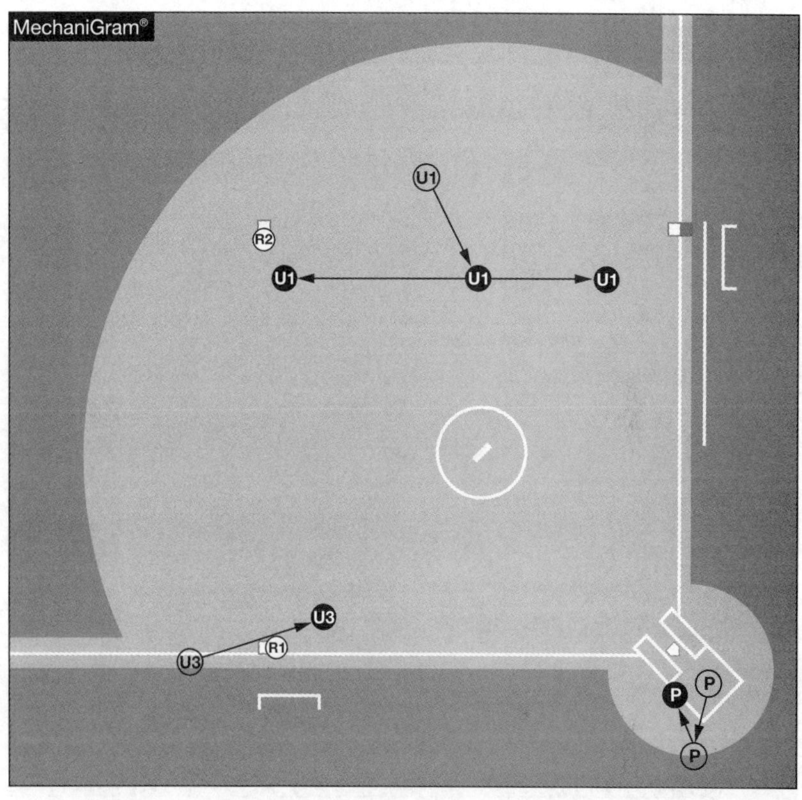

P: When a fly ball is hit from the right fielder up to dead-ball territory, move to the first-base line extended to get the best view and angle of the play. Responsible for fair/foul, catch/no catch and any play at the plate.

U1: Pick up the ball and glance at the runner while hustling inside the diamond to button hook at a minimum depth of 10-12 feet. Continue to alternate between the ball and the runner keeping all four elements in front of you. Be prepared to move as a play develops. Responsible for the runner leaving early on the pitch at second base (R2), the tag up at second base (R2) and any play at first base or second base.

U3: Pick up the ball and glance at the runner while hustling inside the diamond to button hook at a minimum depth of 10-12 feet. Continue to alternate between the ball and the runner keeping all four elements in front of you. Responsible for the runner leaving early on the pitch at third base (R1), the tag up at third base (R1) and any play at third base.

FLY BALL TO THE OUTFIELD, BALL IS NOT CAUGHT, NO UMPIRE CHASES

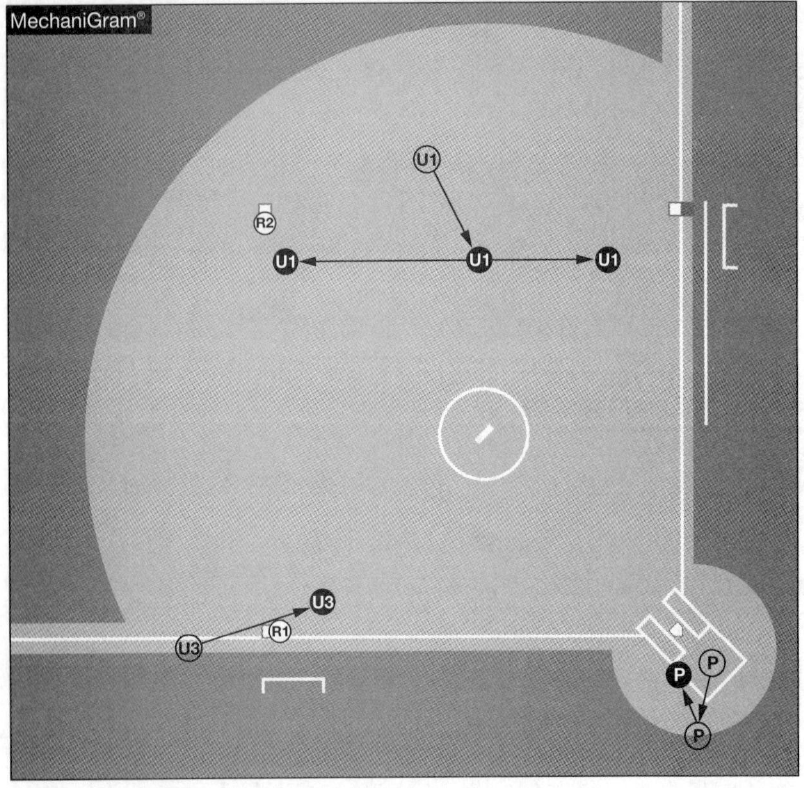

P: When a fly ball is hit from the right fielder up to dead-ball territory, move to the first-base line extended to get the best view and angle of the play. Responsible for fair/foul, catch/no catch and any play at the plate.

U1: Pick up the ball and glance at the runner while hustling inside the diamond to button hook at a minimum depth of 10-12 feet. Continue to alternate between the ball and the runner keeping all four elements in front of you. Be prepared to move parallel to the baseline staying ahead of the runner (batter-runner). Responsible for the runner leaving early on the pitch at second base (R2), the tag up at second base (R2) and any play at first base or second base.

U3: Pick up the ball and glance at the runner while hustling inside the diamond to button hook at a minimum depth of 10-12 feet. Continue to alternate between the ball and the runner keeping all four elements in front of you. Responsible for the runner leaving early on the pitch at third base (R1), the tag up at third base (R1) and any play at third base.

FLY BALL TO THE OUTFIELD, BALL IS CAUGHT, U1 CHASES

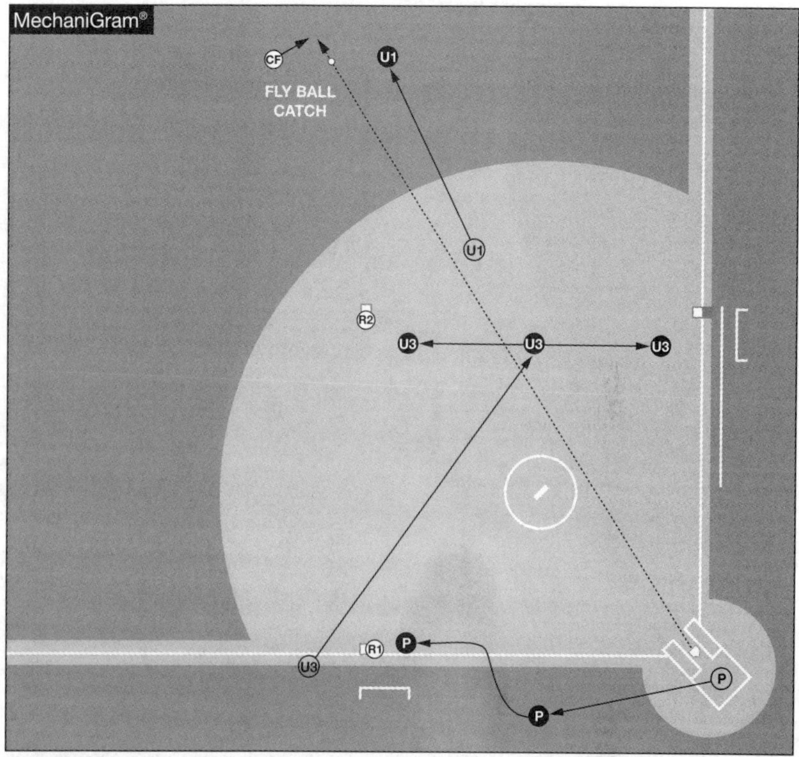

P: When a fly ball is hit and a base umpire goes out, move toward the holding zone about halfway to third base in foul ground to an area where you have an unobstructed view of all four elements. Be prepared to move as the play develops. Responsible for the tag up at third base (R1), any play on a lead runner (R1) at third base and any play at the plate.

U1: Pick up the flight of the ball and glance at your partner. Responsible for any fly ball from the right fielder up to the left fielder. When chasing the fly ball communicate with the crew you are chasing. Move parallel to the flight of the ball, or if necessary to gain a better angle, move away from the fielder; stop facing the player when the play happens. If caught, give the out signal and verbal facing the play. If the ball is dropped and it is not obvious, give the safe/no catch signal. Let the ball turn you back toward the infield and observe the rest of the play from there. Responsible for the runner leaving early on the pitch at second base (R2) and catch/no catch.

U3: When a fly ball is hit and U1 goes out, pick up the ball and glance at the runner while hustling across the diamond toward first base to a position about halfway between second base and first base. Continue to alternate between the ball and the runner keeping all four elements in front of you. Be prepared to move parallel to the baseline staying ahead of the runner (R2). Responsible for the runner leaving early on the pitch at third base (R1), the tag up at second base (R2) and any play at first base or second base and the last runner to third base (R2).

FLY BALL TO THE OUTFIELD, BALL IS NOT CAUGHT, U1 CHASES

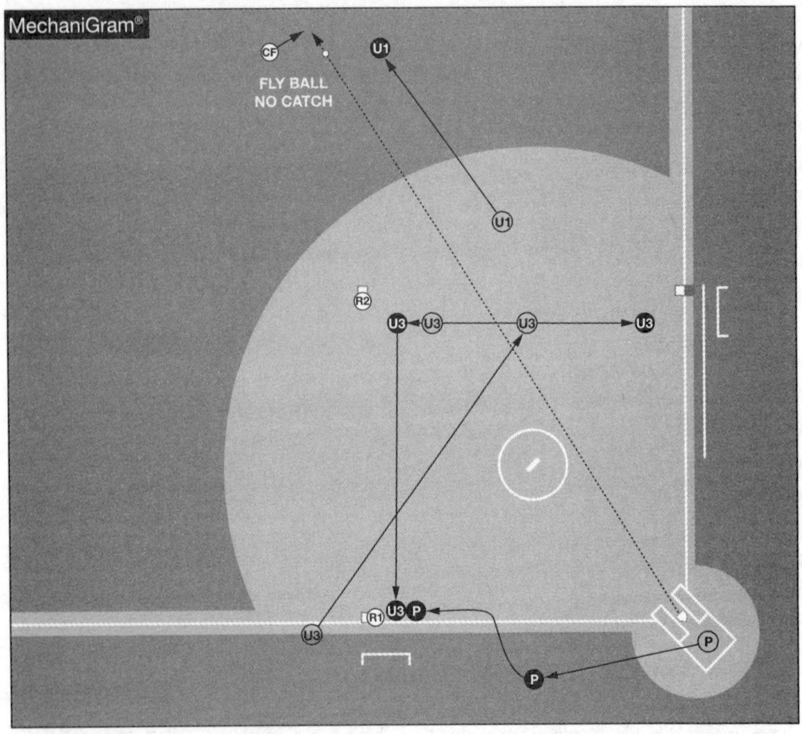

P: When a fly ball is hit and a base umpire goes out, move toward the holding zone about halfway to third base in foul ground to an area where you have an unobstructed view of all four elements. Be prepared to move as the play develops. Responsible for the tag up at third base (R1), any play on a lead runner (R1 and R2) at third base and any play at the plate.

U1: Pick up the flight of the ball and glance at your partner. Responsible for any fly ball from the right fielder up to the left fielder. When chasing the fly ball communicate with the crew you are chasing. Move parallel to the flight of the ball, or if necessary to gain a better angle, move away from the fielder; stop facing the player when the play happens. If the ball is dropped and it is not obvious, give the safe/no catch signal. Let the ball turn you back toward the infield and observe the rest of the play from there. Responsible for the runner leaving early on the pitch at first base (R2) and catch/no catch.

U3: When a fly ball is hit and U1 goes out, pick up the ball and glance at the runner while hustling across the diamond toward first base to a position about halfway between second base and first base. Continue to alternate between the ball and the runners keeping all four elements in front of you. Be prepared to move parallel to the baseline staying ahead of the runner. Responsible for the runner leaving early on the pitch at third base (R1), the tag up at second base (R2) and any play at first base or second base and the last runner to third base (batter-runner).

FLY BALL TO THE OUTFIELD, BALL IS CAUGHT, U3 CHASES

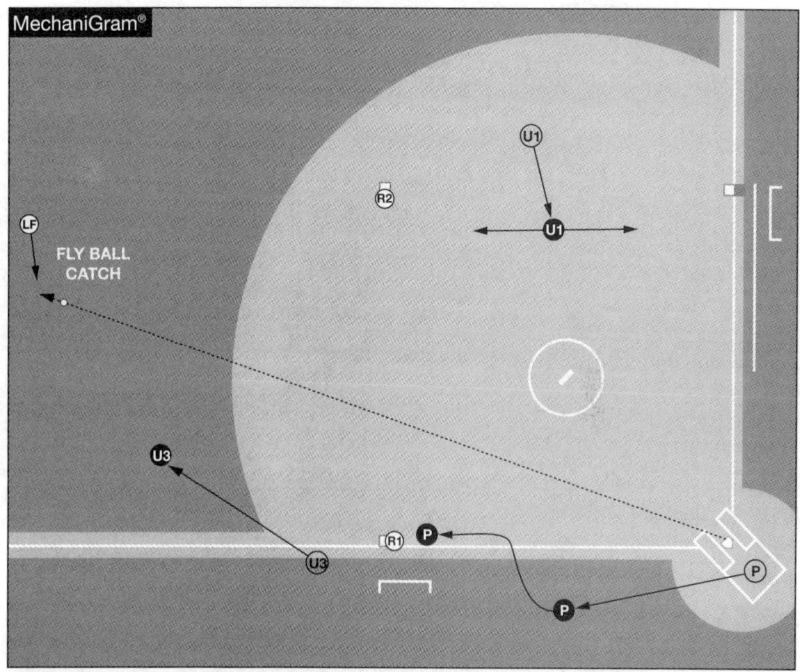

P: When a fly ball is hit and a base umpire goes out, move toward the holding zone about halfway to third base in foul ground to an area where you have an unobstructed view of all four elements. Be prepared to move as the play develops. Responsible for the tag up at third base (R1), any play on the lead runner (R1) at third base and any play at the plate.

U1: When a fly ball is hit and U3 goes out, pick up the ball and glance at the runner while hustling inside the diamond to button hook at a minimum depth of 10-12 feet. Continue to alternate between the ball and the runner (R2) keeping all four elements in front of you. Be prepared to move parallel to the baseline staying ahead of the runner. Responsible for the runner leaving early on the pitch at second base (R2) the tag-up at second base (R2), any play at first base or second base and the last runner (R2) at third base.

U3: Pick up the flight of the ball and glance at your partner. Responsible for any fly ball hit from the left fielder up to dead-ball territory. When chasing the fly ball communicate with the crew you are chasing. Move parallel to the flight of the ball, or if necessary to gain a better angle, move away from the fielder; stop facing the player when the play happens. If caught, give the out signal and verbal facing the play. If the ball is dropped and it is not obvious, give the safe/no catch signal. Let the ball turn you back toward the infield and observe the rest of the play from there. Responsible for the runner leaving early on the pitch at third base (R1), fair/foul, catch/no catch.

FLY BALL TO THE OUTFIELD, BALL IS NOT CAUGHT, U3 CHASES

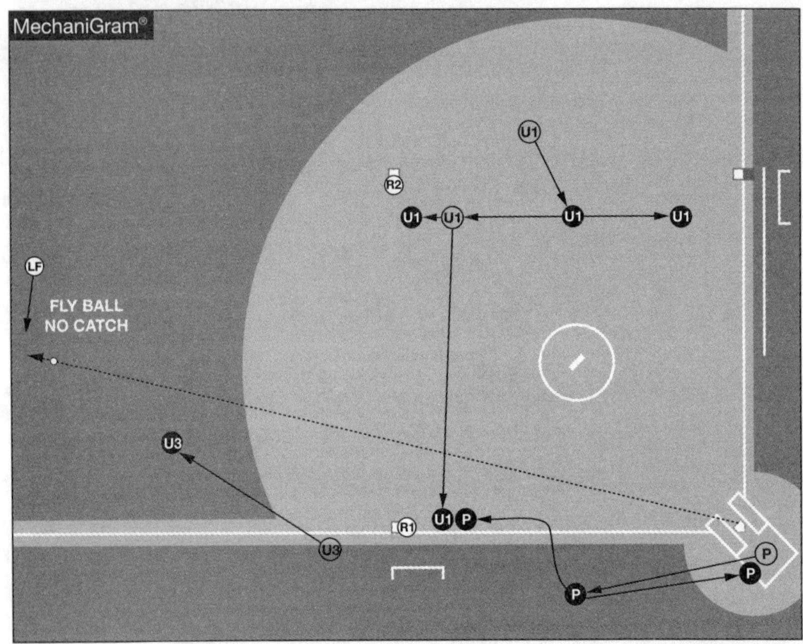

P: When a fly ball is hit and a base umpire goes out, move toward the holding zone about halfway to third base in foul ground to an area where you have an unobstructed view of all four elements. Be prepared to move as the play develops. Responsible for the tag up at third base (R1), any play on the lead runners at third base (R1 and R2) and any play at the plate.

U1: When a fly ball is hit and U3 goes out, pick up the ball and glance at the runner while hustling inside the diamond to button hook at a minimum depth of 10-12 feet. Continue to alternate between the ball and the runner (batter-runner) keeping all four elements in front of you. Be prepared to move parallel to the baseline staying ahead of the runner. Responsible for the runner leaving early on the pitch at second base (R2) the tag-up at second base (R2), any play at first base or second base and the last runner (batter-runner) at third base.

U3: Pick up the flight of the ball and glance at your partner. Responsible for any fly ball hit from the left fielder up to dead-ball territory. When chasing the fly ball communicate with the crew you are chasing. Move parallel to the flight of the ball, or if necessary to gain a better angle, move away from the fielder; stop facing the player when the play happens. If caught, give the out signal and verbal facing the play. If the ball is dropped and it is not obvious, give the safe/no catch signal. Let the ball turn you back toward the infield and observe the rest of the play from there. Responsible for the runner leaving early on the pitch at third base (R1), fair/foul, catch/no catch.

Three-Umpire System

Part 8.6

Runner on Second Base

- Ground Ball in the Infield

- Base Hit to the Outfield

- Fly Ball to the Outfield, Ball is Caught, No Umpire Chases

- Fly Ball to the Outfield, Ball is Not Caught, No Umpire Chases

- Fly Ball to the Outfield, Ball is Caught, U1 Chases

- Fly Ball to the Outfield, Ball is Not Caught, U1 Chases

- Fly Ball to the Outfield, Ball is Caught, U3 Chases

- Fly Ball to the Outfield, Ball is Not Caught, U3 Chases

GROUND BALL IN THE INFIELD

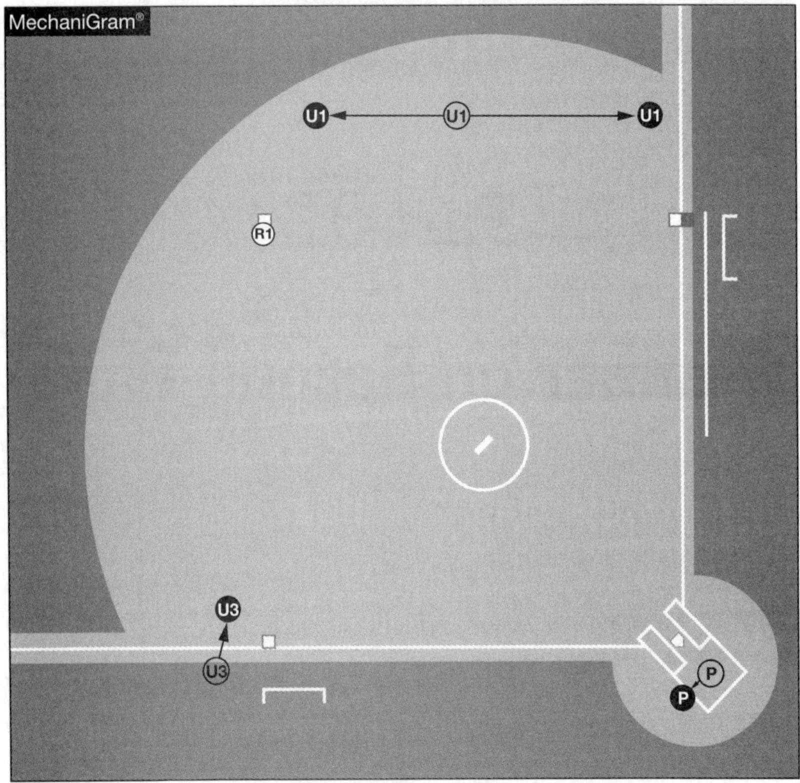

P: Move out from behind the plate and read the play. Responsible for fair/foul and any play at the plate.

U1: Let the ball take you to the play. Responsible for the runner at second base (R1) leaving early on the pitch and any play at first base or second base.

U3: Step into fair territory and read the play. Responsible for any play at third base.

BASE HIT TO THE OUTFIELD

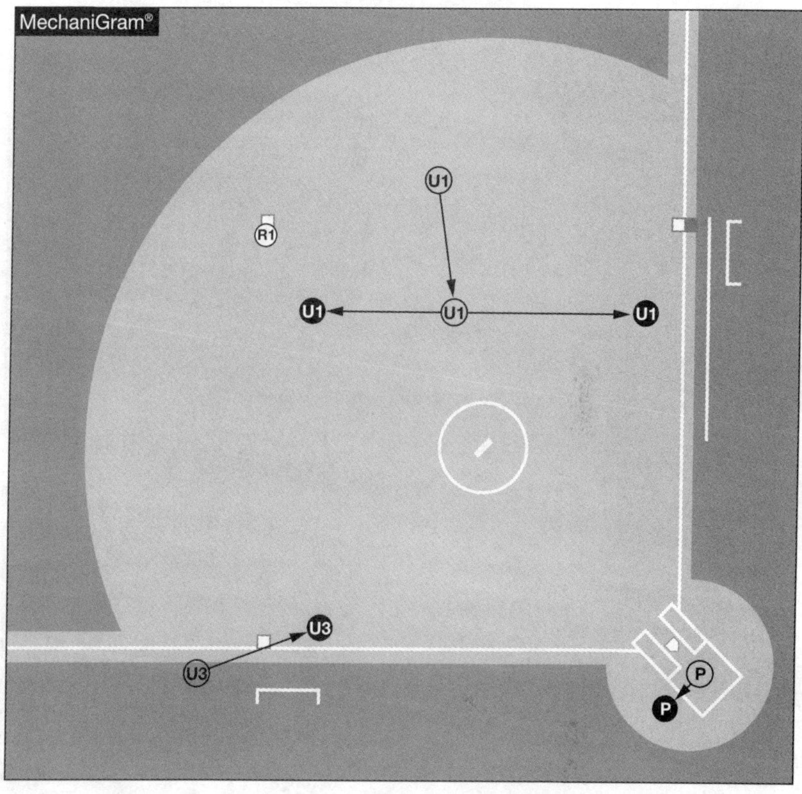

P: Move out from behind the plate and read the play. Responsible for fair/foul and any play at the plate.

U1: Pick up the ball and glance at the runner while hustling inside the diamond to button hook at a minimum depth of 10-12 feet. Continue to alternate between the ball and the runners keeping all four elements in front of you. Be prepared to move parallel to the baseline staying ahead of the runner. Responsible for the runner at second base (R1) leaving early on the pitch, any play at first base and second base.

U3: Pick up the ball and glance at the runner while hustling inside the diamond to button hook at a minimum depth of 10-12 feet. Continue to alternate between the ball and the runner keeping all four elements in front of you. Responsible for any play at third base.

FLY BALL TO THE OUTFIELD, BALL IS CAUGHT, NO UMPIRE CHASES

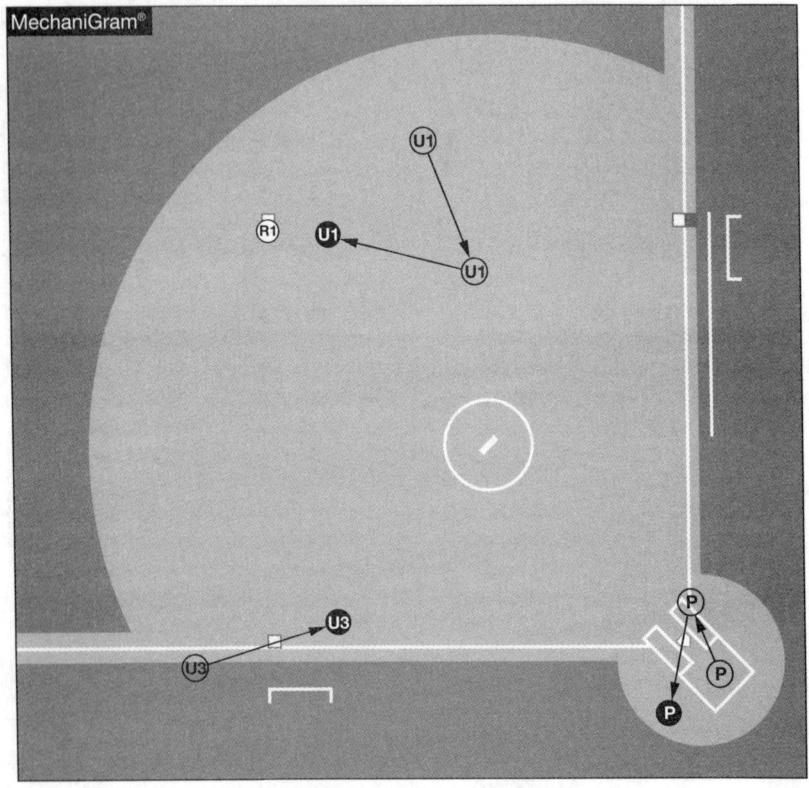

P: When a fly ball is hit from the right fielder up to dead-ball territory, step out from behind the plate and move up the first-base line one or two steps to get an unobstructed view of the play. Responsible for fair/foul, catch/no catch and any play at the plate.

U1: Pick up the ball and glance at the runner while hustling inside the diamond to button hook at a minimum depth of 10-12 feet. Continue to alternate between the ball and the runner keeping all four elements in front of you. Be prepared to move parallel to the baseline staying ahead of the runner. Responsible for the runner at second base (R1) leaving early on the pitch, the tag up at second base (R1) and any play at first base and second base.

U3: Pick up the ball and glance at the runner while hustling inside the diamond to button hook at a minimum depth of 10-12 feet. Continue to alternate between the ball and the runner keeping all four elements in front of you. Responsible for any play at third base.

FLY BALL TO THE OUTFIELD, BALL IS NOT CAUGHT, NO UMPIRE CHASES

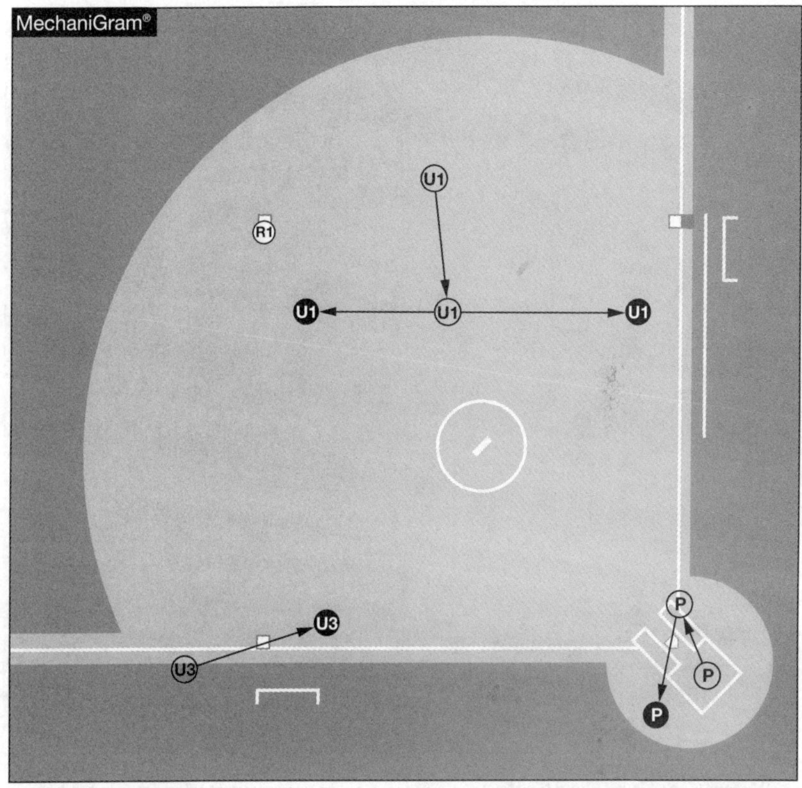

P: When a fly ball is hit from the right fielder up to dead-ball territory, step out from behind the plate and move up the first-base line one or two steps to get an unobstructed view of the play. Responsible for fair/foul, catch/no catch and any play at the plate.

U1: Pick up the ball and glance at the runner while hustling inside the diamond to button hook at a minimum depth of 10-12 feet. Continue to alternate between the ball and the runner keeping all four elements in front of you. Be prepared to move parallel to the baseline staying ahead of the runner. Responsible for the runner at second base (R1) leaving early on the pitch, the tag up at second base (R1) and any play at first base and second base.

U3: Pick up the ball and glance at the runner while hustling inside the diamond to button hook at a minimum depth of 10-12 feet. Continue to alternate between the ball and the runner keeping all four elements in front of you. Responsible for any play at third base.

FLY BALL TO THE OUTFIELD, BALL IS CAUGHT, U1 CHASES

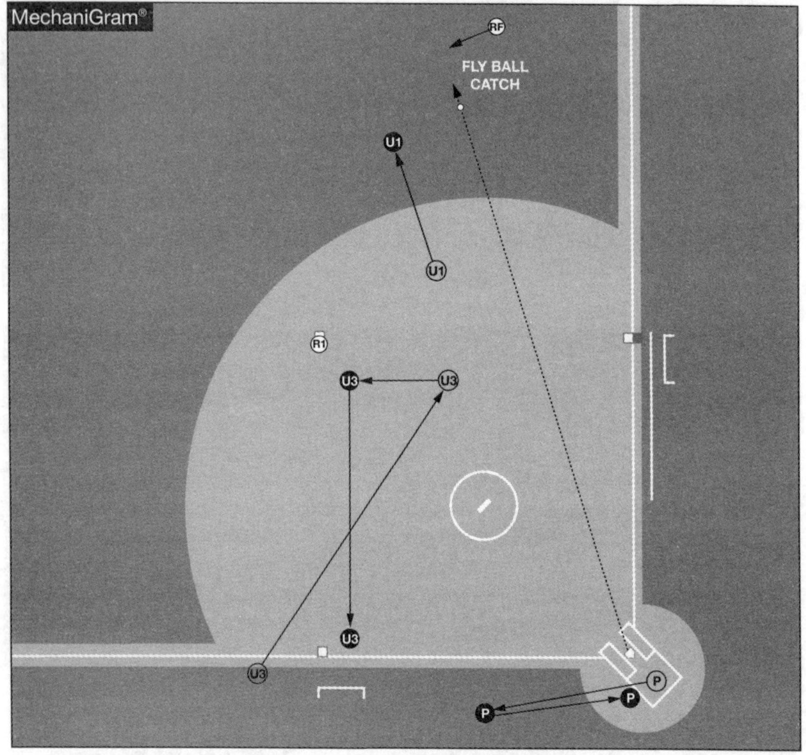

P: When a fly ball is hit and a base umpire goes out, move toward the holding zone about halfway to third base in foul ground to an area where you have an unobstructed view of all four elements. Be prepared to move as the play develops. Responsible for any play at the plate.

U1: Pick up the flight of the ball and glance at your partner. Responsible for any fly ball from the right fielder up to left fielder. When chasing the fly ball communicate with the crew you are chasing. Move parallel to the flight of the ball or if necessary to gain a better angle, move away from the fielder; stop facing the player when the play happens. If caught, give the out signal and verbal facing the play. If the ball is dropped and it is not obvious, give the safe/no catch signal. Let the ball turn you back toward the infield and observe the rest of the play from there. Responsible for the runner at second base (R1) leaving early on the pitch, catch/no catch.

U3: When a fly ball is hit and U1 goes out, pick up the ball and glance at the runner while hustling across the diamond toward first base to a position about halfway between second base and first base. Continue to alternate between the ball and the runner keeping all four elements in front of you. Be prepared to move parallel to the baseline staying ahead of the runner (R1). Responsible for the tag-up at second base (R1), any play at first base or second base and the last runner (R1) at third base.

FLY BALL TO THE OUTFIELD, BALL IS NOT CAUGHT, U1 CHASES

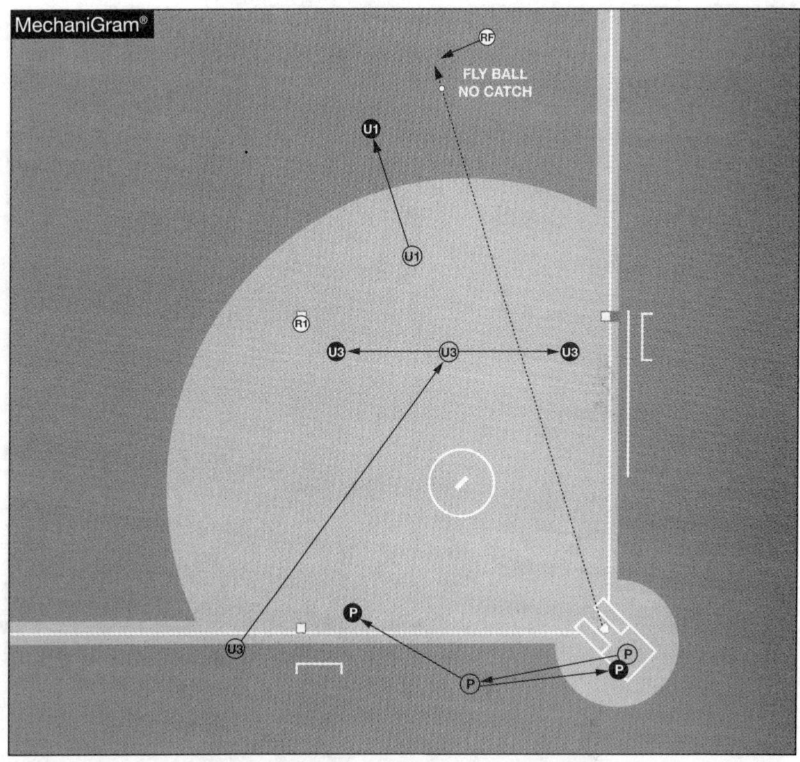

P: When a fly ball is hit and a base umpire goes out, move toward the holding zone about halfway to third base in foul ground to an area where you have an unobstructed view of all four elements. Be prepared to move as the play develops. Responsible for any play on the lead runner at third base (R1) and any play at the plate.

U1: Pick up the flight of the ball and glance at your partner. Responsible for any fly ball from the right fielder up to left fielder. When chasing the fly ball communicate with the crew you are chasing. Move parallel to the flight of the ball, or if necessary to gain a better angle, move away from the fielder; stop facing the player when the play happens. If caught, give the out signal and verbal facing the play. If the ball is dropped and it is not obvious, give the safe/no catch signal. Let the ball turn you back toward the infield and observe the rest of the play from there. Responsible for the runner at second base (R1) leaving early on the pitch, catch/no catch.

U3: When a fly ball is hit and U1 goes out, pick up the ball and glance at the runner while hustling across the diamond toward first base to a position about halfway between second base and first base. Continue to alternate between the ball and the runner keeping all four elements in front of you. Be prepared to move parallel to the baseline staying ahead of the runner (batter-runner). Responsible for the tag-up at second base (R1), any play at first base or second base and the last runner (batter-runner) at third base.

FLY BALL TO THE OUTFIELD, BALL IS CAUGHT, U3 CHASES

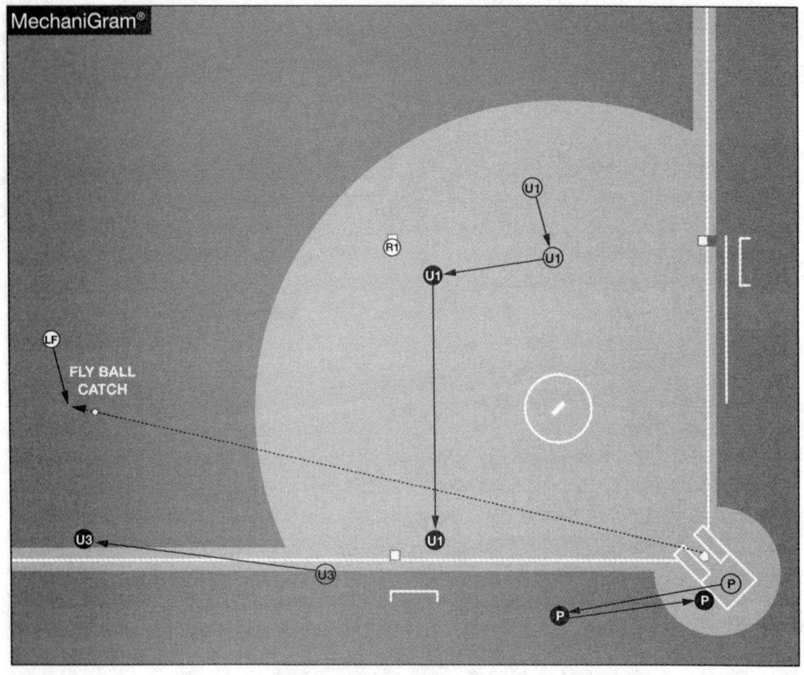

P: When a fly ball is hit and a base umpire goes out, move toward the holding zone about halfway to third base in foul ground to an area where you have an unobstructed view of all four elements. Be prepared to move as the play develops. Responsible for any play at the plate.

U1: When a fly ball is hit and U3 goes out, pick up the ball and glance at the runner while hustling inside the diamond to button hook at a minimum depth of 10-12 feet. Continue to alternate between the ball and the runner (R1) keeping all four elements in front of you. Be prepared to move parallel to the baseline staying ahead of the runner. Responsible for the runner at second base (R1) leaving early on the pitch, the tag-up at second base (R1), any play at first base or second base and the last runner (R1) at third base.

U3: Pick up the flight of the ball and glance at your partner. Responsible for any fly ball hit from the left fielder up to dead-ball territory. When chasing the fly ball communicate with the crew you are chasing. Move parallel to the flight of the ball, or if necessary to gain a better angle, move away from the fielder; stop facing the player when the play happens. If caught, give the out signal and verbal facing the play. If the ball is dropped and it is not obvious, give the safe/no catch signal. Let the ball turn you back toward the infield and observe the rest of the play from there. Responsible for fair/foul, catch/no catch.

FLY BALL TO THE OUTFIELD, BALL IS NOT CAUGHT, U3 CHASES

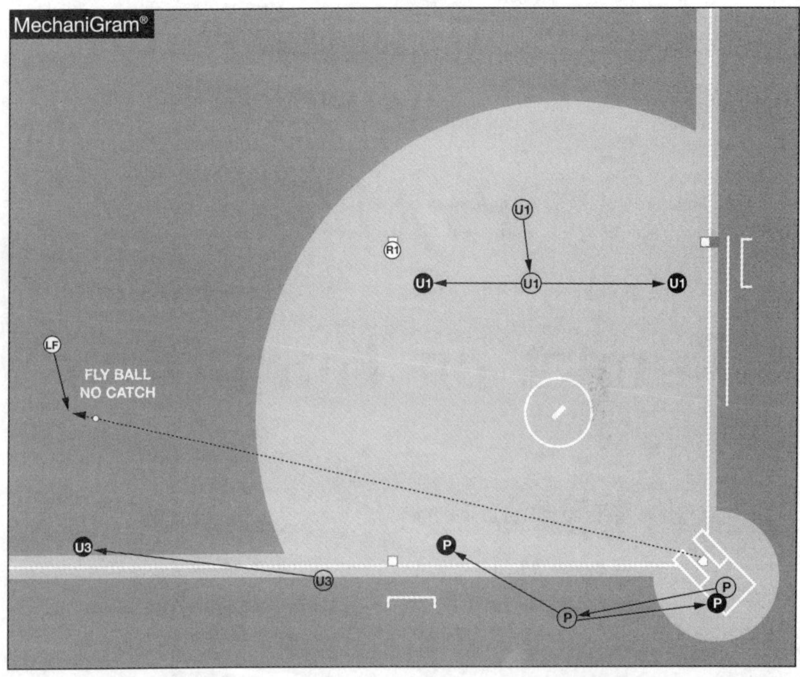

P: When a fly ball is hit and a base umpire goes out, move toward the holding zone about halfway to third base in foul ground to an area where you have an unobstructed view of all four elements. Be prepared to move as the play develops. Responsible for any play on the lead runner at third base (R1) and any play at the plate.

U1: When a fly ball is hit and U3 goes out, pick up the ball and glance at the runner while hustling inside the diamond to button hook at a minimum depth of 10-12 feet. Continue to alternate between the ball and the runners keeping all four elements in front of you. Be prepared to move parallel to the baseline staying ahead of the runner. Responsible for the runner at second base (R1) leaving early on the pitch, the tag-up at second base (R1), any play at first base or second base and the last runner (batter-runner) at third base.

U3: Pick up the flight of the ball and glance at your partner. Responsible for any fly ball hit from the left fielder up to dead-ball territory. When chasing the fly ball communicate with the crew you are chasing. Move parallel to the flight of the ball, or if necessary to gain a better angle, move away from the fielder; stop facing the player when the play happens. If caught, give the out signal and verbal facing the play. If the ball is dropped and it is not obvious, give the safe/no catch signal. Let the ball turn you back toward the infield and observe the rest of the play from there. Responsible for fair/foul, catch/no catch.

Three-Umpire System

Part 8.7

Runner on Third Base

- ◆ Ground Ball in the Infield
- ◆ Base Hit to the Outfield
- ◆ Fly Ball to the Outfield, Ball is Caught, U1 Chases
- ◆ Fly Ball to the Outfield, Ball is Not Caught, U1 Chases
- ◆ Fly Ball to the Outfield, Ball is Caught, U3 Chases
- ◆ Fly Ball to the Outfield, Ball is Not Caught, U3 Chases

GROUND BALL IN THE INFIELD

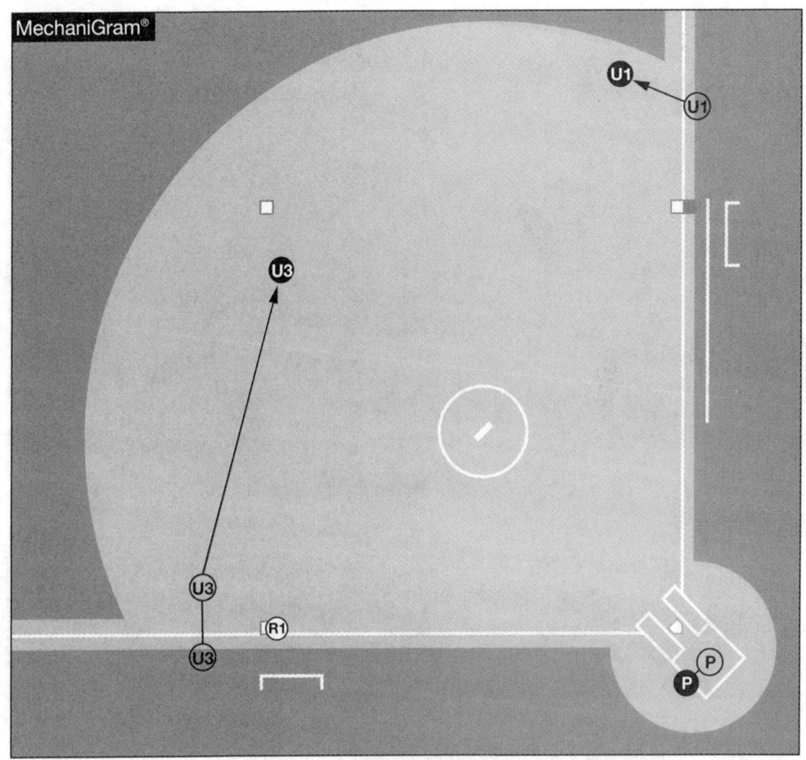

P: Move out from behind the plate and read the play. See the runner from third base (R1) touch the plate and as the batter-runner approaches second base, rotate to third base in fair territory to a 90-degree angle at a minimum depth of 10-12 feet from third base. Responsible for the lead runner (R1) at the plate and the last runner (batter-runner) at third base.

U1: Step into fair territory, at an angle of 90 degrees to the path of the throw, no more than a 45-degree angle from the foul line, and let the ball take you to the play. Responsible for any play at first base when at first base and any play at the plate when rotated to the plate. If the runner (R1) at third base does not advance to the plate, you are also responsible for any play at second base.

U3: Step inside the diamond and read the play. If the runner at third advances to the plate, hustle into the diamond to a 90-degree angle at a minimum depth of 10-12 feet from second base. Responsible for the runner at third base (R1) leaving early on the pitch, any play on that runner at third base (R1) and any play at second base if the runner at third base (R1) advances to the plate.

BASE HIT TO THE OUTFIELD

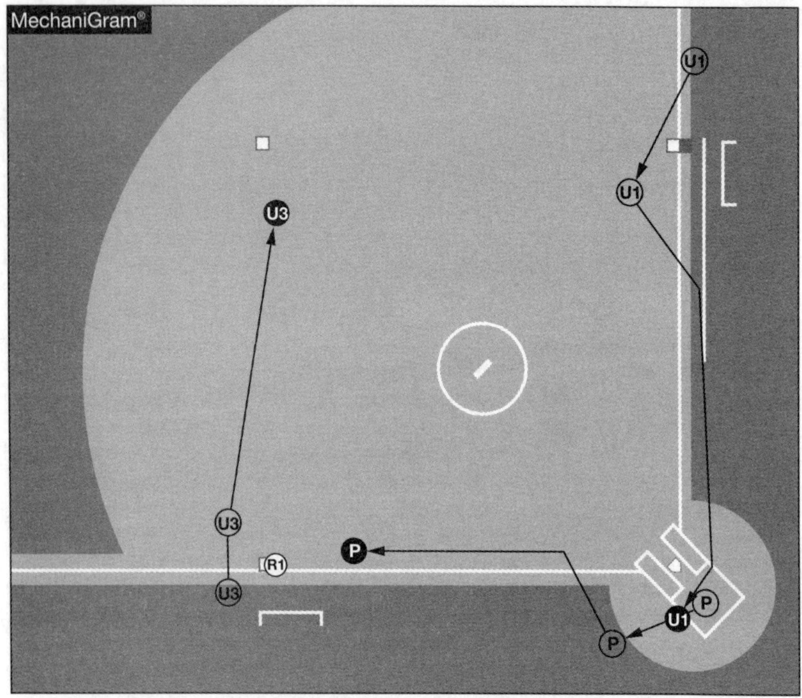

P: Move out from behind the plate and read the play. Observe the runner from third base (R1) touch the plate and as the batter-runner approaches second base rotate to third base in fair territory to a 90 degree angle at a minimum depth of 10-12 feet from third base. When the runner (batter-runner) reaches third base, visually confirm that U1 has rotated into position at home plate. Responsible for the lead runner (R1) at the plate and the last runner (batter-runner) at third base.

U1: Pick up the ball and glance at the runner while hustling inside the diamond to button hook at a minimum depth of 10-12 feet. Continue to alternate between the ball and the runner keeping all four elements in front of you. If the runner continues on to second base, visually confirm U3 has rotated to second base. As the runner commits to second base, rotate to home in foul ground to the farthest back corner of the right-hand batter's box, at a minimum of 10-12 feet from the plate, for any possible play at home plate. Responsible for any play at first base when at first base and any play at the plate when rotated to the plate.

U3: Pick up the ball and glance at the runner while hustling into the diamond to a 90-degree angle at a minimum depth of 10-12 feet from second base. Continue to alternate between the ball and the runner keeping all four elements in front of you. Responsible for any play at second base and any play at first base when U1 has rotated to the plate.

FLY BALL TO THE OUTFIELD, BALL IS CAUGHT, U1 CHASES

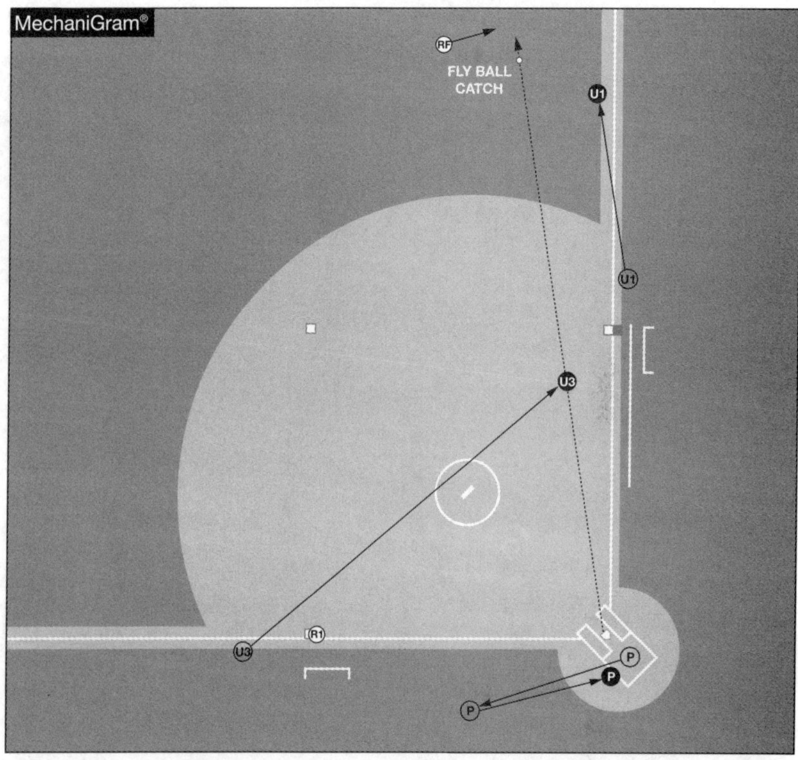

P: When a fly ball is hit and a base umpire goes out, move toward the holding zone about halfway to third base in foul ground to an area where you have an unobstructed view of all four elements. Be prepared to move as the play develops. Responsible for the tag up at third base (R1), any play on that runner (R1) at third base and any play at the plate.

U1: Pick up the flight of the ball and glance at your partner. Responsible for any fly ball from the center fielder to the right fielder and up to dead-ball territory. When chasing the fly ball communicate with the crew you are chasing. Move parallel to the flight of the ball, or if necessary to gain a better angle, move away from the fielder; stop facing the player when the play happens. If caught, give the out signal and verbal facing the play. If the ball is dropped and it is not obvious, give the safe/no catch signal. Let the ball turn you back toward the infield and observe the rest of the play from there. Responsible for fair/foul, catch/no catch.

U3: When a fly ball is hit and U1 goes out, pick up the ball and glance at the runner while hustling across the diamond toward first base to see the play at first base. Continue to alternate between the ball and the runner (batter-runner) keeping all four elements in front of you. Be prepared to move parallel to the baseline staying ahead of the runner. Responsible for the runner leaving early on the pitch at third base (R1), any play at first base or second base and the last runner (batter-runner) at third base.

FLY BALL TO THE OUTFIELD, BALL IS NOT CAUGHT, U1 CHASES

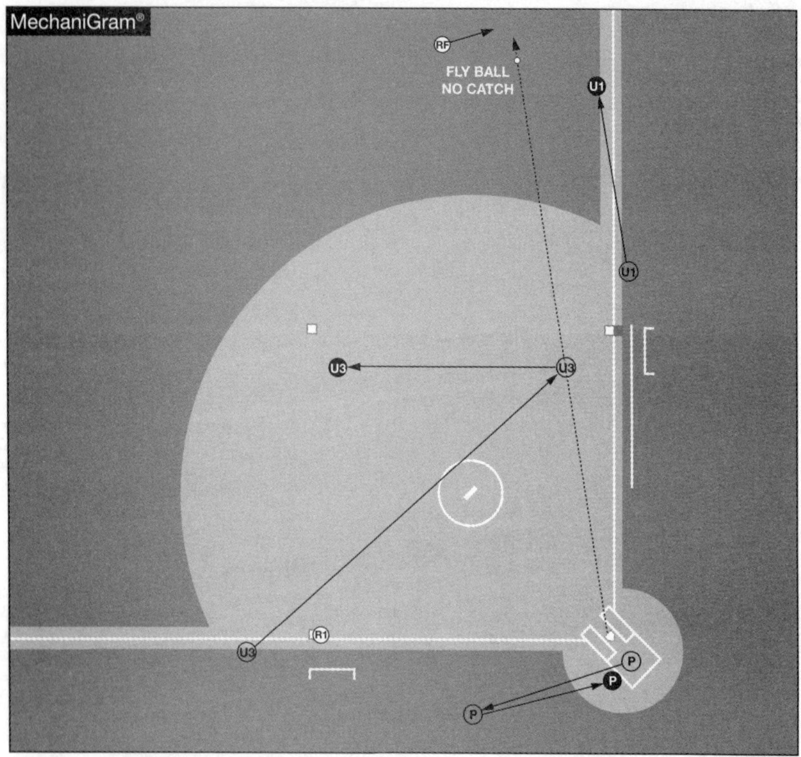

P: When a fly ball is hit and a base umpire goes out, move toward the holding zone about halfway to third base in foul ground to an area where you have an unobstructed view of all four elements. Be prepared to move as the play develops. Responsible for the tag up at third base (R1), any play on that runner (R1) at third base and any play at the plate.

U1: Pick up the flight of the ball and glance at your partner. Responsible for any fly ball from the center fielder to right fielder and up to dead-ball territory. When chasing the fly ball communicate with the crew you are chasing. Move parallel to the flight of the ball, or if necessary to gain a better angle, move away from the fielder; stop facing the player when the play happens. If caught, give the out signal and verbal facing the play. If the ball is dropped and it is not obvious, give the safe/no catch signal. Let the ball turn you back toward the infield and observe the rest of the play from there. Responsible for fair/foul, catch/no catch.

BWhen a fly ball is hit and U1 goes out, pick up the ball and glance at the runner while hustling across the diamond toward first base to see the play at first base. Continue to alternate between the ball and the runner (batter-runner) keeping all four elements in front of you. Be prepared to move parallel to the baseline staying ahead of the runner. Responsible for the runner leaving early on the pitch at third base (R1), any play at first base or second base and the last runner (batter-runner) at third base.

FLY BALL TO THE OUTFIELD, BALL IS CAUGHT, U3 CHASES

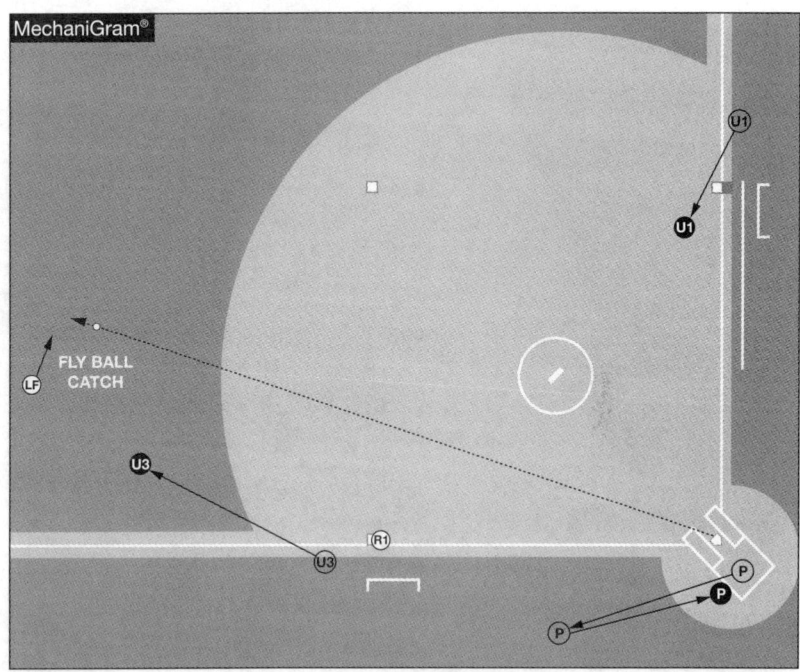

P: When a fly ball is hit and a base umpire goes out, move toward the holding zone about halfway to third base in foul ground to an area where you have an unobstructed view of all four elements. Be prepared to move as the play develops. Responsible for the tag up at third base (R1), any play on that runner (R1) at third base and any play at the plate.

U1: When a fly ball is hit and U3 goes out, pick up the ball and glance at the runner while hustling inside the diamond to button hook at a minimum depth of 10-12 feet. Continue to alternate between the ball and the runner (batter-runner) keeping all four elements in front of you. Be prepared to move parallel to the baseline staying ahead of the runner. Responsible for any play at first base or second base and the last runner (batter-runner) at third base.

U3: Pick up the flight of the ball and glance at your partner. Responsible for any fly ball hit from the center fielder to left fielder and up to dead-ball territory. When chasing the fly ball communicate with the crew you are chasing. Move parallel to the flight of the ball, or if necessary to gain a better angle, move away from the fielder; stop facing the player when the play happens. If caught, give the out signal and verbal facing the play. If the ball is dropped and it is not obvious, give the safe/no catch signal. Let the ball turn you back toward the infield and observe the rest of the play from there. Responsible for the runner leaving early on the pitch at third base (R1), fair/foul, catch/no catch.

FLY BALL TO THE OUTFIELD, BALL IS NOT CAUGHT, U3 CHASES

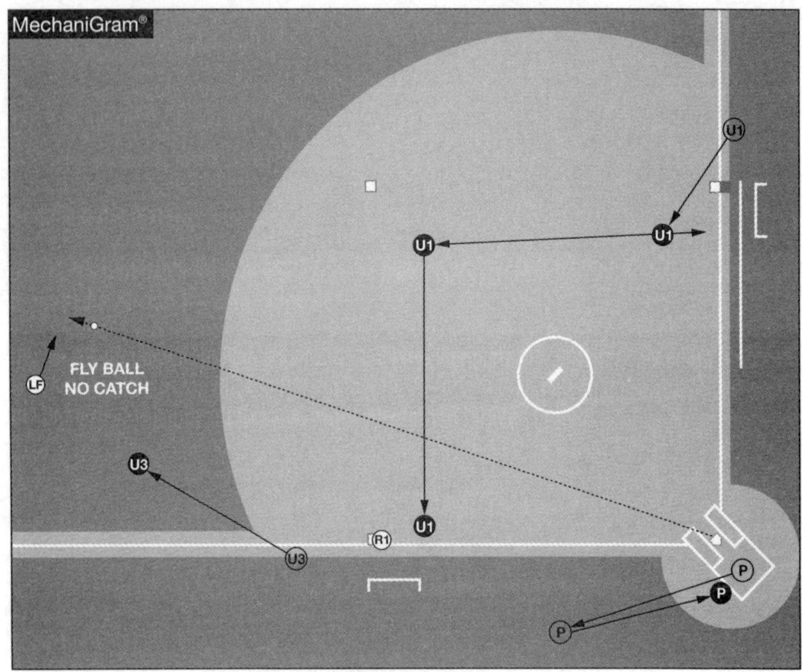

P: When a fly ball is hit and a base umpire goes out, move toward the holding zone about halfway to third base in foul ground to an area where you have an unobstructed view of all four elements. Be prepared to move as the play develops. Responsible for the tag up at third base (R1), any play on that runner (R1) at third base and any play at the plate.

U1: When a fly ball is hit and U3 goes out, pick up the ball and glance at the runner while hustling inside the diamond to button hook at a minimum depth of 10-12 feet. Continue to alternate between the ball and the runner (batter-runner) keeping all four elements in front of you. Be prepared to move parallel to the baseline staying ahead of the runner. Responsible for any play at first base or second base and the last runner (batter-runner) at third base.

U3: Pick up the flight of the ball and glance at your partner. Responsible for any fly ball hit from the center fielder to the left fielder and up to dead-ball territory. When chasing the fly ball communicate with the crew you are chasing. Move parallel to the flight of the ball, or if necessary to gain a better angle, move away from the fielder; stop facing the player when the play happens. If caught, give the out signal and verbal facing the play. If the ball is dropped and it is not obvious, give the safe/no catch signal. Let the ball turn you back toward the infield and observe the rest of the play from there. Responsible for the runner leaving early on the pitch at third base (R1), fair/foul, catch/no catch.

Three-Umpire System

Part 8.8

Runners on First, Second and Third Base

- ◆ Ground Ball in the Infield

- ◆ Base Hit to the Outfield

- ◆ Fly Ball to the Outfield, Ball is Caught, No Umpire Chases

- ◆ Fly Ball to the Outfield, Ball is Not Caught, No Umpire Chases

- ◆ Fly Ball to the Outfield, Ball is Caught, U1 Chases

- ◆ Fly Ball to the Outfield, Ball is Not Caught, U1 Chases

- ◆ Fly Ball to the Outfield, Ball is Caught, U3 Chases

- ◆ Fly Ball to the Outfield, Ball is Not Caught, U3 Chases

GROUND BALL IN THE INFIELD

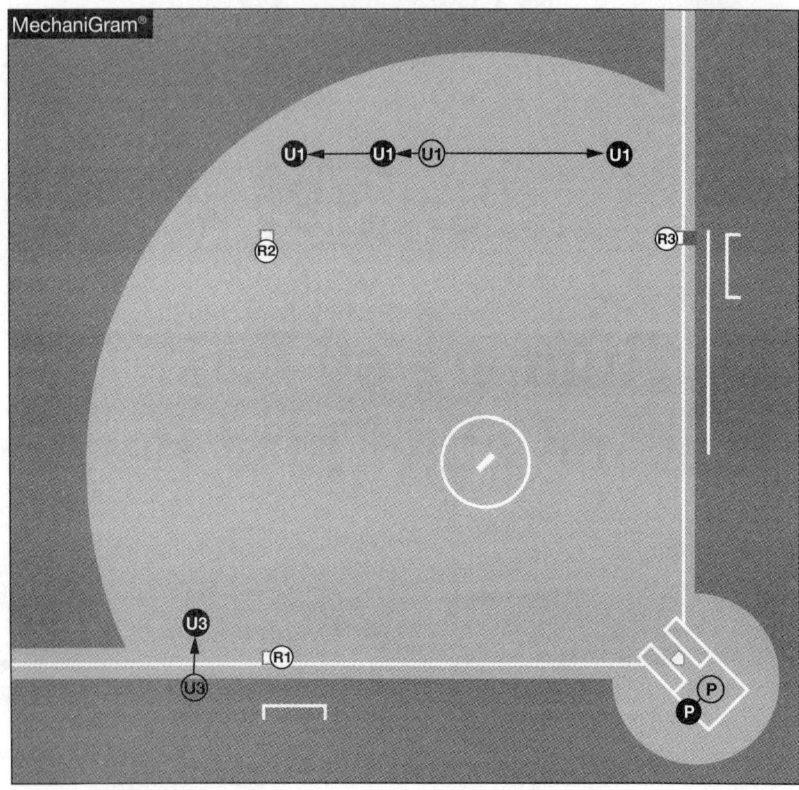

P: Move out from behind the plate and read the play. Responsible for fair/foul and any play at the plate.

U1: Let the ball take you to the play. Responsible for the runner leaving early on the pitch at second base (R2) and any play at first base or second base.

U3: Step into fair territory and read the play. Responsible for the runners leaving early on the pitch at third base and first base (R1 and R3) and any play at third base.

BASE HIT TO THE OUTFIELD

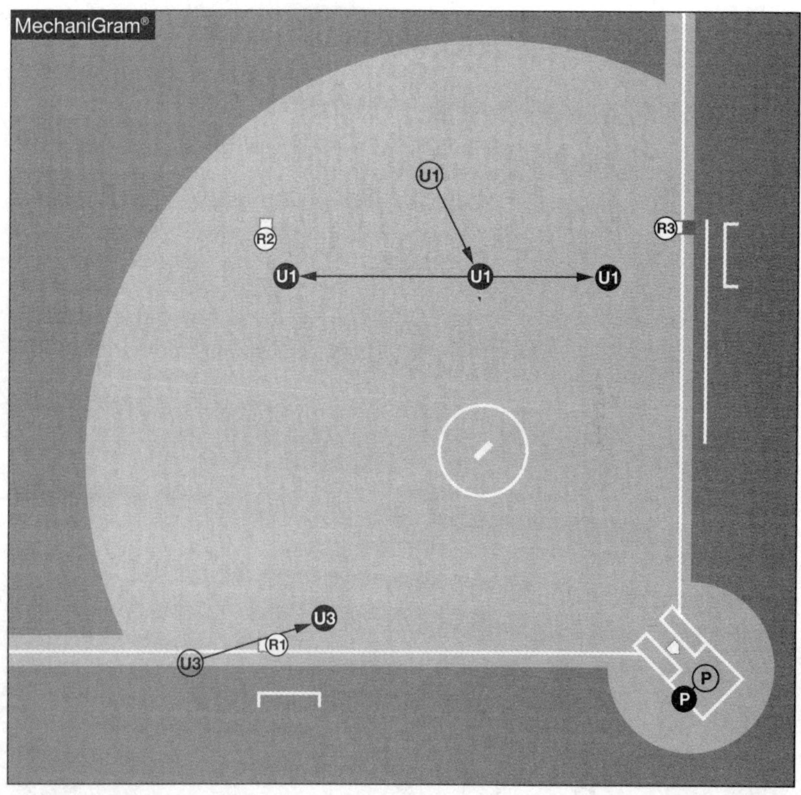

P: Move out from behind the plate and read the play. Responsible for fair/foul and any play at the plate.

U1: Pick up the ball and glance at the runner while hustling inside the diamond to button hook at a minimum depth of 10-12 feet. Continue to alternate between the ball and the runners (R1 and batter-runner) keeping all four elements in front of you. Be prepared to move parallel to the baseline staying ahead of the runner. Responsible for the runner leaving early on the pitch at second base (R2) and any play at first base or second base.

U3: Pick up the ball and glance at the runner while hustling inside the diamond to button hook at a minimum depth of 10-12 feet. Continue to alternate between the ball and the runners keeping all four elements in front of you. Responsible for the runners leaving early on the pitch at third base and first base (R1 and R3) and any play at third base.

FLY BALL TO THE OUTFIELD, BALL IS CAUGHT, NO UMPIRE CHASES

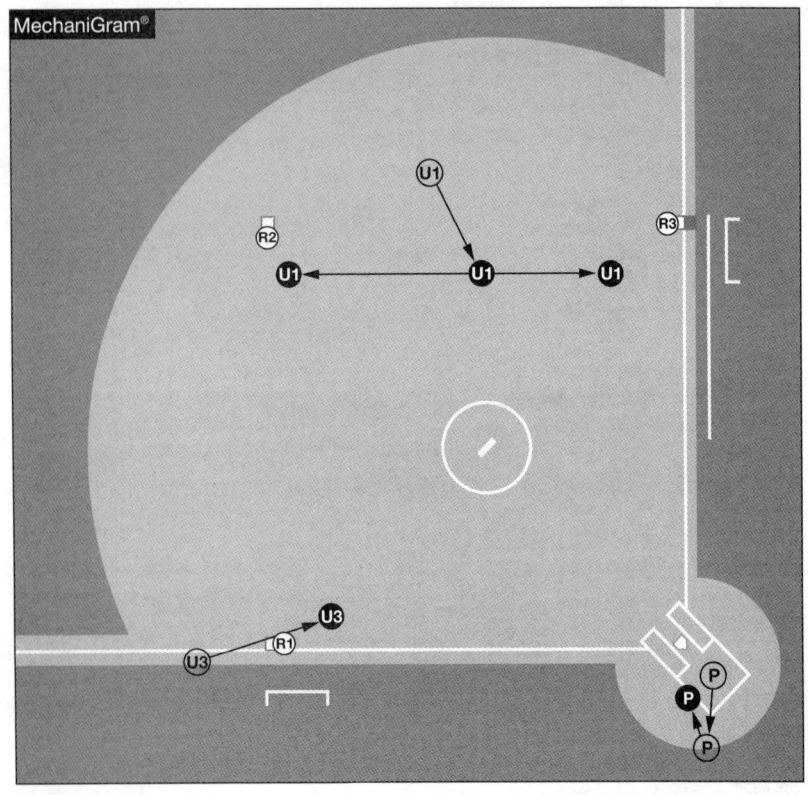

P: When a fly ball is hit from the right fielder up to dead-ball territory, move to the first-base line extended to get the best view and angle of the play. Responsible for fair/foul, catch/no catch and any play at the plate.

U1: Pick up the ball and glance at the runner while hustling inside the diamond to button hook at a minimum depth of 10-12 feet. Continue to alternate between the ball and the runners (R2 and R3) keeping all four elements in front of you. Be prepared to move as a play develops. Responsible for the runner leaving early on the pitch at second base (R2), the tag up at first base and second base (R2 and R3) and any play at first base or second base.

U3: Pick up the ball and glance at the runner while hustling inside the diamond to button hook at a minimum depth of 10-12 feet. Continue to alternate between the ball and the runner keeping all four elements in front of you. Responsible for the runners leaving early on the pitch at third base and first base (R1 and R3), the tag up at third base (R1) and any play at third base.

FLY BALL TO THE OUTFIELD, BALL IS NOT CAUGHT, NO UMPIRE CHASES

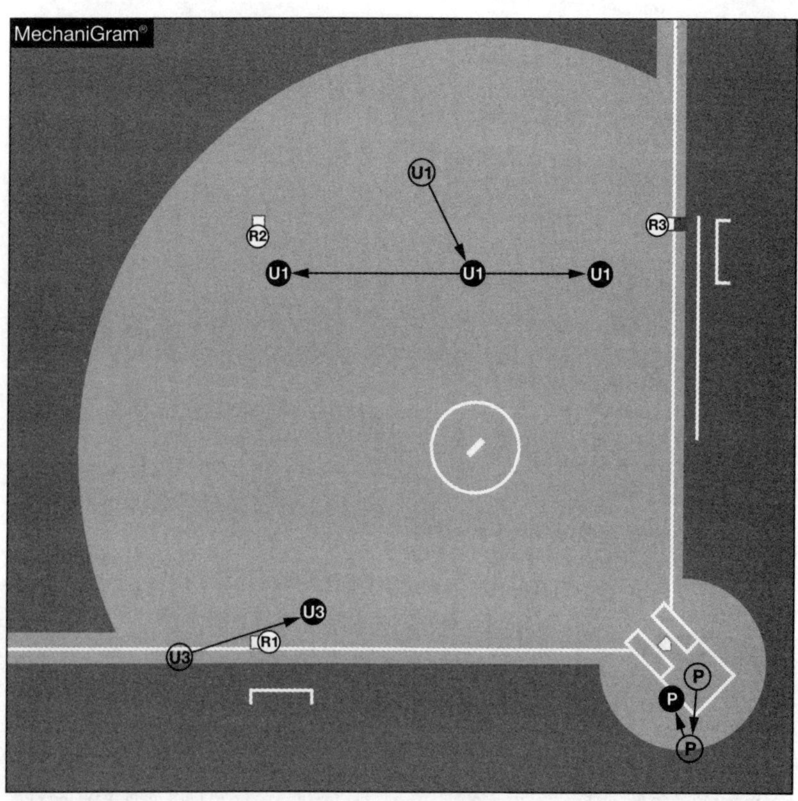

P: When a fly ball is hit from the right fielder up to dead-ball territory, move to the first-base line extended to get the best view and angle of the play. Responsible for fair/foul, catch/no catch and any play at the plate.

U1: Pick up the ball and glance at the runner while hustling inside the diamond to button hook at a minimum depth of 10-12 feet. Continue to alternate between the ball and the runner keeping all four elements in front of you. Be prepared to move parallel to the baseline staying ahead of the runners (R3 and batter-runner). Responsible for the runner leaving early on the pitch at second base (R2), the tag up at second base and first base (R2 and R3) any play at first base or second base.

U3: Pick up the ball and glance at the runner while hustling inside the diamond to button hook at a minimum depth of 10-12 feet. Continue to alternate between the ball and the runner keeping all four elements in front of you. Responsible for the runners leaving early on the pitch at third base and first base (R1 and R3), the tag up at third base (R1) and any play at third base.

FLY BALL TO THE OUTFIELD, BALL IS CAUGHT, U1 CHASES

P: When a fly ball is hit and a base umpire goes out, move toward the holding zone about halfway to third base in foul ground to an area where you have an unobstructed view of all four elements. Be prepared to move as the play develops. Responsible for the tag up at third base (R1), any play on a lead runner (R1 and R2) at third base and any play at the plate.

U1: Pick up the flight of the ball and glance at your partner. Responsible for any fly ball from the right fielder up to the left fielder. When chasing the fly ball communicate with the crew you are chasing. Move parallel to the flight of the ball, or if necessary to gain a better angle, move away from the fielder; stop facing the player when the play happens. If caught, give the out signal and verbal facing the play. If the ball is dropped and it is not obvious, give the safe/no catch signal. Let the ball turn you back toward the infield and observe the rest of the play from there. Responsible for the runner leaving early on the pitch at second base (R2) and catch/no catch.

U3: When a fly ball is hit and U1 goes out, pick up the ball and glance at the runner while hustling across the diamond toward first base to a position about halfway between second base and first base. Continue to alternate between the ball and the runner keeping all four elements in front of you. Be prepared to move parallel to the baseline staying ahead of the runner (R3). Responsible for the runners leaving early on the pitch at third base and first base (R1 and R3), the tag up at second base and first base (R2 and R3) and any play at first base or second base and the last runner to third base (R3).

FLY BALL TO THE OUTFIELD, BALL IS NOT CAUGHT, U1 CHASES

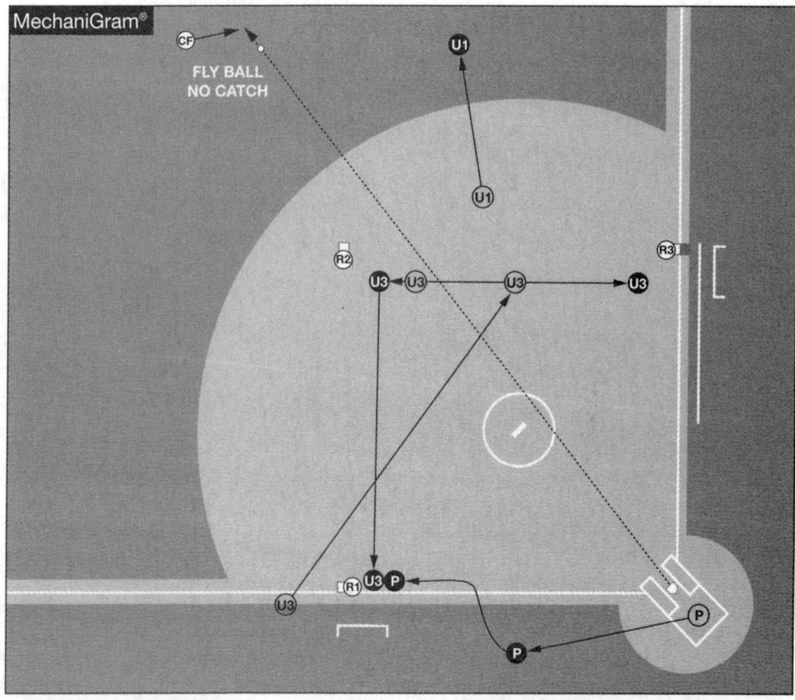

P: When a fly ball is hit and a base umpire goes out, move toward the holding zone about halfway to third base in foul ground to an area where you have an unobstructed view of all four elements. Be prepared to move as the play develops. Responsible for the tag up at third base (R1), any play on a lead runner (R1, R2 and R3) at third base and any play at the plate.

U1: Pick up the flight of the ball and glance at your partner. Responsible for any fly ball from the right fielder up to the left fielder. When chasing the fly ball communicate with the crew you are chasing. Move parallel to the flight of the ball, or if necessary to gain a better angle, move away from the fielder; stop facing the player when the play happens. If the ball is dropped and it is not obvious, give the safe/no catch signal. Let the ball turn you back toward the infield and observe the rest of the play from there. Responsible for the runner leaving early on the pitch at first base (R2) and catch/no catch.

U3: When a fly ball is hit and U1 goes out, pick up the ball and glance at the runner while hustling across the diamond toward first base to a position about halfway between second base and first base. Continue to alternate between the ball and the runners keeping all four elements in front of you. Be prepared to move parallel to the baseline staying ahead of the runners (R3 and batter-runner). Responsible for the runners leaving early on the pitch at third base and first base (R1 and R3), the tag up at second base and first base (R2 and R3) and any play at first base or second base and the last runner to third base (batter-runner).

FLY BALL TO THE OUTFIELD, BALL IS CAUGHT, U3 CHASES

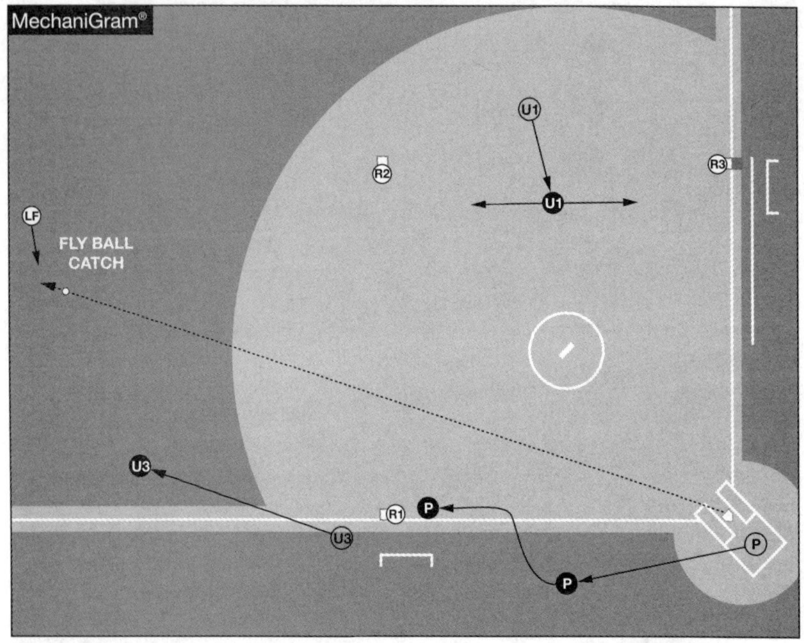

P: When a fly ball is hit and a base umpire goes out, move toward the holding zone about halfway to third base in foul ground to an area where you have an unobstructed view of all four elements. Be prepared to move as the play develops. Responsible for the tag up at third base (R1), any play on a lead runner (R1 and R2) at third base and any play at the plate.

U1: When a fly ball is hit and U3 goes out, pick up the ball and glance at the runner while hustling inside the diamond to button hook at a minimum depth of 10-12 feet. Continue to alternate between the ball and the runner (R2 and R3) keeping all four elements in front of you. Be prepared to move parallel to the baseline staying ahead of the runner (R3). Responsible for the runner leaving early on the pitch at second base (R2) the tag-up at second base and first base (R2 and R3), any play at first base or second base and the last runner (R3) at third base.

U3: Pick up the flight of the ball and glance at your partner. Responsible for any fly ball hit from the left fielder up to dead-ball territory. When chasing the fly ball communicate with the crew you are chasing. Move parallel to the flight of the ball, or if necessary to gain a better angle, move away from the fielder; stop facing the player when the play happens. If caught, give the out signal and verbal facing the play. If the ball is dropped and it is not obvious, give the safe/no catch signal. Let the ball turn you back toward the infield and observe the rest of the play from there. Responsible for the runners leaving early on the pitch at third base and first base (R1 and R3), fair/foul, catch/no catch.

FLY BALL TO THE OUTFIELD, BALL IS NOT CAUGHT, U3 CHASES

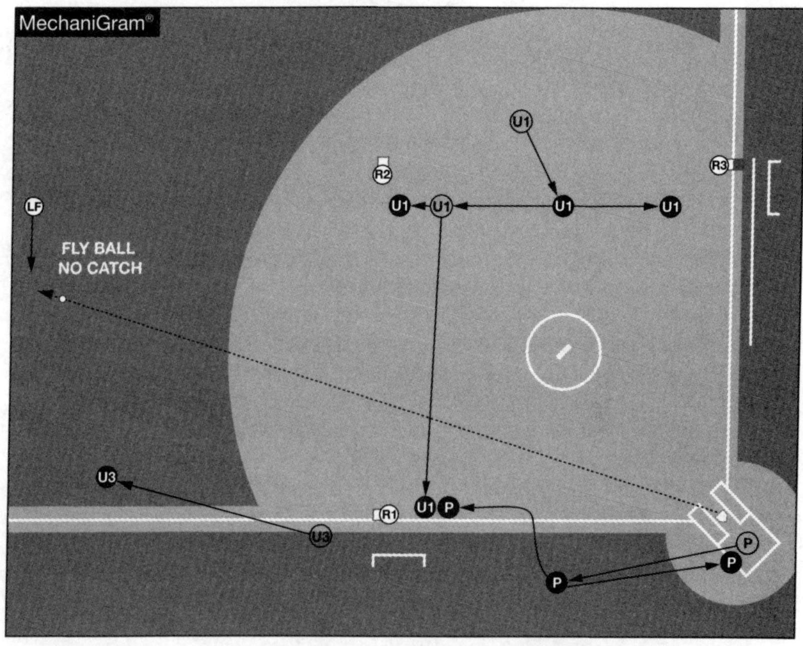

P: When a fly ball is hit and a base umpire goes out, move toward the holding zone about halfway to third base in foul ground to an area where you have an unobstructed view of all four elements. Be prepared to move as the play develops. Responsible for the tag up at third base (R1), any play on a lead runner (R1, R2 and R3) at third base and any play at the plate.

U1: When a fly ball is hit and U3 goes out, pick up the ball and glance at the runner while hustling inside the diamond to button hook at a minimum depth of 10-12 feet. Continue to alternate between the ball and the runner (batter-runner) keeping all four elements in front of you. Be prepared to move parallel to the baseline staying ahead of the runners (R3 and batter-runner). Responsible for the runner leaving early on the pitch at second base (R2) the tag-up at second base and first base (R2 and R3), any play at first base or second base and the last runner (batter-runner) at third base.

U3: Pick up the flight of the ball and glance at your partner. Responsible for any fly ball hit from the left fielder up to dead-ball territory. When chasing the fly ball communicate with the crew you are chasing. Move parallel to the flight of the ball, or if necessary to gain a better angle, move away from the fielder; stop facing the player when the play happens. If caught, give the out signal and verbal facing the play. If the ball is dropped and it is not obvious, give the safe/no catch signal. Let the ball turn you back toward the infield and observe the rest of the play from there. Responsible for the runners leaving early on the pitch at third base and first base (R1 and R3), fair/foul, catch/no catch.

OFFICIALS
CODE OF ETHICS

Officials at an interscholastic athletic event are participants in the educational development of high school students. As such, they must exercise a high level of self-discipline, independence and responsibility. The purpose of this Code is to establish guidelines for ethical standards of conduct for all interscholastic officials.

- **Officials** shall master both the rules of the game and the mechanics necessary to enforce the rules, and shall exercise authority in an impartial, firm and controlled manner.

- **Officials** shall work with each other and their state associations in a constructive and cooperative manner.

- **Officials** shall uphold the honor and dignity of the profession in all interaction with student-athletes, coaches, athletic directors, school administrators, colleagues, and the public. This includes, but is not limited to, positive verbal and nonverbal communication with coaches, bench personnel and players.

- **Officials** shall avoid the use of alcohol, drugs, and tobacco products beginning with the arrival at the competition site until departure following the completion of the contest.

- **Officials** shall prepare themselves both physically and mentally, shall dress neatly and appropriately, and shall comport themselves in a manner consistent with the high standards of the profession.

- **Officials** shall be punctual and professional in the fulfillment of all contractual obligations.

- **Officials** shall remain mindful that their conduct influences the respect that student-athletes, coaches and the public hold for the profession.

- **Officials** shall, while enforcing the rules of play, remain aware of the inherent risk of injury that competition poses to student-athletes. Where appropriate, officials shall inform event management of conditions or situations that appear unreasonably hazardous.

- **Officials** shall take reasonable steps to educate themselves in the recognition of emergency conditions that might arise during the course of competition.

- **Officials** shall maintain an ethical approach while participating in forums, chat rooms and all forms of social media.

Signal Chart

Out

Punch Out

Overhand Out

Safe, No Catch, No Tag

Sell Safe

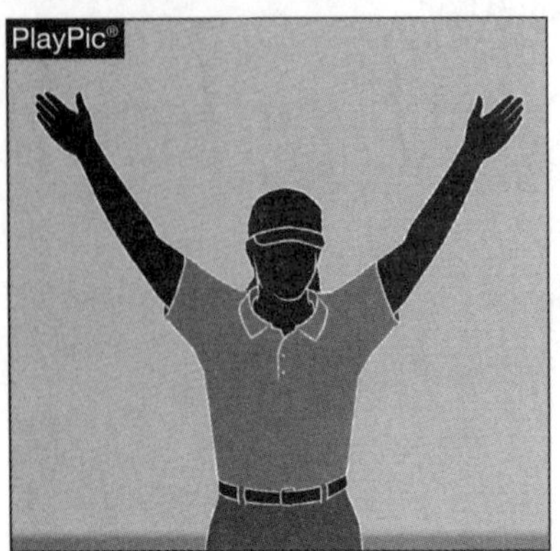

Dead Ball, Foul Ball, No Pitch, Time

Fair Ball

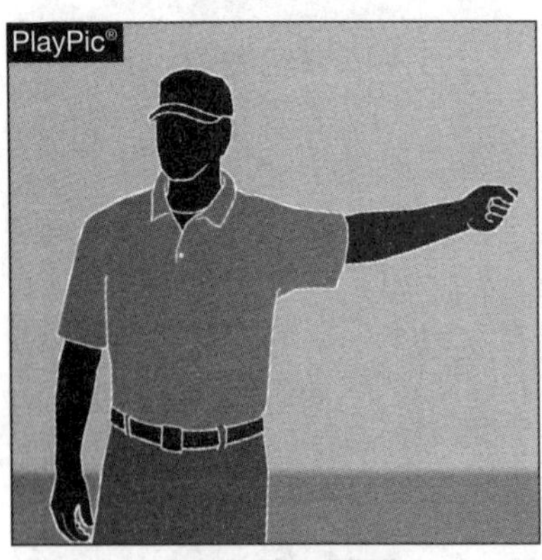

Delayed Dead Ball

Infield Fly

Point

Home Run

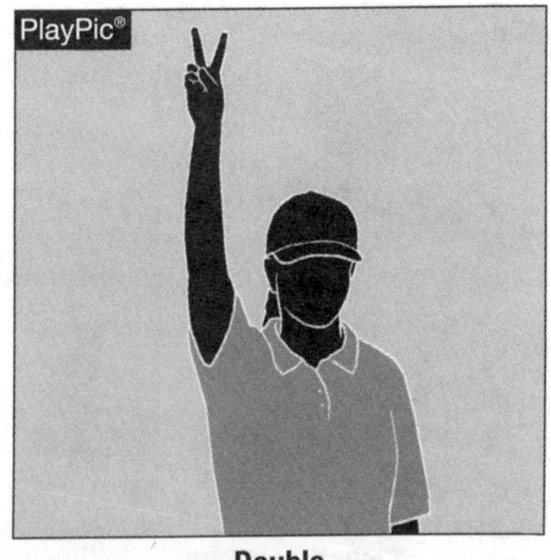

Double

Ejection

The Run Scores

The Run Does Not Score

Play Ball

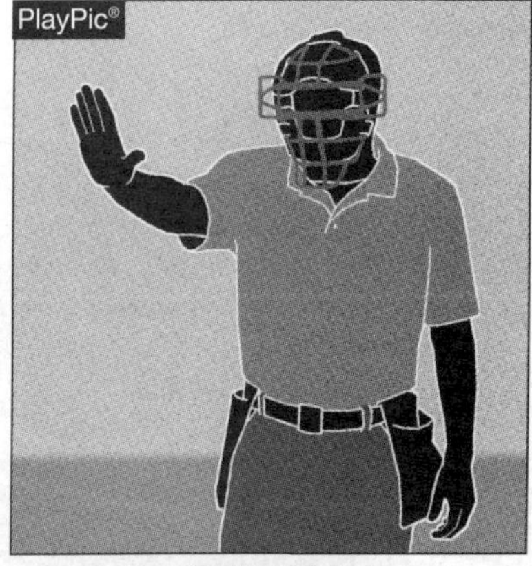

Do Not Pitch

Strike

Called Third Strike

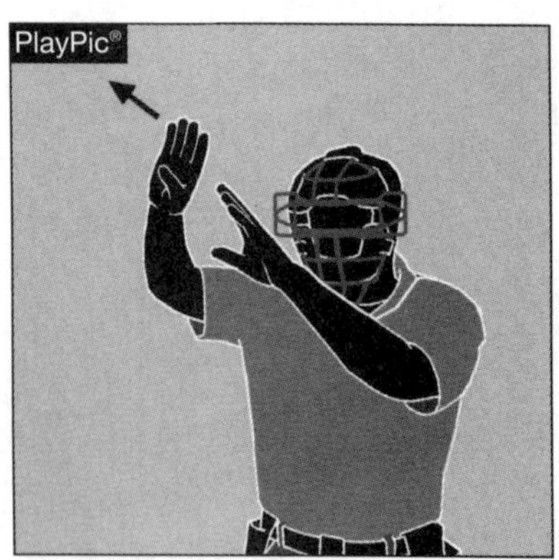

Foul Tip

Ball

Count

Umpire-to-Umpire Signals

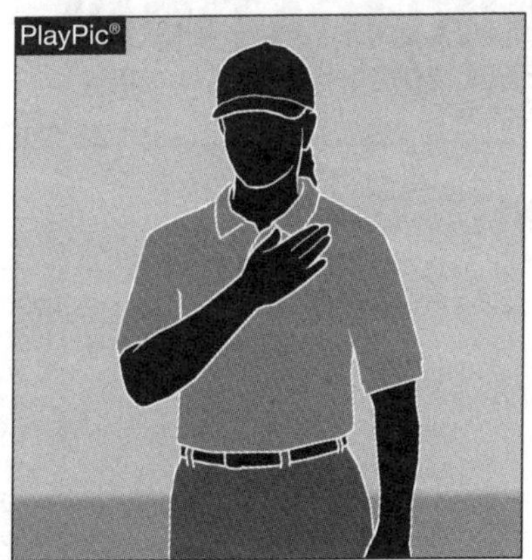

Infield Fly Situation is On

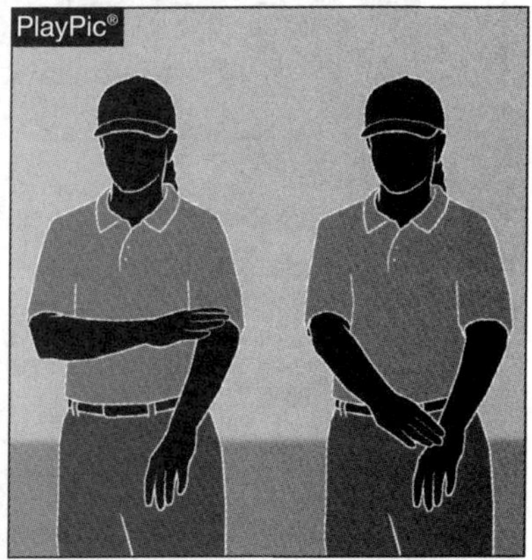

Infield Fly Situation is Off or Not On

NFHS PUBLICATIONS

Prices effective April 1, 2023 — March 31, 2024

RULES PUBLICATIONS

Baseball Rules Book.................................$12.00	Boys Lacrosse Rules Book............................$12.00
Baseball Case Book...................................$12.00	Girls Lacrosse Rules Book............................$12.00
Baseball Umpires Manual (2023 & 2024).....$12.00	Soccer Rules Book......................................$12.00
Baseball Simplified & Illustrated Rules $15.95	Softball Rules Book.....................................$12.00
Basketball Rules Book...............................$12.00	Softball Case Book......................................$12.00
Basketball Case Book................................$12.00	Softball Umpires Manual (2024 & 2025)......$12.00
Basketball Simplified & Illustrated Rules $15.95	Softball Simplified & Illustrated Rules $15.95
Basketball Officials Manual (2023-25) $12.00	Spirit Rules Book..$12.00
Basketball Handbook (2022-24)....................$12.00	Swimming & Diving Rules Book....................$12.00
Field Hockey Rules Book............................$12.00	Track & Field Rules Book.............................$12.00
Football Rules Book $12.00	Track & Field Case Book $12.00
Football Case Book....................................$12.00	Track & Field Manual (2023 & 2024)............$12.00
Football Simplified & Illustrated Rules..........$15.95	Volleyball Rules Book..................................$12.00
Football Handbook (2023 & 2024)................$12.00	Volleyball Case Book & Manual....................$12.00
Football Game Officials Manual (2022 & 2023).$12.00	Volleyball Simplified & Illustrated Rules $15.95
Girls Gymnastics Rules Book & Manual	Water Polo Rules Book (2022-24) $12.00
(2022-24)....................................$12.00	Wrestling Rules Book...................................$12.00
Ice Hockey Rules Book $12.00	Wrestling Case Book & Manual....................$12.00

MISCELLANEOUS ITEMS

NFHS Statisticians' Manual $8.25
Scorebooks: Baseball-Softball, Basketball, Swimming & Diving, Cross Country, Soccer,
  Track & Field, Volleyball, Wrestling and Field Hockey $13.00
Diving Scoresheets (pad of 100)..$11.00
Volleyball Team Rosters & Lineup Sheets (pads of 100) $11.00
Libero Tracking Sheet (pads of 50)...$11.00
Baseball/Softball Lineup Sheets – 3-Part NCR (sets/100)..$11.00
Wrestling Tournament Match Cards (sets/100) $11.00
Competitors Numbers (Track and Gymnastics – Waterproof, nontearable, black numbers and
  six colors of backgrounds numbers are 1-1000 sold in sets of 100 ....$15.00/set

MISCELLANEOUS SPORTS ITEMS

Court and Field Diagram Guide $25.25	From Chicago to Indy – The First 100 Years...$29.95
NFHS Handbook (2023-24)..........................$15.00	Rules PowerPoints......................................$60.00
Let's Make It Official $5.25	Rules Changes Videos $60.00

ORDERING

Individuals ordering NFHS publications and other products and materials
are requested to order online at **www.nfhs.com**.

Visit NFHS Officials Store

www.nfhsofficialsstore.com

OFFICIALS APPAREL AND EQUIPMENT SUCH AS:

- Shirts
- Shorts
- Pants
- Jackets
- Compression Products
- Ball Bags
- Bean Bags
- Belts
- Game Cards/Holders
- Hats
- Lanyards/Whistles
- Penalty Flags
- Travel Bags

PRODUCTS ARE AVAILABLE IN THE SPORTS OF:

- Baseball/Softball
- Basketball
- Football
- Lacrosse
- Soccer
- Volleyball
- Wrestling

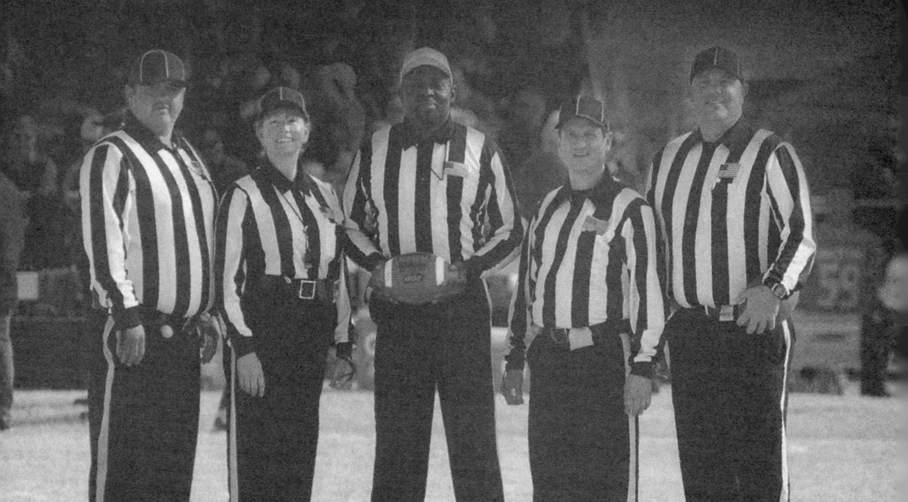

NFHS
LEARNING CENTER
NFHSLearn.com